Rick Steves'
French
Phrase Book & Dictionary
Fifth Edition

**AVALON
TRAVEL**

Avalon Travel Publishing, 1400 65th Street, Suite 250,
Emeryville, CA 94608, USA

Avalon Travel Publishing is a member of
the Perseus Books Group.

Printed in the United States of America by Worzalla.
Fifth edition. Ninth printing October 2007.

ISBN-10: 1-56691-517-1
ISBN-13: 978-1-56691-517-5

Europe Through the Back Door Managing Editor:
  Risa Laib
Europe Through the Back Door Editor:
  Cameron Hewitt
Avalon Travel Publishing Editor: Matt Orendorff
Translation: Scott Bernhard, Paul Desloover,
  Sabine Leteinturier, Steve Smith
Phonetics: Risa Laib, Cameron Hewitt
Production & Typesetting: Matt Orendorff
Cover Design: Kari Gim
Maps & Graphics: David C. Hoerlein, Zoey Platt
Photography: Rick Steves
Front cover photos:
  foreground–Paris © Getty Images, Inc.
  background–Eiffel Tower, Paris © Getty Images, Inc.

Distributed to the book trade by
Publishers Group West, Berkeley, California

Other ATP travel guidebooks by Rick Steves

Rick Steves' Best of Europe
Rick Steves' Europe 101: History and Art for the Traveler
  (with Gene Openshaw)
Rick Steves' Europe Through the Back Door
Rick Steves' Best European City Walks & Museums
  (with Gene Openshaw)
Rick Steves' Postcards from Europe
Rick Steves' France (with Steve Smith)
Rick Steves' Germany & Austria
Rick Steves' Great Britain
Rick Steves' Ireland (with Pat O'Connor)
Rick Steves' Italy
Rick Steves' Portugal
Rick Steves' Scandinavia
Rick Steves' Spain
Rick Steves Switzerland
Rick Steves' Provence & the French Riviera
Rick Steves' Amsterdam, Bruges & Brussels
  (with Gene Openshaw)
Rick Steves' Florence & Tuscany (with Gene Openshaw)
Rick Steves' London (with Gene Openshaw)
Rick Steves' Paris
  (with Steve Smith and Gene Openshaw)
Rick Steves' Rome (with Gene Openshaw)
Rick Steves' Venice (with Gene Openshaw)
Rick Steves' Phrase Books: German, Italian, Portuguese,
Spanish, and French/Italian/German

For the latest on Rick's lectures, guidebooks, tours, and public
television series, contact Europe Through the Back Door, Box
2009, Edmonds, WA 98020, tel. 425/771-8303, fax 425/771-
0833, www.ricksteves.com, or e-mail: rick@ricksteves.com.

CONTENTS

Getting Started 1–3

French Basics 4–13
  Meeting and Greeting . . . 4   Struggling with French . . . 8
  Essentials 5   Handy Questions 9
  Where? 6   Le Yin et le Yang 11
  How Much? 6   Big Little Words 12
  How Many? 7   Quintessentially
  When? 7   French Expressions 13

Counting 14–25
  Numbers 14
  Money 17
  Money Words 19
  Time 20
  Timely Expressions 21   The Month 23
  About Time 22   The Year 24
  The Day 22   Holidays and Happy Days . 24
  The Week 23

  KEY PHRASES: MONEY 19
  KEY PHRASES: TIME 20

Traveling 26–53
  Flights 26
  Making a Reservation . . 26   Getting to/from the Airport . 27
  At the Airport 27
  Trains 28
  The Train Station 28   On the Platform 33
  Getting a Ticket 29   On the Train 34
  Reservations, Supplements,   Reading Train and Bus
    and Discounts 31   Schedules 36
  Ticket Talk 32   Going Places 37
  Changing Trains 33   Places within France 37
  Buses and Subways 39
  At the Bus Station or   Taking Buses and Subways . 40
    Métro Stop 39

I

Illustrations

Maps

Hi, I'm Rick Steves.

I'm the only monolingual speaker I know who's had the nerve to design a series of European phrase books. But that's one of the things that makes them better.

You see, after 25 summers of travel through Europe, I've learned first hand: (1) what's essential for communication in another country, and (2) what's not. I've assembled the most important words and phrases in a logical, no-frills format, and I've worked with native Europeans and seasoned travelers to give you the simplest, clearest translation possible.

But this book is more than just a pocket translator. The words and phrases have been carefully selected to help you have a smarter, smoother trip in France. The key to getting more out of every travel dollar is to get closer to the local people, and to rely less on entertainment, restaurants, and hotels that cater only to foreign tourists. This book will not only help you order a meal at a locals-only Parisian restaurant—but it will also help you talk with the family who runs the place . . . about their kids, travel dreams, politics, and favorite *fromage*. Long after your memories of châteaux have faded, you'll still treasure the personal encounters you had with your new French friends.

A good phrase book should help you enjoy your French experience—not just survive it—so I've added a healthy dose of humor. A few phrases are just for fun and aren't meant to be used at all. Most of the phrases are for real and should be used with "please." I know you can tell the difference.

To get the most out of this book, take the time to internalize and put into practice my French pronunciation tips. Don't worry too much about memorizing grammatical rules, like the gender of a noun—forget about sex, and communicate!

You'll notice this book has a handy dictionary and a nifty menu decoder. You'll also find tongue twisters, international words, telephone tips, and a tear-out "cheat sheet." Tear it out and tuck it in your beret, so you can easily memorize key phrases during otherwise idle moments. As you prepare for your trip, you may want to read this year's edition of my *Rick Steves' France* guidebook.

Your French experience will be enriched by a basic understanding of French etiquette. This causes lots of needless frustration among Americans. Here's the situation in a nutshell. Americans feel that informality is friendly and formality is cold. The French feel that informality is rude and formality is polite. So, ironically, as the Americans and French are both doing their best to be nice, they accidentally offend one another. Remember you're the outsider, so watch the locals and try to incorporate some French-syle politeness into your routine. Walk into any shop in France and you will hear a cheery, *"Bonjour, Monsieur / Madame."* As you leave, you'll hear a lilting, *"Au revoir, Monsieur / Madame."* Always address a man as *Monsieur*, a woman as *Madame,* and an unmarried young woman or a girl as *Mademoiselle* (leaving this out is like addressing a French person as "Hey, you!"). For good measure, toss in *s'il vous plaît* (please) whenever you can.

Adjust those cultural blinders. If you come to France expecting rudeness, you are sure to find it. If you respect the fine points of French culture and make an attempt to speak their language, you'll find the French as warm and friendly as anyone in Europe.

My goal is to help you become a more confident, extroverted traveler. If this phrase book helps make that happen, or if you have suggestions for making it better, I'd love to hear from you. I personally read and value all feedback. You can reach me at Europe Through the Back Door, P.O. Box 2009, Edmonds, WA 98020, tel. 425/771-8303, fax 425/771-0833, e-mail: rick@ricksteves.com.

Happy travels, and *bonne chance* (good luck) as you hurdle the language barrier!

Rick Steves

GETTING
STARTED

Challenging, Romantic French

...is spoken throughout Europe and thought to be one of the most beautiful languages in the world. Half of Belgium speaks French, and French rivals English as the handiest second language in Spain, Portugal, and Italy. Even your U.S. passport is translated into French. You're probably already familiar with this poetic language. Consider: *bonjour, c'est la vie, bon appétit, merci, au revoir,* and *bon voyage!* The most important phrase is *s'il vous plaît* (please), pronounced see voo play. Use it liberally. The French will notice and love it.

As with any language, the key to communicating is to go for it with a mixture of bravado and humility. Try to sound like Maurice Chevalier or Inspector Clouseau.

French has some unusual twists to its pronunciation:

Ç sounds like S in sun.
CH sounds like SH in shine.
G usually sounds like G in get.
    But G followed by E or I sounds like S in treasure.
GN sounds like NI in onion.
H is always silent.

1

J sounds like S in treasure.
R sounds like an R being swallowed.
I sounds like EE in seed.
È and Ê sound like E in let.
É and EZ sound like AY in play.
ER, at the end of a word, sounds like AY in play.
Ô sounds like O in note.

In a Romance language, sex is unavoidable. A man is
content (happy), a woman is *contente.* In this book,
when you see a pair of words like "*content / contente,*"
use the second word when talking about a woman.

French has accents. The cedilla makes Ç sound
like "s" (*façade*). The circumflex makes Ê sound like
"eh" (*crêpe*), but has no effect on Â, Î, Ô, or Û. The
grave accent stifles È into "eh" (*crème*), but doesn't
change the stubborn À (*à la carte*). The acute accent
opens É into "ay" (*café*).

French is tricky because the spelling and pronunciation seem to have little to do with each other.
Qu'est-ce que c'est? (What is that?) is pronounced: kehs
kuh say.

The final letters of many French words are silent,
so *Paris* sounds like pah-ree. The French tend to stress
every syllable evenly: pah-ree. In contrast, Americans
say **Par**-is, emphasizing the first syllable.

In French, if a word that ends in a consonant is
followed by a word that starts with a vowel, the consonant is frequently linked with the vowel. *Mes amis* (my
friends) is pronounced: may-zah-mee. Some words are
linked with an apostrophe. *Ce est* (It is) becomes *C'est,*
as in *C'est la vie* (That's life). *Le* and *la* (the masculine
and feminine "the") are intimately connected to words
starting with a vowel. *La orange* becomes *l'orange.*

French has a few sounds that are unusual in
English: the French *u* and the nasal vowels. To say the
French *u,* round your lips to say "oh," but say "ee."
Vowels combined with either *n* or *m* are often nasal

vowels. As you nasalize a vowel, let the sound come through your nose as well as your mouth. The vowel is the important thing. The *n* or *m*, represented in this book by <u>n</u> for nasal, is not pronounced.

There are a total of four nasal sounds, all contained in the phrase *un bon vin blanc* (a good white wine).

Nasal vowels:	Phonetics:	To make the sound:
un	uh<u>n</u>	nasalize the U in lung.
bon	boh<u>n</u>	nasalize the O in bone.
vin	va<u>n</u>	nasalize the A in sack.
blanc	blah<u>n</u>	nasalize the A in want.

If you practice saying *un bon vin blanc,* you'll learn how to say the nasal vowels . . . and order a fine wine.

Here's a guide to the rest of the phonetics in this book:

ah	like A in father.
ay	like AY in play.
eh	like E in let.
ee	like EE in seed.
ehr, air	sounds like "air" (in *merci* and *extraordinaire*).
ew	pucker your lips and say "ee."
g	like G in go.
ī	like I in light.
or	like OR in core.
oh	like O in note.
oo	like OO in too.
s	like S in sun.
uh	like U in but.
ur	like UR in purr.
zh	like S in treasure.

FRENCH
BASICS

In 1945, American G.I.s helped liberate Paris using only these phrases.

Meeting and Greeting

Good day.	*Bonjour.*	boh<u>n</u>-zhoor
Good morning.	*Bonjour.*	boh<u>n</u>-zhoor
Good evening.	*Bonsoir.*	boh<u>n</u>-swar
Good night.	*Bonne nuit.*	buhn nwee
Hi / Bye. (informal)	*Salut.*	sah-lew
Welcome!	*Bienvenue!*	bee-a<u>n</u>-vuh-new
Mr.	*Monsieur*	muhs-yur
Mrs.	*Madame*	mah-dahm
Miss	*Mademoiselle*	mahd-mwah-zehl
How are you?	*Comment allez-vous?*	koh-mah<u>nt</u> ah-lay-voo
Very well, thank you.	*Très bien, merci.*	treh bee-a<u>n</u> mehr-see
And you?	*Et vous?*	ay voo
My name is___.	*Je m'appelle___.*	zhuh mah-pehl
What's your name?	*Quel est votre nom?*	kehl ay voh-truh noh<u>n</u>
Pleased to meet you.	*Enchanté.*	ah<u>n</u>-shah<u>n</u>-tay
Where are you from?	*D'où êtes-vous?*	doo eht voo
I am / We are...	*Je suis /*	zhuh swee /
	Nous sommes...	noo suhm

4

Are you...?	*Êtes-vous...?*	eht-vooz
...on vacation	*...en vacances*	ah<u>n</u> vah-kah<u>n</u>s
...on business	*...en voyage d'affaires*	ah<u>n</u> voy-yahzh dah-fair
See you later.	*À bientôt.*	ah bee-a<u>n</u>-toh
So long! (informal)	*Salut!*	sah-lew
Goodbye.	*Au revoir.*	oh reh-vwar
Good luck!	*Bonne chance!*	buhn shah<u>n</u>s
Have a good trip!	*Bon voyage!*	boh<u>n</u> voy-yahzh

The greeting "*Bonjour*" (Good day) turns to "*Bonsoir*" (Good evening) at sundown.

Essentials

Good day.	*Bonjour.*	boh<u>n</u>-zhoor
Do you speak English?	*Parlez-vous anglais?*	par-lay-voo ah<u>n</u>-glay
Yes. / No.	*Oui. / Non.*	wee / noh<u>n</u>
I don't speak French.	*Je ne parle pas français.*	zhuh nuh parl pah frah<u>n</u>-say
I'm sorry.	*Désolé.*	day-zoh-lay
Please.	*S'il vous plaît.*	see voo play
Thank you.	*Merci.*	mehr-see
Thank you very much.	*Merci beaucoup.*	mehr-see boh-koo
No problem.	*Pas de problème.*	pah duh proh-blehm
Good. / Very good. / Excellent.	*Bien. / Très bien. / Excellent.*	bee-a<u>n</u> / treh bee-a<u>n</u> / ehk-sehl-ah<u>n</u>
You are very kind.	*Vous êtes très gentil.*	vooz eht treh zhah<u>n</u>-tee
Excuse me. (to pass)	*Pardon.*	par-doh<u>n</u>
Excuse me. (to get attention)	*Excusez-moi.*	ehk-skew-zay-mwah
It doesn't matter.	*Ça m'est égal.*	sah meht ay-gal
You're welcome.	*Je vous en prie.*	zhuh vooz ah<u>n</u> pree
Sure.	*Bien sûr.*	bee-a<u>n</u> suhr

BASICS

O.K.	D'accord.	dah-kor
Let's go.	Allons-y.	ahl-loh<u>n</u>-zee
Goodbye.	Au revoir.	oh reh-vwar

Where?

Where is...?	Où est...?	oo ay
...the tourist information office	...l'office du tourisme	loh-fees dew too-reez-muh
...a cash machine	...un distributeur automatique	uh<u>n</u> dee-stree-bew-tur oh-toh-mah-teek
...the train station	...la gare	lah gar
...the bus station	...la gare routière	lah gar root-yehr
Where are the toilets?	Où sont les toilettes?	oo soh<u>n</u> lay twah-leht
men / women	hommes / dames	ohm / dahm

You'll find some French words are similar to English if you're looking for a *banque, pharmacie, hôtel,* or *restaurant.*

How Much?

How much is it, please?	Combien, s'il vous plaît?	koh<u>n</u>-bee-a<u>n</u> see voo play
Write it?	Ecrivez?	ay-kree-vay
Is it free?	C'est gratuit?	say grah-twee
Included?	Inclus?	a<u>n</u>-klew
Do you have...?	Avez-vous...?	ah-vay-voo
Where can I buy...?	Où puis-je acheter...?	oo pwee-zhuh ah-shuh-tay
I would like...	Je voudrais...	zhuh voo-dray
We would like...	Nous voudrions...	noo voo-dree-oh<u>n</u>
...this.	...ceci.	suh-see
...just a little.	...un petit peu.	uh<u>n</u> puh-tee puh
...more.	...plus.	plew
...a ticket.	...un billet.	uh<u>n</u> bee-yay
...a room.	...une chambre.	ewn shah<u>n</u>-bruh
...the bill.	...l'addition.	lah-dee-see-oh<u>n</u>

How Many?

one	*un*	uh<u>n</u>
two	*deux*	duh
three	*trois*	twah
four	*quatre*	kah-truh
five	*cinq*	sa<u>n</u>k
six	*six*	sees
seven	*sept*	seht
eight	*huit*	weet
nine	*neuf*	nuhf
ten	*dix*	dees

You'll find more to count on in the Numbers section (page 14).

When?

At what time?	*À quelle heure?*	ah kehl ur
open / closed	*ouvert / fermé*	oo-vehr / fehr-may
Just a moment.	*Un moment.*	uh<u>n</u> moh-mah<u>n</u>
Now.	*Maintenant.*	ma<u>n</u>-tuh-nah<u>n</u>
Soon.	*Bientôt.*	bee-a<u>n</u>-toh
Later.	*Plus tard.*	plew tar
Today.	*Aujourd'hui.*	oh-zhoor-dwee
Tomorrow.	*Demain.*	duh-ma<u>n</u>

Be creative! You can combine these phrases to say: "Two, please," or "No, thank you," or "Open tomorrow?" or "Please, where can I buy a ticket?" Please is a magic word in any language, but especially in French. The French love to hear it. If you want to buy something and you don't know the word for it, just point and say, "*S'il vous plaît*" (Please). If you know the word for what you want, such as the bill, simply say, "*L'addition, s'il vous plaît*" (The bill, please).

Struggling with French

Do you speak English?	*Parlez-vous anglais?*	par-lay-voo ah<u>n</u>-glay
A teeny weeny bit?	*Un tout petit peu?*	uh<u>n</u> too puh-tee puh
Please speak English.	*Parlez anglais, s'il vous plaît.*	par-lay ah<u>n</u>-glay see voo play
You speak English well.	*Vous parlez bien anglais.*	voo par-lay bee-a<u>n</u> ah<u>n</u>-glay
I don't speak French.	*Je ne parle pas français.*	zhuh nuh parl pah frah<u>n</u>-say
We don't speak French.	*Nous ne parlons pas français.*	noo nuh par-lo<u>n</u> pah frah<u>n</u>-say
I speak a little French.	*Je parle un petit peu français.*	zhuh parl uh<u>n</u> puh-tee puh frah<u>n</u>-say
Sorry, I speak only English.	*Désolé, je ne parle qu'anglais.*	day-zoh-lay zhuh nuh parl kah<u>n</u>-glay
Sorry, we speak only English.	*Désolé, nous ne parlons qu'anglais.*	day-zoh-lay noo nuh par-lo<u>n</u> kah<u>n</u>-glay
Does somebody nearby speak English?	*Quelqu'un près d'ici parle anglais?*	kehl-kuh<u>n</u> preh dee-see parl ah<u>n</u>-glay
Who speaks English?	*Qui parle anglais?*	kee parl ah<u>n</u>-glay
What does this mean?	*Qu'est-ce-que ça veut dire?*	kehs-kuh sah vuh deer
How do you say this in French / English?	*Comment dit-on en français / anglais?*	koh-mah<u>n</u> dee-toh<u>n</u> ah<u>n</u> frah<u>n</u>-say / ah<u>n</u>-glay
Repeat?	*Répétez?*	ray-pay-tay
Speak slowly, please.	*Parlez lentement, s'il vous plaît.*	par-lay lah<u>n</u>-tuh-mah<u>n</u> see voo play
Slower.	*Plus lentement.*	plew lah<u>n</u>-tuh-mah<u>n</u>
I understand.	*Je comprends.*	zhuh koh<u>n</u>-prah<u>n</u>
I don't understand.	*Je ne comprends pas.*	zhuh nuh koh<u>n</u>-prah<u>n</u> pah
Do you understand?	*Vous comprenez?*	voo koh<u>n</u>-preh-nay
Write it?	*Ecrivez?*	ay-kree-vay

A French person who is asked, "Do you speak English?"
assumes you mean, "Do you speak English fluently?"
and will likely answer no. But if you just keep on struggling in French, you'll bring out the English in most any
French person.

Handy Questions

How much?	*Combien?*	kohn-bee-an
How many?	*Combien?*	kohn-bee-an
How long...?	*Combien de temps...?*	kohn-bee-an duh tahn
...is the trip	*...dure le voyage*	dewr luh voy-yahzh
How many minutes?	*Combien de minutes?*	kohn-bee-an duh mee-newt
How many hours?	*Combien d'heures?*	kohn-bee-an dur
How far?	*C'est loin?*	say lwan
How?	*Comment?*	koh-mahn
Can you help me?	*Vous pouvez m'aider?*	voo poo-vay may-day
Can you help us?	*Vous pouvez nous aider?*	voo poo-vay nooz ay-day
Can I...?	*Puis-je...?*	pwee-zhuh
Can we...?	*Pouvons-nous...?*	poo-vohn-noo
...have one	*...avoir un*	ah-vwar uhn
...go free	*...aller gratuitement*	ah-lay grah-tweet-mahn
...borrow that for a moment / an hour	*...emprunter ça pour un moment / une heure*	ahn-pruhn-tay sah poor uhn moh-mahn / ewn ur
...use the toilet	*...utiliser les toilettes*	oo-tee-lee-zay lay twah-leht
What? (didn't hear)	*Comment?*	koh-mahn
What is this?	*Qu'est-ce que c'est?*	kehs kuh say
What is better?	*Qu'est-ce qui vaut mieux?*	kehs kee voh mee-uh
What's going on?	*Qu'est-ce qui se passe?*	kehs kee suh pahs
When?	*Quand?*	kahn
What time is it?	*Quelle heure est-il?*	kehl ur ay-teel

BASICS

At what time?	*À quelle heure?*	ah kehl ur
On time? / Late?	*A l'heure? / En retard?*	ah lur / ahn ruh-tar
How long will it take?	*Ça prend combien de temps?*	sah prahn kohn-bee-an duh tahn
At what time does this open / close?	*À quelle heuere c'est ouvert / fermé?*	ah kehl ur say oo-vehr / fehr-may
Is this open daily?	*C'est ouvert tous les jours?*	say oo-vehr too lay zhoor
What day is this closed?	*C'est fermé quel jour?*	say fehr-may kehl zhoor
Do you have...?	*Avez-vous...?*	ah-vay-voo
Where is...?	*Où est...?*	oo ay
Where are...?	*Où sont...?*	oo sohn
Where can I find / buy...?	*Où puis-je trouver / acheter...?*	oo pwee-zhuh troo-vay / ah-shuh-tay
Where can we find / buy...?	*Où pouvons-nous trouver / acheter...?*	oo poo-vahn-noo troo-vay / ah-shuh-tay
Is it necessary?	*C'est nécessaire?*	say nay-suh-sair
Is it possible...?	*C'est possible...?*	say poh-see-bluh
...to enter	*...d'entrer*	dahn-tray
...to picnic here	*...de pique-niquer ici*	duh peek-neek-ay ee-see
...to sit here	*...de s'assoir ici*	duh sah-swar ee-see
...to look	*...de regarder*	duh ray-gar-day
...to take a photo	*...de prendre une photo*	duh prahn-druh ewn foh-toh
...to see a room	*...de voir une chambre*	duh vwar ewn shahn-bruh
Who?	*Qui?*	kee
Why?	*Pourquoi?*	poor-kwah
Why not?	*Pourquoi pas?*	poor-kwah pah
Yes or no?	*Oui ou non?*	wee oo nohn

To prompt a simple answer, ask, "*Oui ou non?*" (Yes or no?). To turn a word or sentence into a question, ask it in a questioning tone. "*C'est bon*" (It's good) becomes "*C'est bon?*" (Is it good?). An easy way to say, "Where is the toilet?" is to ask, "*Toilette?*"

Le Yin et le Yang

cheap / expensive	*bon marché / cher*	bohn mar-shay / shehr
big / small	*grand / petit*	grahn / puh-tee
hot / cold	*chaud / froid*	shoh / frwah
warm / cool	*tiede / frais*	tee-ehd / fray
cool (nice) /not cool	*sympa / pas sympa*	sahn-pah / pah sahn-pah
open / closed	*ouvert / fermé*	oo-vehr / fehr-may
entrance / exit	*entrée / sortie*	ahn-tray / sor-tee
push / pull	*pousser / tirer*	poo-say / tee-ray
arrive / depart	*arriver / partir*	ah-ree-vay / par-teer
early / late	*tôt / tard*	toh / tar
soon / later	*bientôt / plus tard*	bee-an-toh / plew tar
fast / slow	*vite / lent*	veet / lahn
here / there	*ici / là-bas*	ee-see / lah-bah
near / far	*près / loin*	preh / lwan
indoors / outdoors	*l'intérieur / dehors*	lan-tay-ree-yoor / duh-or
good / bad	*bon / mauvais*	bohn / moh-vay
best / worst	*le meilleur / le pire*	luh meh-yur / luh peer
a little / lots	*un peu / beaucoup*	uhn puh / boh-koo
more / less	*plus / moins*	plew / mwan
mine / yours	*le mien / le vôtre*	luh mee-an / luh voh-truh
this / that	*ce / cette*	suh / seht
everybody / nobody	*tout le monde / personne*	too luh mohnd / pehr-suhn
easy / difficult	*facile / difficile*	fah-seel / dee-fee-seel
left / right	*à gauche / à droite*	ah gohsh / ah dwaht
up / down	*en haut / en bas*	ahn oh / ahn bah
above / below	*au-dessus / en-dessous*	oh-duh-sew / ahn-duh-soo
young / old	*jeune / vieux*	zhuhn / vee-uh
new / old	*neuf / vieux*	nuhf / vee-uh
heavy / light	*lourd / léger*	loor / lay-zhay
dark / light	*sombre / clair*	sohn-bruh / klair
happy (m, f) / sad	*content, contente / triste*	kohn-tahn, kohn-tahnt / treest
beautiful / ugly	*beau / laid*	boh / leh

nice / mean	*gentil / méchant*	zhah<u>n</u>-tee / may-shah<u>n</u>
intelligent / stupid	*intelligent / stupide*	a<u>n</u>-teh-lee-zhah<u>n</u> / stew-peed
vacant / occupied	*libre / occupé*	lee-bruh / oh-kew-pay
with / without	*avec / sans*	ah-vehk / sah<u>n</u>

Big Little Words

I	*je*	zhuh
you (formal)	*vous*	voo
you (informal)	*tu*	tew
we	*nous*	noo
he	*il*	eel
she	*elle*	ehl
they	*ils*	eel
and	*et*	ay
at	*à*	ah
because	*parce que*	pars kuh
but	*mais*	may
by (via)	*par*	par
for	*pour*	poor
from	*de*	duh
here	*ici*	ee-see
if	*si*	see
in	*en*	ah<u>n</u>
it (m / f)	*le / la*	luh / lah
not	*pas*	pah
now	*maintenant*	ma<u>n</u>-tuh-nah<u>n</u>
only	*seulement*	suhl-mah<u>n</u>
or	*ou*	oo
this / that	*ce / cette*	suh / seht
to	*à*	ah
very	*très*	treh

Quintessentially French Expressions

Bon appétit!	*bohn ah-pay-tee*	Enjoy your meal!
Ça va?	*sah vah*	How are you? (informal)
Ça va. (response to Ça va?)	*sah vah*	I'm fine.
Sympa. / Pas sympa.	*Sahn-pah / pah sahn-pah*	Nice. / Not nice.
C'est chouette. (literally: That's a female owl.)	*Say shweht*	That's cool.
Ce n'est pas vrai!	*suh nay pah vray*	It's not true!
C'est comme ça.	*say kohm sah*	That's the way it is.
Comme ci, comme ça.	*kohm see kohm sah*	So so.
D'accord.	*dah-kor*	O.K.
Formidable!	*for-mee-dah-bluh*	Great!
Mon Dieu!	*mohn dee-uh*	My God!
Tout de suite.	*toot sweet*	Right away.
Voilà.	*vwah-lah*	Here it is.

COUNTING

Numbers

0	*zéro*	zay-roh
1	*un*	uh<u>n</u>
2	*deux*	duh
3	*trois*	twah
4	*quatre*	kah-truh
5	*cinq*	sa<u>nk</u>
6	*six*	sees
7	*sept*	seht
8	*huit*	weet
9	*neuf*	nuhf
10	*dix*	dees
11	*onze*	oh<u>nz</u>
12	*douze*	dooz
13	*treize*	trehz
14	*quatorze*	kah-torz
15	*quinze*	ka<u>nz</u>
16	*seize*	sehz
17	*dix-sept*	dee-seht
18	*dix-huit*	deez-weet
19	*dix-neuf*	deez-nuhf
20	*vingt*	va<u>n</u>

21	*vingt et un*	vant ay uhn
22	*vingt-deux*	vant-duh
23	*vingt-trois*	vant-twah
30	*trente*	trahnt
31	*trente et un*	trahnt ay uhn
40	*quarante*	kah-rahnt
41	*quarante et un*	kah-rahnt ay uhn
50	*cinquante*	san-kahnt
51	*cinquante et un*	san-kahnt ay uhn
60	*soixante*	swah-sahnt
61	*soixante et un*	swah-sahnt ay uhn
70	*soixante-dix*	swah-sahnt-dees
71	*soixante et onze*	swah-sahnt ay ohnz
72	*soixante-douze*	swah-sahnt-dooz
73	*soixante-treize*	swah-sahnt-trehz
74	*soixante-quatorze*	swah-sahnt-kah-torz
75	*soixante-quinze*	swah-sahnt-kanz
76	*soixante-seize*	swah-sahnt-sehz
77	*soixante-dix-sept*	swah-sahnt-dee-seht
78	*soixante-dix-huit*	swah-sahnt-deez-weet
79	*soixante-dix-neuf*	swah-sahnt-deez-nuhf
80	*quatre-vingts*	kah-truh-van
81	*quatre-vingt-un*	kah-truh-van-uhn
82	*quatre-vingt-deux*	kah-truh-van-duh
83	*quatre-vingt-trois*	kah-truh-van-twah
84	*quatre-vingt-quatre*	kah-truh-van-kah-truh
85	*quatre-vingt-cinq*	kah-truh-van-sank
86	*quatre-vingt-six*	kah-truh-van-sees
87	*quatre-vingt-sept*	kah-truh-van-seht
88	*quatre-vingt-huit*	kah-truh-van-weet
89	*quatre-vingt-neuf*	kah-truh-van-nuhf
90	*quatre-vingt-dix*	kah-truh-van-dees
91	*quatre-vingt-onze*	kah-truh-van-ohnz
92	*quatre-vingt-douze*	kah-truh-van-dooz
93	*quatre-vingt-treize*	kah-truh-van-trehz
94	*quatre-vingt-quatorze*	kah-truh-van-kah-torz
95	*quatre-vingt-quinze*	kah-truh-van-kanz

COUNTING

96	*quatre-vingt-seize*	kah-truh-van-sehz
97	*quatre-vingt-dix-sept*	kah-truh-van-dee-seht
98	*quatre-vingt-dix-huit*	kah-truh-van-deez-weet
99	*quatre-vingt-dix-neuf*	kah-truh-van-deez-nuhf
100	*cent*	sahn
101	*cent un*	sahn uhn
102	*cent deux*	sahn duh
200	*deux cents*	duh sahn
1000	*mille*	meel
2000	*deux mille*	duh meel
2001	*deux mille un*	duh meel uhn
2002	*deux mille deux*	duh meel duh
2003	*deux mille trois*	duh meel twah
2004	*deux mille quatre*	duh meel kah-truh
2005	*deux mille cinq*	duh meel sank
2006	*deux mille six*	duh meel sees
2007	*deux mille sept*	duh meel seht
2008	*deux mille huit*	duh meel weet
2009	*deux mille neuf*	duh meel nuhf
2010	*deux mille dix*	duh meel dees
million	*million*	meel-yohn
billion	*milliard*	meel-yar
number one	*numéro un*	new-may-roh uhn
first	*premier*	pruhm-yay
second	*deuxième*	duhz-yehm
third	*troisième*	twahz-yehm
once / twice	*une fois / deux fois*	ewn fwah / duh fwah
a quarter	*un quart*	uhn kar
a third	*un tiers*	uhn tee-ehr
half	*demi*	duh-mee
this much	*comme ça*	kohm sah
a dozen	*une douzaine*	ewn doo-zayn
some	*quelques*	kehl-keh
enough	*suffisament*	soo-fee-zah-mahn
a handful	*une poignée*	ewn pwahn-yay
50%	*cinquante pour cent*	san-kahnt poor sahn
100%	*cent pour cent*	sahn poor sahn

French numbering is a little quirky from the seventies through the nineties. Let's pretend momentarily that the French speak English. Instead of saying 70, 71, 72, up to 79, the French say, "sixty ten," "sixty eleven," "sixty twelve" up to "sixty nineteen." Instead of saying 80, the French say, "four twenties." The numbers 81 and 82 are literally "four twenty one" and "four twenty two." It gets stranger. The number 90 is "four twenty ten." To say 91, 92, up to 99, the French say, "four twenty eleven," "four twenty twelve" on up to "four twenty nineteen." But take heart. If little French children can learn these numbers, so can you. Besides, didn't Abe Lincoln say, "Four score and seven..."

Money

Where is a cash machine?	*Où est un distributeur automatique?*	oo ay uhn dee-stree-bew-tur oh-toh-mah-teek
My ATM card has been...	*Ma carte a été...*	mah kart ah ay-tay
...demagnetized.	*... démagnétisée.*	day-mag-neht-ee-zay
...stolen.	*... volée.*	voh-lay
...eaten by the machine.	*... avalée par la machine.*	ah-vah-lee par lah mah-sheen
My card doesn't work.	*Ma carte ne marche pas.*	mah kart neh marsh pah
Do you accept credit cards?	*Vous prenez les cartes de crédit?*	voo preh-nay lay kart duh kray-dee
Can you change dollars?	*Pouvez-vous changer les dollars?*	poo-vay-voo shahn-zhay lay doh-lar
What is your exchange rate for dollars...?	*Quel est le cours du dollar...?*	kehl ay luh koor dew doh-lar

...in traveler's checks	...en cheques de voyage	ahn shehk duh voy-yahzh
What is the commission?	Quel est la commission?	kehl ay lah koh-mee-see-ohn
Any extra fee?	Il y a d'autre frais?	eel yah doh-truh fray
Can you break this? (large into small bills)	Vous pouvez casser ça?	voo poo-vay kas-ay sah
I would like...	Je voudrais...	zhuh voo-dray
...small bills.	...des petits billets.	day puh-tee bee-yay
...large bills.	...des gros billets.	day groh bee-yay
...coins.	...des pièces.	day pee-ehs
€ 50	cinquante euros	seeng-kwayn-tah eh-oo-roo
Is this a mistake?	C'est une erreur?	sayt ewn er-ror
This is incorrect.	C'est incorrect.	say in-koh-rehkt
Did you print these today?	Vous les avez imprimés aujourd'hui?	voo layz ah-vay an-pree-may oh-zhoor-dwee
I'm broke / poor / rich.	Je suis fauché / pauvre / riche.	zhuh swee foh-shay / poh-vruh / reesh
I'm Bill Gates.	Je suis Bill Gates.	zhuh swee "Bill Gates"
Where is the nearest casino?	Où se trouve le casino le plus proche?	oo suh troov luh kah-see-noh luh plew prohsh

France uses the euro currency. Euros (€) are divided into 100 cents. Use your common cents—cents are like pennies, and the currency has coins like nickels, dimes, and quarters.

Money Words

euro (€)	euro	eh-oo-roo
cents	centimes	sahn-teem
money	argent	ar-zhahn
cash	liquide	lee-keed

cash machine	*distributeur automatique*	dee-stree-bew-tur oh-toh-mah-teek
bank	*banque*	bahnk
credit card	*carte de crédit*	kart duh kray-dee
change money	*changer de l'argent*	shahn-zhay duh ar-zhahn
exchange	*bureau de change*	bew-roh duh shahnzh
buy / sell	*acheter / vendre*	ah-shuh-tay / vahn-druh
commission	*commission*	koh-mee-see-ohn
traveler's check	*cheque de voyage*	shehk duh voy-yahzh
cash advance	*crédit de caisse*	kray-dee duh kehs
cashier	*caisse*	kehs
bills	*billets*	bee-yay
coins	*pièces*	pee-ehs
receipt	*reçu*	ruh-sew

At French banks, you may encounter a security door that allows one person to enter at a time. Push the *entrez* (enter) button, then *attendez* (wait), and *voilà!*, the door opens. Every *distributeur automatique* (cash machine) is multilingual, but if you'd like to learn French under pressure, look for these three buttons: *annuler* (cancel), *modifier* (change), *valider* (affirm). Your PIN number is a *code*.

COUNTING

KEY PHRASES: MONEY

euro (€)	*euro*	eh-oo-roo
money	*argent*	ar-zhahn
cash	*liquide*	lee-keed
credit card	*carte de crédit*	kart duh kray-dee
bank	*banque*	bahnk
cash machine	*distributeur automatique*	dee-stree-bew-tur oh-toh-mah-teek
Where is a cash machine?	*Oú est un distributeur automatique?*	oo ay uhn dee-stree-bew-tur oh-toh-mah-teek
Do you accept credit cards?	*Vous prenez les cartes de crédit?*	voo preh-nay lay kart duh kray-dee

Time

What time is it?	*Quelle heure est-il?*	kehl ur ay-teel
It's...	*Il est...*	eel ay
...8:00 in the morning.	*...huit heures du matin.*	weet ur doo mah-tah<u>n</u>
...16:00.	*...seize heures.*	sehz ur
...4:00 in the afternoon.	*...quatre heures de l'après-midi.*	kah-truh ur duh lah-preh-mee-dee
...10:30 in the evening.	*...dix heures et demie du soir.*	deez ur ayd-mee dew swar
...a quarter past nine.	*...neuf heures et quart.*	nuhv ur ay kar
...a quarter to eleven.	*...onze heures moins le quart.*	oh<u>nz</u> ur mwa<u>n</u> luh kar
...noon.	*...midi.*	mee-dee
...midnight.	*...minuit.*	meen-wee
...early / late.	*...tôt / tard.*	toh / tar
...on time.	*...à l'heure.*	ah lur
...sunrise.	*...l'aube.*	lohb
...sunset.	*...le coucher de soleil.*	luh koo-shay duh soh-lay
It's my bedtime.	*C'est l'heure où je me couche.*	say lur oo zhuh muh koosh

KEY PHRASES: TIME		
minute	*minute*	mee-newt
hour	*heure*	ur
day	*jour*	zhoor
week	*semaine*	suh-mehn
What time is it?	*Quelle heure est-il?*	kehl ur ay-teel
It's...	*Il est...*	eel ay
...8:00.	*...huit heures.*	weet ur
...16:00.	*...seize heures.*	sehz ur
At what time does this open / close?	*À quelle heuere c'est ouvert / fermé?*	ah kehl ur say oo-vehr / fehr-may

COUNTING

Timely Expressions

I'll return / We'll return...	*Je reviens / Nous revenons...*	zhuh reh-vee-an / noo ruh-vuh-nohn
...at 11:20.	*...à onze heures vingt.*	ah ohnz ur van
I'll be / We'll be...	*Je serai / Nous serons...*	zhuh suh-ray / noo suh-rohn
...there by 18:00.	*...là avant dix huit heures.*	lah ah-vahn deez-weet ur
When is checkout time?	*À quelle heure on doit libérer la chambre?*	ah kehl ur ohn dwah lee-bay-ray lah shahn-bruh
At what time does...?	*À quelle heure...?*	ah kehl ur
...this open / close	*...c'est ouvre / ferme*	say oov-reh / fehrm
...this train / bus leave for ___	*...ce train / bus part pour ___*	seh tran / bews par poor
...the next train / bus leave for ___	*...le prochain train / bus part pour ___*	luh proh-shan tran / bews par poor
...the train / bus arrive in ___	*...le train / bus arrive à ___*	luh tran / bews ah-reev ah
I want / We want...	*Je veux / Nous voulons...*	zhuh vuh / noo voo-lohn
...to take the 16:30 train.	*...prendre le train de seize heures trente.*	prahn-druh luh tran duh sehz ur trahnt
Is the train...?	*Le train est...?*	luh tran ay
Is the bus...?	*Le bus est...?*	luh bews ay
...early / late	*...en avance / en retard*	ahn ah-vahns / ahn ruh-tar
...on time	*...à l'heure*	ah lur

COUNTING

In France, the 24-hour clock (military time) is used by hotels and stores, and for train, bus, and ferry schedules. Informally, the French use the 24-hour clock and "our clock" interchangeably—17:00 is also 5:00 *de l'après-midi* (in the afternoon).

About Time

minute	*minute*	mee-newt
hour	*heure*	ur
in the morning	*dans le matin*	dahn luh mah-tan
in the afternoon	*dans l'après-midi*	dahn lah-preh-mee-dee
in the evening	*dans le soir*	dahn luh swar
night	*nuit*	nwee
at 6:00 sharp	*à six heures précises*	ah sees ur preh-see
from 8:00 to 10:00	*de huit heures à dix heures*	duh weet ur ah dees ur
in half an hour	*dans une demie heure*	dahnz ewn duh-mee ur
in one hour	*dans une heure*	dahnz ewn ur
in three hours	*dans trois heures*	dahn twah ur
anytime	*n'importe quand*	nan-port kahn
immediately	*immédiatement*	ee-may-dee-aht-mahn
every hour	*toutes les heures*	toot layz ur
every day	*tous les jours*	too lay zhoor
last	*dernier*	dehrn-yay
this (m / f)	*ce / cette*	suh / seht
next	*prochain*	proh-shan
May 15	*le quinze mai*	luh kanz may
high season	*haute saison*	oht say-zohn
low season	*basse saison*	bahs say-zohn
in the future	*dans l'avenir*	dahn lah-vahn-eer
in the past	*dans le passé*	dahn luh pah-say

The Day

day	*jour*	zhoor
today	*aujourd'hui*	oh-zhoor-dwee
yesterday	*hier*	yehr
tomorrow	*demain*	duh-man
tomorrow morning	*demain matin*	duh-man mah-tan
day after tomorrow	*après demain*	ah-preh duh-man

The Week

week	*semaine*	suh-mehn
last week	*la semaine dernière*	lah suh-mehn dehrn-yehr
this week	*cette semaine*	seht suh-mehn
next week	*la semaine d'avance*	lah suh-mehn dah-vahns
Monday	*lundi*	luhn-dee
Tuesday	*mardi*	mar-dee
Wednesday	*mercredi*	mehr-kruh-dee
Thursday	*jeudi*	zhuh-dee
Friday	*vendredi*	vahn-druh-dee
Saturday	*samedi*	sahm-dee
Sunday	*dimanche*	dee-mahnsh

The Month

month	*mois*	mwah
January	*janvier*	zhahn-vee-yay
February	*février*	fay-vree-yay
March	*mars*	mars
April	*avril*	ahv-reel
May	*mai*	may
June	*juin*	zhwan
July	*juillet*	zhwee-yay
August	*août*	oot
September	*septembre*	sehp-tahn-bruh
October	*octobre*	ohk-toh-bruh
November	*novembre*	noh-vahn-bruh
December	*décembre*	day-sahn-bruh

COUNTING

The Year

year	*année*	ah-nay
spring	*printemps*	pra<u>n</u>-tah<u>n</u>
summer	*été*	ay-tay
fall	*automne*	oh-tuhn
winter	*hiver*	ee-vehr

Holidays and Happy Days

holiday	*jour férié*	zhoor fay-ree-ay
national holiday	*fête nationale*	feht nah-see-oh-nahl
school holiday	*vacance scolaire*	vah-kah<u>n</u>s skoh-lair
religious holiday	*fête religieuse*	feht ruh-lee-zhuhz
Independence Day (July 14)	*le quatorze juillet*	luh kah-torz zhwee-yay
Is it a holiday today / tomorrow?	*C'est un jour férié aujourd'hui / demain?*	say tuh<u>n</u> zhoor fay-ree-ay oh-zhoor-dwee / duh-ma<u>n</u>
What is the holiday?	*C'est quel jour férié?*	say kehl zhoor fay-ree-ay
Is a holiday coming up soon?	*C'est bientôt un jour férié?*	say bee-a<u>n</u>-toh uh<u>n</u> zhoor fay-ree-ay
When?	*Quand?*	kah<u>n</u>
Merry Christmas!	*Joyeux Noël!*	zhwah-yuh noh-ehl
Happy New Year!	*Bonne année!*	buhn ah-nay
Easter	*Pâques*	pahk
Happy anniversary!	*Bon anniversaire de mariage!*	boh<u>n</u> ah-nee-vehr-sair duh mah-ree-yahzh
Happy birthday!	*Bon anniversaire!*	boh<u>n</u> ah-nee-vehr-sair

The French sing "Happy Birthday" to the same tune we do. Here are the words: *Joyeux anniversaire, joyeux anniversaire, joyeux anniversaire* (fill in name), *nos voeux les plus sincères*.

Other celebrations include May 1 (Labor Day), May 8 (Liberation Day), and August 15 (Assumption of Mary). France's biggest holiday is on July 14, Bastille Day. Festivities begin on the evening of the 13th and rage throughout the country.

If a holiday falls on a Thursday, many get Friday off as well: The Friday is called *le pont*, or the bridge, between the holiday and the weekend. On school holidays (*vacances scolaires*), families head for the beach, jamming resorts.

COUNTING

TRAVELING

Flights

All airports have bilingual signage with the local language and English. Also, nearly all airport service personnel and travel agents speak English these days. Still, these words and phrases could conceivably come in handy.

Making a Reservation

I'd like to...	*Je voudrais...*	zhuh voo-dray
my reservation /	*ma réservation /*	mah ray-zehr-vah-see-oh<u>n</u> /
my ticket.	*mon billet.*	moh<u>n</u> bee-yay
We'd like to...	*Nous voudrions...*	noo voo-dree-oh<u>n</u>
our reservation /	*notre réservation /*	noh-truh ray-zehr-vah-see-
our tickets.	*nos billet.*	oh<u>n</u> / noh bee-yay
...confirm	*...confirmer*	koh<u>n</u>-feer-may
...reconfirm	*...reconfirmer*	ray-koh<u>n</u>-feer-may
...change	*...modifier*	moh-dee-fee-ay
...cancel	*...annuler*	ah-noo-lay
a seat near the	*un siège côté*	uh<u>n</u> see-ehzh koh-tay
aisle / window	*couloir / fenêtre*	kool-wahr / fuh-neh-truh

At the Airport

Which terminal?	*Quel terminal?*	kehl tehr-mee-nahl
international flights	*vols internationaux*	vohl een-tehr-nah-see-ohn-oh
domestic flights	*vols domestiques*	vohl doh-mehs-teek
arrival	*arrivée*	ah-ree-vay
departure	*départ*	day-par
baggage check	*inspection des bagages*	een-spehk-see-ohn day bah-gahzh
baggage claim	*caroussel des bagages*	kah-roo-sehl day bah-gahzh
Nothing to declare.	*Rien à déclarer.*	ree-an ah day-klah-ray
I have only carry-on luggage.	*J'ai juste un bagage en cabine.*	zhay zhoost uhn bah-gahzh ahn kah-been
flight number	*numéro de vol*	noo-mehr-oh duh vohl
departure gate	*la porte de départ*	lah port duh day-par
duty free	*hors taxe*	or tahks
luggage cart	*chariot à bagages*	shah-ree-oh ah bah-gahzh
jet lag	*décalage horaire*	day-kah-lahzh oh-rair

Getting to/from the Airport

Approximately how much is a taxi ride to...?	*C'est combien environ un taxi pour...?*	say kohn-bee-an ahn-vee-rohn uhn tahk-see poor
...downtown	*...le centre-ville*	luh sahn-truh-veel
...the train station	*...la gare*	lah gar
...the airport	*...l'aéroport*	lah-ay-roh-por
Is there a bus (or train)...?	*Il y a un bus (ou un train)...?*	eel yah uhn bews (oo uhn tran)
...from the airport to downtown	*...de l'aéroport au centre-ville*	duh lah-ay-roh-por oh sahn-truh-veel
...from downtown to the airport	*...du centre-ville à l'aéroport*	dew sahn-truh-veel ah lah-ay-roh-por

How much is it?	*C'est combien?*	say kohn-bee-an
Where does it leave from...?	*Il part d'où...?*	eel par doo
Where does it arrive...?	*Il arrive où...?*	eel ah-ree-vay oo
...at the airport	*...à l'aéroport*	ah lah-ay-roh-por
...downtown	*...au centre-ville*	oh sahn-truh-veel
How often does it run?	*Quand est-ce qu'il circule?*	kahn ehs keel seer-kewl

Trains

The Train Station

Where is...?	*Où est... ?*	oo ay
...the train station	*...la gare*	lah gar
French State Railways	*SNCF*	S N say F
train information	*renseignements SNCF*	rahn-sehn-yuh-mahn S N say F
train	*train*	tran
high-speed train	*TGV*	tay zhay vay
fast / faster	*rapide / plus rapide*	rah-peed / plew rah-peed
arrival	*arrivée*	ah-ree-vay
departure	*départ*	day-par
delay	*retard*	ruh-tar
toilet	*toilette*	twah-leht
waiting room	*salle d'attente*	sahl dah-tahnt
lockers	*consigne automatique*	kohn-seen-yuh oh-toh-mah-teek
baggage check room	*consigne de bagages*	kohn-seen-yuh duh bah-gahzh
lost and found office	*bureau des objets trouvés*	bew-roh dayz ohb-zhay troo-vay
tourist information	*office du tourisme*	oh-fees dew too-reez-muh

platform	*quai*	kay
to the platforms	*accès aux quais*	ahk-seh oh kay
track	*voie*	vwah
train car	*voiture*	vwah-tewr
dining car	*voiture*	vwah-tewr
	restaurant	rehs-toh-rah<u>n</u>
sleeper car	*voiture-lit*	vwah-tewr-lee
conductor	*conducteur*	koh<u>n</u>-dewk-tur

You'll encounter several types of trains in France. Along with the various local and milk-run trains, there are:

- the slow *Regionale* trains
- the medium-speed *Trains Express Regionaux*
- the fast *EuroCity* international trains
- the super-fast trains: *TGV* (within France and to Switzerland), *Thalys* (to BeNeLux), and *Artesia* (to Italy).

Railpasses cover travel on all of these trains, but you'll be required to pay for a reservation (about $4 per trip) on *TGV* and *Artesia* trains. On *Thalys* trains, you'll pay a Passholder Fare (about $15 second class or $30 first class) if your railpass covers all of the countries on the route you'll be taking. The Eurostar train that connects Paris with London and Brussels requires a separate ticket— a railpass can help you get a discount, but usually only if you book in advance.

Getting a Ticket

Where can I buy a ticket?	*Où puis-j'acheter un billet?*	oo pweezh ah-shuh-tay uh<u>n</u> bee-yay
A ticket to ___.	*Un billet pour ___.*	uh<u>n</u> bee-yay poor
Where can we buy tickets?	*Où pouvons-nous acheter les billets?*	oo poo-voh<u>n</u>-nooz ah-shuh-tay lay bee-yay
Two tickets to ___.	*Deux billets pour ___.*	duh bee-yay poor
Is this the line for...?	*C'est la file pour...?*	say lah feel poor
...tickets	*...les billets*	lay bee-yay

TRAVELING

English	French	Pronunciation
...reservations	...les réservations	lay ray-zehr-vah-see-ohn
How much is the fare to ___?	C'est combien pour aller à ___?	say kohn-bee-an poor ah-lay ah
Is this ticket valid for ___?	Ce billet est bon pour ___?	suh bee-yay ay bohn poor
How long is this ticket valid?	Ce billet est bon pour combien de temps?	suh bee-yay ay bohn poor kohn-bee-an duh tahn
When is the next train?	Le prochain train part á quelle heure?	luh proh-shan tran par ah kehl ur
Do you have a schedule for all trains departing for ___ today / tomorrow?	Avez-vous un horaire pour tous les trains qui partent pour ___ aujourd'hui / demain?	ah-vay-vooz uhn oh-rair poor too lay tran kee par-tahn poor ___ oh-zhoor-dwee / duh-man
I'd like to leave...	Je voudrais partir...	zhuh voo-dray par-teer
We'd like to leave...	Nous voudrions partir...	noo voo-dree-ohn par-teer
I'd like to arrive...	Je voudrais arriver...	zhuh voo-dray ah-ree-vay
We'd like to arrive...	Nous voudrions arriver...	noo voo-dree-ohn ah-ree-vay
...by ___.	...avant ___.	ah-vahn
...in the morning.	...le matin.	luh mah-tan
...in the afternoon.	...l'après-midi.	lah-preh-mee-dee
...in the evening.	...le soir.	luh swahr
Is there a...?	Il y a un...?	eel yah uhn
...earlier train	...train plus tôt	tran plew toh
...later train	...train plus tard	tran plew tar
...overnight train	...train de nuit	tran duh nwee
...cheaper train	...train moins cher	tran mwahn shehr
...cheaper option	...solution meilleure marché	soh-lew-see-ohn may-ur mar-shay
...local train	...T.E.R. (train express régional)	tay ay ehr (tran ehk-sprehs ray-zhee-oh-nahl)
...express train	...train direct	tran dee-rehkt
What track does the train leave from?	Le train part de quel voie?	luh tran par duh kel vwah
On time?	À l'heure?	ah lur
Late?	En retard?	ahn ruh-tar

KEY PHRASES: TRAINS

train station	*gare*	gar
train	*train*	tra<u>n</u>
ticket	*billet*	bee-yay
transfer (n)	*correspondance*	kor-rehs-poh<u>n</u>-dah<u>ns</u>
supplement	*supplément*	sew-play-mah<u>n</u>
arrival	*arrivée*	ah-ree-vay
departure	*départ*	day-par
platform	*quai*	kay
track	*voie*	vwah
train car	*voiture*	vwah-tewr
A ticket to ___.	*Un billet pour ___.*	uh<u>n</u> bee-yay poor
Two tickets to ___.	*Deux billets pour ___.*	duh bee-yay poor
When is the next train?	*Le prochain train part á quelle heure?*	luh proh-sha<u>n</u> tra<u>n</u> par ah kehl ur
Where does the train leave from?	*Il le train part d'où?*	eel luh tra<u>n</u> par doo
Which train to ___?	*Quel train pour ___?*	kehl tra<u>n</u> poor

Reservations, Supplements, and Discounts

Is a reservation required?	*Une réservation est obligatoire?*	ewn ray-zehr-vah-see-oh<u>n</u> ay oh-blee-gah-twahr
I'd like to reserve...	*Je voudrais réserver...*	zhuh voo-dray ray-zehr-vay
...a seat.	*...une place.*	ewn plahs
...a berth.	*...une couchette.*	ewn koo-sheht
...a sleeper.	*...un compartiment privé.*	uh<u>n</u> koh<u>n</u>-par-tuh-mah<u>n</u> pree-vay
...the entire train.	*...le train entier.*	luh tra<u>n</u> ah<u>n</u>-tee-ay
We'd like to reserve...	*Nous voudrions réserver...*	noo voo-dree-oh<u>n</u> ray-zehr-vay
...two seats.	*...deux places.*	duh plahs
...two couchettes.	*...deux couchettes.*	duh koo-sheht

...two sleepers.	...un compartiment privé pour deux personnes.	uhn kohn-par-tuh-mahn pree-vay poor duh pehr-suhn
Is there a supplement?	Il y a un supplément?	eel yah uhn sew-play-mahn
Does my railpass cover the supplement?	Le supplément est inclus dans mon pass?	luh sew-play-mahn ay an-klew dahn mohn pahs
Is there a discount for...?	Il y a une réduction pour les...?	eel yah ewn ray-dewk-see-ohn poor lay
...youth	...jeunes	zhuhn
...seniors	...gens âgés	zhahn ah-zhay
...families	...familles	fah-mee

Ticket Talk

ticket window	guichet	gee-shay
reservations window	comptoir des réservations	kohn-twahr day ray-zehr-vah-see-ohn
national	en France	ahn frahns
international	internationaux	een-tehr-nah-see-ohn-oh
ticket	billet	bee-yay
one way	aller simple	ah-lay san-pluh
round trip	aller retour	ah-lay-ruh-toor
first class	première classe	pruhm-yehr klahs
second class	deuxième classe	duhz-yehm klahs
non-smoking	non fumeur	nohn few-mur
validate	composter	kohn-poh-stay
schedule	horaire	oh-rair
departure	départ	day-par
direct	direct	dee-rehkt
transfer (n)	correspondance	kor-rehs-pohn-dahns
with supplement	avec supplément	ah-vehk sew-play-mahn
reservation	réservation	ray-zehr-vah-see-ohn
seat...	place...	plahs
...by the window	...côté fenêtre	koh-tay fuh-neh-truh
...on the aisle	...côté couloir	koh-tay kool-wahr

berth...	*couchette...*	koo-sheht
...upper	*...en haut*	ah<u>n</u> oh
...middle	*...milieu*	meel-yuh
...lower	*...en bas*	ah<u>n</u> bah
refund	*remboursement*	rah<u>n</u>-boor-suh-mah<u>n</u>
reduced fare	*tarif réduit*	tah-reef ray-dwee

Changing Trains

Is it direct?	*C'est direct?*	say dee-rehkt
Must I /	*Je dois /*	zhuh dwah /
Must we...?	*Nous devons...?*	noo duh-voh<u>n</u>
...make a transfer	*...prendre une*	prah<u>n</u>-druh ewn
	correspondance	kor-rehs-poh<u>n</u>-dah<u>n</u>s
When? / Where?	*À quelle heure? / Où?*	ah kehl ur / oo
Do I change	*Je transfère*	zhuh trah<u>n</u>s-fehr
here for ___?	*ici pour ___?*	ee-see poor
Do we change	*Nous transférons*	noo trah<u>n</u>s-fehr-oh<u>n</u>
here for ___?	*ici pour ___?*	ee-see poor
Where do I	*Où je transfère*	oo zhuh trah<u>n</u>s-fehr
change for ___?	*pour ___?*	poor
Where do we	*Où nous transférons*	oo noo trah<u>n</u>s-fehr-oh<u>n</u>
change for ___?	*pour ___?*	poor
At what time?	*À quelle heure?*	ah kehl ur
From what track	*Le train part de*	luh tra<u>n</u> par duh
does the train	*quelle voie?*	kehl vwah
leave?		
How many	*Combien de*	koh<u>n</u>-bee-a<u>n</u> duh
minutes in ___ to	*minutes à ___ pour*	mee-newt ah ___ poor
change trains?	*changer de train?*	shah<u>n</u>-zhay duh tra<u>n</u>

On the Platform

Where is...?	*Où est...?*	oo ay
Is this...?	*C'est...?*	say
...the train to ___	*...le train pour ___*	luh tra<u>n</u> poor
Which train to ___?	*Quel train pour ___?*	kehl tra<u>n</u> poor

Which train car to ___?	*Quelle voiture pour ___?*	kehl vwah-tewr poor
Where is first class?	*Où est la première classe?*	oo ay lah pruhm-yehr klahs
front	*à l'avant*	ah lah-vah<u>n</u>
middle	*au milieu*	oh meel-yuh
back	*au fond*	oh foh<u>n</u>

Arrive at the station well before your departure to find the right platform. In small towns, your train may depart before the station opens; go directly to the tracks and find the overhead sign that confirms your train stops at that track.

For security reasons, all luggage (including day packs) must carry a tag with the traveler's first and last name and current address. Free tags are available at all trains stations in France.

On the Train

Is this seat free?	*C'est libre?*	say lee-bruh
May I...?	*Je peux...?*	zhuh puh
May we...?	*Nous pouvons...?*	noo poo-voh<u>n</u>
...sit here	*...s'asseoir ici*	sah-swar ee-see
...open the window	*...ouvrir la fenêtre*	oo-vreer lah fuh-neh-truh
...eat your meal	*...manger votre repas*	mah<u>n</u>-zhay voh-truh ruh-pah
Save my place?	*Garder ma place?*	gar-day mah plahs
Save our places?	*Garder nos places?*	gar-day noh plahs
That's my seat.	*C'est ma place.*	say mah plahs
These are our seats.	*Ce sont nos places.*	suh soh<u>n</u> noh plahs
Where are you going?	*Où allez-vous?*	oo ah-lay-voo
I'm going to ___.	*Je vais à ___.*	zhuh vay ah
We're going to ___.	*Nous allons à ___.*	nooz ah-loh<u>n</u> ah
Tell me when to get off?	*Dîtes-moi quand je descends?*	deet-mwah kah<u>n</u> zhuh day-sah<u>n</u>
Tell us when to get off?	*Dîtes-nous quand on descend?*	deet-noo kah<u>n</u> ohn day-sah<u>n</u>

Where is a (good-looking) conductor?	*Où est un (beau) conducteur?*	oo ay uh<u>n</u> (boh) koh<u>n</u>-dewk-tur
Does this train stop in ___?	*Ce train s'arrête à ___?*	suh tra<u>n</u> sah-reht ah
When will it arrive in ___?	*Il va arriver à ___ à quelle heure?*	eel vah ah-ree-vay ah ___ ah kehl ur
When will it arrive?	*Il va arriver à quelle heure?*	eel vah ah-ree-vay ah kehl ur

Major Rail Lines in France

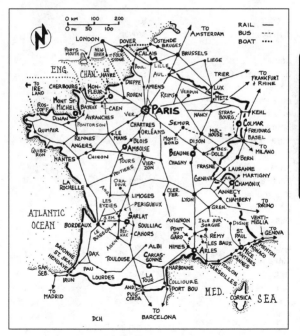

Reading Train and Bus Schedules

French schedules use the 24-hour clock. It's like American time until noon. After that, subtract twelve and add p.m. So, 13:00 is 1 p.m., 20:00 is 8 p.m., and 24:00 is midnight. One minute after midnight is 00:01.

Train schedules show blue (quiet), white (normal), and red (peak and holiday) times. You can save money if you get the blues (travel during off-peak hours).

à, pour	to
arrivée	arrival
de	from
départ	departure
dimanche	Sunday
en retard	late
en semaine	workdays (Monday-Saturday)
et	and
heure	hour
horaire	timetable
jour férié	holiday
jours	days
jusqu'à	until
la semaine	weekdays
par	via
pas	not
samedi	Saturday
sauf	except
seulement	only
tous	every
tous les jours	daily
vacances	holidays
voie	track
1–5	Monday–Friday
6, 7	Saturday, Sunday

Going Places

France	la France	lah frah<u>ns</u>
Belgium	la Belgique	lah behl-zheek
English Channel	la Manche	lah mah<u>ns</u>h
Austria	l'Autriche	loh-treesh
Czech Republic	la République Tcheque	lah reh-poob-leek chehk
Great Britain	la Grande-Bretagne	lah grah<u>n</u> breh-tahn-yuh
Germany	l'Allemagne	lahl-mahn-yuh
Greece	la Grèce	lah grehs
Ireland	l'Irlande	leer-lahnd
Italy	l'Italie	lee-tah-lee
Netherlands	les Pays-Bas	lay peh-ee-bah
Portugal	le Portugal	luh por-tew-gal
Scandinavia	la Scandinavie	lah skah<u>n</u>-dee-nah-vee
Spain	l'Espagne	luh-spahn-yuh
Switzerland	la Suisse	lah swees
Turkey	la Turquie	lah tehr-kee
Europe	l'Europe	lur-rohp
EU	UE	ew uh
(European	(l'Union	(lewn-yoh<u>n</u>
Union)	Européenne)	ur-oh-pay-ehn)
Russia	la Russie	lah roo-see
Africa	l'Afrique	laf-reek
United States	les États-Unis	layz ay-tah-zew-nee
Canada	le Canada	luh kah-nah-dah
world	le monde	luh moh<u>n</u>d

Places Within France

If you're using the *Rick Steves' France* guidebook, here are more place names you'll recognize. When French clerks at train stations and train conductors don't understand your pronunciation, write the town name on a piece of paper.

Alsace	ahl-sahs
Amboise	ahm-bwahz
Annecy	ah<u>n</u>-see

TRAVELING

Antibes	ahn-teeb
Arles	arl
Arromanches	ah-roh-mahnsh
Avignon	ah-veen-yohn
Bayeux	bah-yuh
Beaune	bohn
Beynac	bay-nak
Bordeaux	bor-doh
Calais	kah-lay
Carcassonne	kar-kah-suhn
Chambord	shahn-bor
Chamonix	shah-moh-nee
Chartres	shart
Chenonceau	shuh-nohn-soh
Cherbourg	shehr-boor
Chinon	shee-nohn
Collioure	kohl-yoor
Colmar	kohl-mar
Côte d'Azur	koht dah-zewr
Dijon	dee-zhohn
Dordogne	dor-dohn-yuh
Giverny	zhee-vehr-nee
Grenoble	gruh-noh-bluh
Honfleur	ohn-floor
Le Havre	luh hah-vruh
Loire	lwar
Lyon	lee-ohn
Marseille	mar-say
Mont Blanc	mohn blahn
Mont St. Michel	mohn san mee-shehl
Nantes	nahnt
Nice	nees
Normandy	nor-mahn-dee
Paris	pah-ree
Provence	proh-vahns
Reims	rans (rhymes with France)

Rouen		roo-ah<u>n</u>
Roussillon		roo-see-yoh<u>n</u>
Sarlat		sar-lah
Strasbourg		strahs-boorg
Verdun		vehr-duh<u>n</u>
Versailles		vehr-sī
Villefranche		veel-frah<u>n</u>sh

Buses and Subways

At the Bus Station or Métro Stop

ticket	*ticket*	tee-kay
city bus	*bus*	bews
long-distance bus	*car*	kar
bus stop	*arrêt de bus*	ah-reh duh bews
bus station	*gare routière*	gar root-yehr
subway	*Métro*	may-troh
subway station	*station de Métro*	stah-see-oh<u>n</u> duh may-troh
subway map	*plan du Métro*	plah<u>n</u> dew may-troh
subway entrance	*l'entrée du Métro*	lah<u>n</u>-tray dew may-troh
subway stop	*arrêt de Métro*	ah-reh duh may-troh
subway exit	*sortie*	sor-tee
direct	*direct*	dee-rehkt
connection	*correspondance*	kor-rehs-poh<u>n</u>-dah<u>n</u>s
pickpocket	*voleur*	voh-loor
batch of 10 tickets	*carnet*	kar-nay

In Paris, you'll save money by buying a *carnet* (batch of 10 tickets) at virtually any Métro station. The tickets, which are sharable, are valid on the buses, Métro, and R.E.R. (underground rail lines) within the city limits.

Taking Buses and Subways

How do I get to ___?	*Comment je vais à ___?*	koh-mah<u>n</u> zhuh vay ah
How do we get to ___?	*Comment nous allons à ___?*	koh-mah<u>n</u> nooz ah-loh<u>n</u> ah
How much is a ticket?	*C'est combien le ticket?*	say koh<u>n</u>-bee-a<u>n</u> luh tee-kay
Where can I buy a ticket?	*Où puis-je acheter un ticket?*	oo pwee-zhuh ah-shuh-tay uh<u>n</u> tee-kay
Where can we buy tickets?	*Où pouvons-nous acheter les tickets?*	oo poo-voh<u>n</u>-noo ah-shuh-tay lay tee-kay
One ticket, please.	*Un billet, s'il vous plaît.*	uh<u>n</u> bee-yay see voo play
Two tickets.	*Deux billets.*	duh bee-yay
Is this ticket valid (for ___)?	*Ce ticket est bon (pour ___)?*	suh tee-kay ay boh<u>n</u> (poor)
Is there...?	*Il y a...?*	eel yah
...a one-day pass	*...un pass à la journée*	uh<u>n</u> pahs ah lah zhoor-nay
...a discount if I buy more tickets	*...une réduction si j'achet plusieurs tickets*	ewn ray-dewk-see-oh<u>n</u> see zhah-shay plewz-yur tee-kay
Which bus to ___?	*Quel bus pour ___?*	kehl bews poor
Does it stop at ___?	*Il s'arrête à ___?*	eel sah-reht ah
Which bus stop for ___?	*Quel arrêt pour ___?*	kehl ah-reh poor
Which subway stop for ___?	*Quel arrêt de Métro pour ___?*	kehl ah-reh duh may-troh poor
Which direction for ___?	*Quelle direction pour ___?*	kehl dee-rehk-see-oh<u>n</u> poor

Must I /	*Je dois /*	zhuh dwah /
Must we...?	*Nous devons...?*	noo duh-voh<u>n</u>
...transfer	*...prendre une correspondance*	prah<u>n</u>-druh ewn kor-rehs-poh<u>n</u>-dah<u>n</u>s
When does the... leave?	*Le... part quand?*	luh... par kah<u>n</u>
...first / next / last	*...premier / prochain / dernier*	pruhm-yay / proh-sha<u>n</u> / dehrn-yay
...bus / subway	*...bus / Métro*	bews / may-troh
What's the frequency per hour / day?	*Combien de fois par heure / jour?*	koh<u>n</u>-bee-a<u>n</u> duh fwah par ur / zhoor
Where does it leave from?	*D'où il part?*	doo eel par
What time does it leave?	*Il part à quelle heure?*	eel par ah kehl ur
I'm going to ___.	*Je vais à ___.*	zhuh vay ah
We're going to ___.	*Nous allons à ___.*	nooz ah-loh<u>n</u> ah
Tell me when to get off?	*Dîtes-moi quand je descends?*	deet-mwah kah<u>n</u> zhuh day-sah<u>n</u>
Tell us when to get off?	*Dîtes-nous quand on descend?*	deet-noo kah<u>n</u> oh<u>n</u> day-sah<u>n</u>

TRAVELING

KEY PHRASES: BUSES AND SUBWAYS

bus	*bus*	bews
subway	*Métro*	may-troh
ticket	*ticket*	tee-kay
How do I get to ___?	*Comment je vais à ___?*	koh-mah<u>n</u> zhuh vay ah
Which stop for ___?	*Quel arrêt pour ___?*	kehl ah-reh poor
Tell me when to get off?	*Dîtes-moi quand je descends?*	deet-mwah kah<u>n</u> zhuh day-sah<u>n</u>

Taxis

Getting a Taxi

Taxi!	*Taxi!*	tahk-see
Can you call a taxi?	*Pouvez-vous appeler un taxi?*	poo-vay-voo ah-puh-lay uhn tahk-see
Where is a taxi stand?	*Où est une station de taxi?*	oo ay ewn stah-see-ohn duh tahk-see
Where can I get a taxi?	*Où puis-je trouver un taxi?*	oo pwee-zhuh troo-vay uhn tahk-see
Where can we get a taxi?	*Où pouvons-nous trouver un taxi?*	oo poo-vohn-noo troo-vay uhn tahk-see
Are you free?	*Vous êtes libre?*	vooz eht lee-bruh
Occupied.	*Occupé.*	oh-kew-pay
To ___ , please.	*À ___ , s'il vous plaît.*	ah ___ see voo play
To this address.	*À cette adresse.*	ah seht ah-drehs
Take me to ___.	*Amenez-moi à ___.*	ah-muh-nay-mwah ah
Take us to ___.	*Amenez-nous à ___.*	ah-muh-nay-nooz ah
Approximately how much will it cost to go...?	*C'est environ combien d'aller...?*	say ahn-vee-rohn kohn-bee-an dah-lay
...to ___	*...à ___*	ah
...to the airport	*...à l'aéroport*	ah lah-ay-roh-por
...to the train station	*...à la gare*	ah lah gar
...to this address	*...à cette adresse*	ah seht ah-drehs
Any extra supplement?	*Il y a un supplément?*	eel yah uhn sew-play-mahn

TRAVELING

KEY PHRASES: TAXIS

Taxi!	*Taxi!*	tahk-see
Are you free?	*Vous êtes libre?*	vooz eht lee-bruh
To ___ , please.	*À ___ , s'il vous plaît.*	ah ___ see voo play
meter	*compteur*	kohn-tur
Stop here.	*Arrêtez-vous ici.*	ah-reh-tay-voo ee-see
Keep the change.	*Gardez la monnaie.*	gar-day lah moh-nay

It's too much.	C'est trop.	say troh
Can you take ___ people?	Pouvez-vous prendre ___ passagers?	poo-vay-voo prahn-druh ___ pah-sah-zhay
Any extra fee?	Il y a d'autres frais?	eel yah doh-truh fray
Do you have an hourly rate?	Avez-vous un taux par heure?	ah-vay-vooz uhn toh par ur
How much for a one-hour city tour?	Combien pour une visite d'une heure en ville?	kohn-bee-an poor ewn vee-zeet dewn ur ahn veel

So you'll know what to expect, ask your hotelier about typical taxi fares. Fares go up at night (7:00 p.m. to 7:00 a.m.) and on Sundays, and drivers always charge for loading baggage in the trunk. Your fare can nearly double if you're taking a short trip with lots of bags. In smaller towns, cabbies are few and customer satisfaction is important. Strike up a conversation and make a new friend.

If you're having a tough time hailing a taxi, ask for the nearest taxi stand (*station de taxi*). The simplest way to tell a cabbie where you want to go is by stating your destination followed by "please" (*"Louvre, s'il vous plaît"*). Tipping isn't expected, but it's polite to round up. So if the fare is €19, round up to €20.

In the Taxi

The meter, please.	Le compteur, s'il vous plaît.	luh kohn-tur see voo play
Where is the meter?	Où est le compteur?	oo ay luh kohn-tur
I'm in a hurry.	Je suis pressé.	zhuh swee preh-say
We're in a hurry.	Nous sommes pressés.	noo suhm preh-say
Slow down.	Ralentissez.	rah-lahn-tee-say
If you don't slow down, I'll throw up.	Si vous ne ralentissez pas, je vais vomir.	see voo nuh rah-lahn-tee-say pah, zhuh vay voh-meer

Left / Right / Straight.	À gauche / À droite / Tout droit.	ah gohsh / ah dwaht / too dwah
I'd like to stop here for a moment.	J'aimerais m'arrêter ici un moment.	zhehm-uh-ray mah-reh-tay ee-see uhn moh-mahn
We'd like to stop here for a moment.	Nous aimerions nous arrêter ici un moment.	nooz ehm-uh-rohn nooz ah-reh-tay ee-see uhn moh-mahn
Please stop here for ___ minutes.	S'il vous plaît arrêtez-vous ici pour ___ minutes.	see voo play ah-reh-tay-voo ee-see poor ___ mee-newt
Can you wait?	Pouvez-vous attendre?	poo-vay vooz ah-tahn-druh
Crazy traffic, isn't it?	C'est fou, cette circulation, non?	say foo seht seer-kewl-ah-see-ohn nohn
You drive like ...	Vous conduisez comme...	voo kohn-dwee-zay kohm
...a madman!	...un fou!	uhn foo
...Michael Schumacher.	...Michael Schumacher.	"Michael Shumacher"
You drive very well.	Vous conduisez très bien.	voo kohn-dwee-zay treh bee-an
Where did you learn to drive?	Où avez-vous appris à conduire?	oo ah-vay-vooz ah-preez ah kohn-dwee
Stop here.	Arrêtez-vous ici.	ah-reh-tay-voo ee-see
Here is fine.	Ici c'est bien.	ee-see say bee-an
At this corner.	À ce coin.	ah say kwan
The next corner.	Au coin prochain.	oh kwan proh-shan
My change, please.	La monnaie, s'il vous plaît.	lah moh-nay see voo play
Keep the change.	Gardez la monnaie.	gar-day lah moh-nay
This ride is / was more fun than Disneyland.	Ce trajet est / était plus drôle que Disneyland.	suh trah-zhay ay / ay-tay plew drohl kuh "Disneyland"

Driving

Rental Wheels

car rental agency	*agence de location de voiture*	ah-zhah<u>n</u>s duh loh-kah-see-oh<u>n</u> duh vwah-tewr
I'd like to rent...	*Je voudrais louer...*	zhuh voo-dray loo-ay
We'd like to rent...	*Nous voudrions louer...*	noo voo-dree-oh<u>n</u> loo-ay
...a car.	*...une voiture.*	ewn vwah-tewr
...a station wagon.	*...un break.*	uh<u>n</u> brayk
...a van.	*...un van.*	uh<u>n</u> vah<u>n</u>
...a motorcycle.	*...une motocyclette.*	ewn moh-toh-see-kleht
...a motor scooter.	*...un vélomoteur.*	uh<u>n</u> vay-loh-moh-tur
...the Concorde.	*...le Concorde.*	luh koh<u>n</u>-kord
How much per...?	*Combien par...?*	koh<u>n</u>-bee-a<u>n</u> par
...hour	*...heure*	ur
...half day	*...demie-journée*	duh-mee zhoor-nay
...day	*...jour*	zhoor
...week	*...semaine*	suh-mehn
Unlimited mileage?	*Kilométrage illimité?*	kee-loh-may-trahzh eel-lee-mee-tay

---

KEY PHRASES: DRIVING

car	*voiture*	vwah-tewr
gas station	*station service*	stah-see-oh<u>n</u> sehr-vees
parking lot	*parking*	par-keeng
accident	*accident*	ahk-see-dah<u>n</u>
left / right	*à gauche / à droite*	ah gohsh / ah dwaht
straight ahead	*tout droit*	too dwah
downtown	*centre-ville*	sah<u>n</u>-truh-veel
How do I get to ___?	*Comment je vais à ___?*	koh-mah<u>n</u> zhuh vay ah
Where can I park?	*Où puis-je me garer?*	oo pwee-zhuh muh gah-ray

When must I bring it back?	Je dois le ramener à quelle heure?	zhuh dwah luh rah-muh-nay ah kehl ur
Is there...?	Est-ce qu'il y a...?	ehs keel yah
...a helmet	...un casque	uhn kahsk
...a discount	...une réduction	ewn ray-dewk-see-ohn
...a deposit	...une caution	ewn koh-see-ohn
...insurance	...une assurance	ewn ah-sewr-rahns

At the Gas Station

gas station	station service	stah-see-ohn sehr-vees
The nearest gas station?	La plus proche station service?	lah plew prohsh stah-see-ohn sehr-vees
Self-service?	Libre service?	lee-bruh sehr-vees
Fill the tank.	Faites le plein.	feht luh plan
Wash the windows.	Lavez le pare-brise.	lah-vay luh pah-ruh-breez
I need...	Il me faut...	eel muh foh
We need...	Il nous faut...	eel noo foh
...gas.	...de l'essence.	duh leh-sahns
...unleaded.	...sans plomb.	sahn plohn
...regular.	...normale.	nor-mahl
...super.	...du super.	dew sew-pehr
...diesel.	...gazoil.	gah-zoyl
Check...	Vérifiez...	vay-ree-fee-ay
...the oil.	...l'huile.	lweel
...the air in the tires.	...la pression dans les pneus.	lah pruh-see-ohn dahn lay puh-nuh
...the radiator.	...le radiateur.	luh rahd-yah-tur
...the battery.	...la batterie.	lah bah-tuh-ree
...the sparkplugs.	...les bougies.	lay boo-zhee
...the headlights.	...les phares.	lay fahr
...the tail lights.	...les feux arrières.	lay fuh ah-ree-ehr
...the directional signal.	...le clignotant.	luh klee-noh-tahn
...the brakes.	...les freins.	lay fran
...the transmission fluid.	...la liquide de transmission.	lah lee-keed duh trahnz-mee-see-ohn

TRAVELING

...the windshield wipers.	...les essuie-glaces.	layz ehs-wee-glahs
...the fuses.	...les fusibles.	lay few-zee-bluh
...the fanbelt.	...la courroie du ventilateur.	lah koor-wah dew vahn-tee-lah-tur
...my pulse.	...mon poul.	mohn pool
...my husband / my wife.	...mon mari / ma femme.	mohn mah-ree / mah fahm

The cheapest gas in France is sold in *hypermarché* (supermarket) parking lots. Euros and liters replace dollars and gallons. If a euro is equal to a dollar and there are about four liters in a gallon, gas costing €1 per liter = $4 per gallon.

Car Trouble

accident	accident	ahk-see-dahn
breakdown	en panne	ahn pahn
dead battery	batterie morte	bah-tuh-ree mort
funny noise	bruit curieux	brwee kew-ree-uh
electrical problem	problème d'électricité	proh-blehm day-lehk-tree-see-tay
flat tire	pneu crevé	puh-nuh kruh-vay
shop with auto parts	magasin de pièces detachées auto	mah-gah-zan duh pee-ehs duh-tah-shay oh-toh
dealership	concessionaire	kohn-seh-see-oh-nair
My car won't start.	Ma voiture ne démarre pas.	mah vwah-tewr nuh day-mar pah
My car is broken.	Ma voiture est cassée.	mah vwah-tewr ay cah-say
This doesn't work.	Ça ne marche pas.	sah nuh marsh pah
It's overheating.	Le moteur surchauffe.	luh moh-tur sewr-shohf
It's a lemon (rattletrap).	C'est un tas de féraille.	say uhn tah duh fay-ray-yī
I need...	J'ai besoin...	zhay buh-swan
We need...	Nous avons besoin...	nooz ah-vohn buh-swan
...a tow truck.	...d'un dépanneur.	duhn day-pah-nur

| ...a mechanic. | ...d'un mécanicien. | duhn may-kah-nee-see-an |
| ...a stiff drink. | ...d'un bon coup à boire. | duhn bohn koo ah bwahr |

In France, people with car problems go to the dealership. If you're renting a troubled Renault, your rental agency may direct you to the nearest *concessionaire Renault.* For help with repair, look up "Repair" in the Services chapter.

Parking

parking lot	*parking*	par-keeng
parking garage	*garage de stationement*	gah-rahzh duh stah-see-ohn-mahn
parking meter	*horodateur*	oh-roh-dah-tur
Where can I park?	*Où puis-je me garer?*	oo pwee-zhuh muh gah-ray
Is parking nearby?	*Il y a un parking près d'ici?*	eel yah uhn par-keeng preh dee-see
Can I park here?	*Je peux me garer ici?*	zhuh puh muh gah-ray ee-see
Is this a safe place to park?	*C'est prudent de se garer ici?*	say prew-dahn duh suh gah-ray ee-see
How long can I park here?	*Je peux me garer ici pour combien de temps?*	zhuh puh muh gah-ray ee-see poor kohn-bee-an duh tahn
Must I pay to park here?	*Je dois payer pour me garer ici?*	zhuh dwah pay-yay poor muh gah-ray ee-see
How much per hour / day?	*Combien heure / jour?*	kohn-bee-an par ur / zhoor

Many French cities use remote meters for curbside parking. After you park, look for a meter at the street corner and buy a ticket to place on the dash. If you're not certain you need a ticket, look at the dashboards of cars parked nearby. If they have tickets, you'll need one, too. Ask a local for help finding the *horodateur* (parking meter).

TRAVELING

Finding
Your Way

I am going to ___.	Je vais à ___.	zhuh vay ah
We are going to ___.	Nous allons à ___.	nooz ah-lohn ah
How do I get to ___?	Comment je vais à ___?	koh-mahn zhuh vay ah
How do we get to ___?	Comment nous allons à ___?	koh-mahn nooz ah-lohn ah
Do you have...?	Avez-vous...?	ah-vay-vooz
...a city map	...un plan de la ville	uhn plahn duh lah veel
...a road map	...une carte routière	ewn kart root-yehr
How many minutes...?	Combien de minutes...?	kohn-bee-an duh mee-newt
How many hours...?	Combien d'heures...?	kohn-bee-an dur
...on foot	...à pied	ah pee-yay
...by bicycle	...à bicyclette	ah bee-see-kleht
...by car	...en voiture	ahn vwah-tewr
How many kilometers to ___?	Combien de kilomètres à ___?	kohn-bee-an duh kee-loh-meh-truh ah
What's the...	Quelle est la...	kehl eh lah...
route to Paris?	route pour Paris?	root poor pah-ree
...most scenic	...plus belle	plew behl
...fastest	...plus directe	plew dee-rehkt
...most interesting	...plus intéressante	plewz an-tay-reh-sahnt
Point it out?	Montrez-moi?	mohn-tray mwah
I'm lost.	Je suis perdu.	zhuh swee pehr-dew
We're lost.	Nous sommes perdu.	noo suhm pehr-dew
Where am I?	Où suis-je?	oo swee-zhuh
Where is...?	Où est...?	oo ay
The nearest...?	Le plus proche...?	luh plew prohsh
Where is this address?	Où se trouve cette adresse?	oo suh troov seht ah-drehs

Route-Finding Words

city map	*plan de la ville*	plah<u>n</u> duh lah veel
road map	*carte routière*	kart root-yehr
downtown	*centre-ville*	sah<u>n</u>-truh-veel
left	*à gauche*	ah gohsh
right	*à droite*	ah dwaht
straight ahead	*tout droit*	too dwah
first	*premier*	pruhm-yay
next	*prochain*	proh-sha<u>n</u>
intersection	*carrefour*	kar-foor
corner	*au coin*	oh kwa<u>n</u>
block	*paté de maisons*	pah-tay duh may-zoh<u>n</u>
roundabout	*rondpoint*	roh<u>n</u>-pwa<u>n</u>
ring road	*rocade*	roh-kahd
stoplight	*feu*	fuh
square	*place*	plahs
street	*rue*	rew
bridge	*pont*	poh<u>n</u>
tunnel	*tunnel*	tew-nehl
highway	*grande route*	grah<u>n</u>d root
national highway	*route nationale*	root nah-see-oh-nahl
freeway	*autoroute*	oh-toh-root
north	*nord*	nor
south	*sud*	sewd
east	*est*	ehs
west	*ouest*	wehs

TRAVELING

The shortest distance between any two points in
France is the *autoroute,* but the tolls add up. You'll
travel cheaper, but slower, on a *route nationale.* Along
the *autoroute,* electronic signs flash messages to let you
know what's ahead: *bouchon* (traffic jam), *circulation*
(traffic), and *fluide* (no traffic).

The Police

As in any country, the flashing lights of a patrol car are a sure sign that someone's in trouble. If it's you, try this handy phrase: *"Pardon, je suis touriste"* (Sorry, I'm a tourist). Or, for the adventurous: *"Si vous n'aimez pas ma conduite, vous n'avez que descendre du trottoir."* (If you don't like how I drive, get off the sidewalk.)

I'm late for my tour.	*Je suis en retard pour mon tour.*	zhuh swee ah<u>n</u> ruh-tar poor moh<u>n</u> toor
Can I buy your hat?	*Je peux acheter votre chapeau?*	zhuh puh ah-shuh-tay voh-truh shah-poh
What seems to be the problem?	*Quel est le problème?*	kehl ay luh proh-blehm
Sorry, I'm a tourist.	*Pardon, je suis touriste.*	par-doh<u>n</u> zhuh swee too-reest

Reading Road Signs

attention travaux	workers ahead
autres directions (follow when leaving a town)	other directions
céder le passage	yield
centre-ville	to the center of town
déviation	detour
entrée	entrance
péage	toll
prochaine sortie	next exit
ralentir	slow down
réservé aux piétons	pedestrians only
sans issue	dead end
sauf riverains	local access only
sens unique	one-way street
sortie	exit
stationnement interdit	no parking
stop	stop

toutes directions	all directions
(follow when leaving a town)	
travaux	construction
virages	curves

Other Signs You May See

à louer	for rent or for hire
à vendre	for sale
chambre libre	vacancy
chien méchant	mean dog
complet	no vacancy
dames	women
danger	danger
défense de fumer	no smoking
défense de toucher	do not touch
défense d'entrer	keep out
eau non potable	undrinkable water
entrée libre	free admission
entrée interdite	no entry
en panne	out of service
fermé	closed
fermé pour restauration	closed for restoration
fermeture annuelle	closed for vacation
guichet	ticket window
hommes	men
hors service	out of service
interdit	forbidden
occupé	occupied
ouvert	open
ouvert de... à...	open from... to...
poussez / tirez	push / pull
prudence	caution
solde	sale
sortie de secours	emergency exit
tirez / poussez	pull / push
toilettes	toilets
WC	toilet

TRAVELING

Standard Road Signs

AND LEARN THESE ROAD SIGNS

Speed Limit (km/hr)

Yield

No Passing

End of No Passing Zone

One Way

Intersection

Main Road

Freeway

Danger

No Entry

No Entry for Cars

All Vehicles Prohibited

Parking

No Parking

Customs

Peace

SLEEPING

Places to Stay

hotel	*hôtel*	oh-tehl
small hotel	*pension*	pah<u>n</u>-see-oh<u>n</u>
small hotel with restaurant	*auberge*	ow-behrzh
castle hotel	*hôtel-château*	oh-tehl-shah-toh
room in a private home	*chambre d'hôte*	shah<u>n</u>-bruh doht
youth hostel	*auberge de jeunesse*	oh-behrzh duh zhuh-nehs
country home rental	*gîte*	zheet
vacancy	*chambre libre*	shah<u>n</u>-bruh lee-bruh
no vacancy	*complet*	koh<u>n</u>-play

Reserving a Room

I like to reserve rooms a few days in advance as I travel. But if my itinerary is set, I reserve before I leave home. To reserve from the U.S. by fax or e-mail, use the handy form in the appendix (online at www.ricksteves.com/reservation).

KEY PHRASES: SLEEPING

I want to make / confirm a reservation.	*Je veux faire / confirmer une réservation.*	zhuh vuh fair / kohn-feer-may ewn ray-zehr-vah-see-ohn
I'd like a room (for two people), please.	*Je voudrais une chambre (pour deux personnes) s'il vous plaît.*	zhuh voo-dray ewn shahn-bruh (poor duh pehr-suhn) see voo play
...with / without / and	*...avec / sans / et*	ah-vehk / sahn / ay
...toilet	*...WC*	vay say
...shower	*...douche*	doosh
Can I see the room?	*Je peux voir la chambre?*	zhuh puh vwar lah shahn-bruh
How much is it?	*Combien?*	kohn-bee-an
Credit card O.K.?	*Carte de crédit O.K.?*	kart duh kray-dee "O.K."

Hello.	*Bonjour.*	bohn-zhoor
Do you speak English?	*Parlez-vous anglais?*	par-lay-voo ahn-glay
Do you have a room...?	*Avez-vous une chambre...?*	ah-vay-vooz ewn shahn-bruh
...for one person	*...pour une personne*	poor ewn pehr-suhn
...for two people	*...pour deux personnes*	poor duh pehr-suhn
...for tonight	*...pour ce soir*	poor suh swar
...for two nights	*...pour deux nuits*	poor duh nwee
...for this Friday	*...pour ce vendredi*	poor suh vahn-druh-dee
...for June 21	*...pour le vingt et un juin*	poor luh vant ay uhn zhwan
Yes or no?	*Oui ou non?*	wee oo nohn
I'd like...	*Je voudrais...*	zhuh voo-dray
We'd like...	*Nous voudrions...*	noo voo-dree-ohn
...a private bathroom.	*...une salle de bains.*	ewn sahl duh ban
...your cheapest room.	*...la chambre la moins chère.*	lah shahn-bruh lah mwan shehr

SLEEPING

...___ beds for ___ people in ___ rooms.	...___ lits par ___ personnes dans ___ chambres.	___ lee par ___ pehr-suhn dahn ___ shahn-bruh
How much is it?	Combien?	kohn-bee-an
Anything cheaper?	Rien de moins cher?	ree-an duh mwan shehr
I'll take it.	Je la prends.	zhuh lah prahn
My name is ___.	Je m'appelle ___.	zhuh mah-pehl
I'll stay...	Je reste...	zhuh rehst
We'll stay...	Nous restons...	noo rehs-tohn
...one night.	...une nuit.	ewn nwee
...___ nights.	...___ nuits.	___ nwee
I'll come...	J'arrive...	zhah-reev
We'll come...	Nous arrivons...	nooz ah-ree-vohn
...in the morning.	...dans la matinée.	dahn lah mah-tee-nay
...in the afternoon.	...dans l'après-midi.	dahn lah-preh-mee-dee
...in the evening.	...dans la soirée.	dahn lah swah-ray
...in one hour.	...dans une heure.	dahnz ewn ur
...before 4:00 in the afternoon.	...avant quatre heures dans l'après-midi.	ah-vahn kah-truh ur dahn lah-preh-mee-dee
...Friday before 6 p.m.	...vendredi avant six heures du soir.	vahn-druh-dee ah-vahn seez ur dew swar
Thank you.	Merci.	mehr-see

L'Alphabet

If phoning, you can use the code alphabet below to spell out your name if necessary. Unless you're giving the hotelier your name as it appears on your credit card, consider using a shorter version of your name to make things easier.

a	ah	Anatole	ahn-ah-tohl
b	bay	Berthe	behrt
c	say	Célestin	say-luh-steen
d	day	Désiré	day-zee-ray
e	uh	Emile	eh-meel
f	"f"	François	frahn-swah
g	zhay	Gaston	gah-stohn

h	ahsh	Henri	ahn-ree
i	ee	Irma	eer-mah
j	zhee	Joseph	zhoh-zuhf
k	kah	Kléber	klay-behr
l	"l"	Louis	loo-ee
m	"m"	Marcel	mar-sehl
n	"n"	Nicolas	nee-koh-lahs
o	"o"	Oscar	ohs-kar
p	pay	Pierre	pee-yehr
q	kew	Quintal	kween-tahl
r	ehr	Raoul	rah-ool
s	"s"	Suzanne	soo-zahn
t	tay	Thérèse	tay-rehs
u	ew	Ursule	oor-sool
v	vay	Victor	veek-tor
w	doo-bluh vay	William	weel-yahm
x	"x"	Xavier	zhahv-yehr
y	ee grehk	Yvonne	ee-vuhn
z	zehd	Zoé	zoh-ay

Using a Credit Card

If you need to secure your reservation with a credit card, here's the lingo.

Is a deposit required?	*Je dois verser un accompte?*	zhuh dwah vehr-say uhn ah-kohnt
Credit card O.K.?	*Carte de crédit O.K.?*	kart duh kray-dee "O.K."
credit card	*carte de crédit*	kart duh kray-dee
debit card	*carte bancaire*	kart bahn-kair
The name on the card is ___.	*Le nom sur la carte est ___.*	luh nohn sewr lah kart ay
The credit card number is...	*Le numéro de carte de crédit est...*	luh noo-mehr-oh duh kart duh kray-dee ay
0	*zéro*	zay-roh
1	*un*	uhn
2	*deux*	duh
3	*trois*	twah

4	*quatre*	kah-truh
5	*cinq*	sank
6	*six*	sees
7	*sept*	seht
8	*huit*	weet
9	*neuf*	nuhf
The expiration date is...	*La date d'expiration est...*	lah daht dehks-pee-rah-see-ohn ay
January	*janvier*	zhahn-vee-yay
February	*février*	fay-vree-yay
March	*mars*	mars
April	*avril*	ahv-reel
May	*mai*	may
June	*juin*	zhwan
July	*juillet*	zhwee-yay
August	*août*	oot
September	*septembre*	sehp-tahn-bruh
October	*octobre*	ohk-toh-bruh
November	*novembre*	noh-vahn-bruh
December	*décembre*	day-sahn-bruh
2003	*deux mille trois*	duh meel twah
2004	*deux mille quatre*	duh meel kah-truh
2005	*deux mille cinq*	duh meel sank
2006	*deux mille six*	duh meel sees
2007	*deux mille sept*	duh meel seht
2008	*deux mille huit*	duh meel weet
2009	*deux mille neuf*	duh meel nuhf
2010	*deux mille dix*	duh meel dees
Can I reserve with a credit card and pay in cash?	*Je peux réserver avec une carte de crédit et payer en liquide?*	zhuh puh ray-zehr-vay ah-vehk ewn kart duh kray-dee ay pay-yay ahn lee-keed
I have another card.	*J'ai une autre carte.*	zhay ewn oh-truh kart

If your *carte de crédit* is not approved, say, "*J'ai une autre carte*" (I have another card)—if you do.

Just the Fax, Ma'am

If you're booking a room by fax...

I want to send a fax.	J'aimerais vous envoyer un fax.	zhehm-uh-ray vooz ahn-voy-ay uhn fahks
What is your fax number?	Quel est votre numéro de fax?	kehl ay voh-truh noo-mehr-oh duh fahks
Your fax number is not working.	Votre numéro de fax ne marche pas.	voh-truh noo-mehr-oh duh fahks nuh marsh pah
Please turn on your fax machine.	Vous pourriez brancher votre fax, s'il vous plaît.	voo poor-yay brahn-shay voh-truh fahks see voo play

Getting Specific

I'd like a room...	Je voudrais une chambre...	zhuh voo-dray ewn shahn-bruh
We'd like a room...	Nous voudrions une chambre...	noo voo-dree-ohn ewn shahn-bruh
...with / without / and	...avec / sans / et	ah-vehk / sahn / ay
...toilet	...WC	vay say
...shower	...douche	doosh
...sink and toilet	...cabinet de toilette	kah-bee-nay duh twah-leht
...shower and toilet	...salle d'eau	sahl doh
...shower down the hall	...douche sur le palier	doosh sewr luh pahl-yay
...bathtub and toilet	...salle de bains	sahl duh ban
...double bed	...grand lit	grahn lee
...twin beds	...deux petits lits, lits jumeaux	duh puh-tee lee, lee zhew-moh
...balcony	...balcon	bahl-kohn
...view	...vue	vew
...only a sink	...lavabo seulement	lah-vah-boh suhl-mahn
...on the ground floor	...au rez-de-chaussée	oh ray-duh-shoh-say
...television	...télévision	tay-lay-vee-zee-ohn

...telephone	...téléphone	tay-lay-fohn
...air conditioning	...climatisation	klee-mah-tee-zah-see-ohn
...kitchenette	...kitchenette	keet-chehn-eht
Is there an elevator?	Il y a un ascenseur?	eel-yah uhn ah-sahn-sur
Do you have a swimming pool?	Vous avez une piscine?	vooz ah-vay ewn pee-seen
I arrive Monday, depart Wednesday.	J'arrive lundi, et pars mercredi.	zhah-reev luhn-dee ay par mehr-kruh-dee
We arrive Monday, depart Wednesday.	Nous arrivons lundi, et partons mercredi.	nooz ah-ree-vohn luhn-dee ay par-tohn mehr-kruh-dee
I'm desperate.	Je suis désespéré.	zhuh swee day-zuh-spay-ray
We're desperate.	Nous sommes désespérés.	noo suhm day-zuh-spay-ray
I'll sleep anywhere.	Je peux dormir n'importe où.	zhuh puh dor-meer nan-port oo
We'll sleep anywhere.	Nous pouvons dormir n'importe où.	noo poo-vohn dor-meer nan-port oo
I have a sleeping bag.	J'ai un sac de couchage.	zhay uhn sahk duh koo-shahzh
We have sleeping bags.	Nous avons les sacs de couchage.	nooz ah-vohn lay sahk duh koo-shahzh
Will you call another hotel for me?	Vous pourriez contacter un autre hôtel pour moi?	voo poor-yay kohn-tahk-tay uhn oh-truh oh-tehl poor mwah

Offering some of the best budget beds in Europe, French hotels are rated from one to four stars (check the blue & white plaque by the front door). For budget travelers, one or two stars is the best value. Prices vary widely under one roof. A room with a double bed (**grand lit**) is cheaper than a room with twin beds (**deux petits lits**), and a bathroom with a shower (**salle d'eau**) is cheaper than a bathroom with a bathtub (**salle de bains**). Rooms with just a toilet and sink (**cabinet de toilette**, abbreviated C. de T.) are even cheaper, and a room with only a sink (**lavabo seulement**) is the cheapest.

Families

Do you have...?	*Vous avez...?*	vooz ah-vay
...a family room	*...une grande chambre, une suite*	ewn grahn shahn-bruh, ewn sweet
...a family rate	*...un tarif famille*	uhn tah-reef fah-mee-yee
...a discount for children	*...un tarif réduit pour enfants*	uhn tah-reef ray-dwee poor ahn-fahn
I have...	*J'ai...*	zhay
We have...	*Nous avons...*	nooz ah-vohn
...one child, ___ months / years old.	*...un enfant, de ___ mois / ans.*	uhn ahn-fahn duh ___ mwah / ahn
...two children, ___ and ___ years old.	*...deux enfants, de ___ et ___ ans.*	duh ahn-fahn duh ___ ay ___ ahn
I'd like...	*Je voudrais...*	zhuh voo-dray
We'd like...	*Nous voudrions...*	noo voo-dree-ohn
...a crib.	*...un berceau.*	uhn behr-soh
...a cot.	*...un lit de camp.*	uhn lee duh kahn
...bunk beds.	*...lits superposés.*	lee sew-pehr-poh-zay
babysitting service	*service de babysitting*	sehr-vees duh "babysitting"
Is... nearby?	*Il y a... près d'ici?*	eel-yah... preh dee-see
...a park	*...un parc*	uhn park
...a playground	*...un parc avec des jeux*	uhn park ah-vehk day zhuh
...a swimming pool	*...une piscine*	ewn pee-seen

Equivalent to our word "kids," the French say *les gamins* or *les gosses.* Snot-nosed kids are *les morveux* and brats are called *les momes.*

Mobility Issues

Stairs are... for me / us / my husband / my wife.	*Les escaliers sont... pour moi / nous / mon mari / ma femme.*	layz ehs-kahl-yay sohn... poor mwah / noo / mohn mah-ree / mah fahm
...impossible	*...impossible*	an-poh-see-bluh
...difficult	*...difficile*	dee-fee-seel

Do you have...?	*Vous avez...?*	vooz ah-vay
...an elevator	*...un ascenseur*	uh<u>n</u> ah-sah<u>n</u>-sur
...a ground floor room	*...une chambre au rez-de-chaussée*	ewn shah<u>n</u>-bruh oh ray-duh-shoh-say
...a wheelchair-accessible room	*...une chambre accessible à un fauteuil roulant*	ewn shah<u>n</u>-bruh ahk-seh-see-bluh ah uh<u>n</u> foh-toy roo-lah<u>n</u>

Confirming, Changing, and Canceling Reservations

You can use this template for your telephone call.

I have a reservation.	*J'ai une réservation.*	zhay ewn ray-zehr-vah-see-oh<u>n</u>
We have a reservation.	*Nous avons une réservation.*	nooz ah-voh<u>n</u> ewn ray-zehr-vah-see-oh<u>n</u>
My name is ___.	*Je m'appelle ___.*	zhuh mah-pehl
I'd like to... my reservation.	*Je voudrais... ma réservation.*	zhuh voo-dray... mah ray-zehr-vah-see-oh<u>n</u>
...confirm	*...confirmer*	koh<u>n</u>-feer-may
...reconfirm	*...reconfirmer*	ray-koh<u>n</u>-feer-may
...cancel	*...annuler*	ah-noo-lay
...change	*...modifier*	moh-dee-fee-ay
The reservation is / was for...	*La réservation est / était pour...*	lah ray-zehr-vah-see-oh<u>n</u> ay / ay-tay poor
...one person	*...une personne*	ewn pehr-suhn
...two people	*...deux personnes*	duh pehr-suhn
...today / tomorrow	*...aujourd'hui / demain*	oh-zhoor-dwee / duh-ma<u>n</u>
...the day after tomorrow	*...après demain*	ah-preh duh-ma<u>n</u>
...August 13	*...le treize août*	luh trehz oot
...one night / two nights	*...une nuit / deux nuits*	ewn nwee / duh nwee
Did you find my / our reservation?	*Avez-vous trouvé ma / notre réservation?*	ah-vay-voo troo-vay mah / noh-truh ray-zehr-vah-see-oh<u>n</u>

What is your cancellation policy?	Quel est le règlement pour annuler?	kehl ay luh reh-gluh-mah<u>n</u> poor ah-noo-lay
Will I be billed for the first night if I can't make it?	Je dois payer la première nuit si je ne peux pas venir?	zhuh dwah pay-yay lah pruhm-yehr nwee see zhuh nuh puh pah vuh-neer
I'd like to arrive instead on ___.	Je préfère arriver le ___.	zhuh pray-fehr ah-ree-vay luh
We'd like to arrive instead on ___.	Nous préférerions arriver le ___.	noo pray-fay-ree-oh<u>n</u> ah-ree-vay luh
Is everything O.K.?	Ça va marcher?	sah vah mar-shay
Thank you. See you then.	Merci. À bientôt.	mehr-see. ah bee-a<u>n</u>-toh
I'm sorry, I need to cancel.	Je suis désolé, car je dois annuler.	zhuh swee day-zoh-lay kar zhuh dwah ah-noo-lay

Nailing Down the Price

How much is...?	Combien...?	koh<u>n</u>-bee-a<u>n</u>
...a room for ___ people	...une chambre pour ___ personnes	ew<u>n</u> shah<u>n</u>-bruh poor ___ pehr-suh<u>n</u>
...your cheapest room	...la chambre la moins chère	lah shah<u>n</u>-bruh lah mwa<u>n</u> shehr
Is breakfast included?	Le Petit déjeuner est compris?	luh puh-tee day-zhuh-nay ay koh<u>n</u>-pree
Is breakfast required?	Le petit déjeuner est obligatoire?	luh puh-tee day-zhuh-nay ay oh-blee-gah-twar
How much without breakfast?	Combien sans le petit déjeuner?	koh<u>n</u>-bee-a<u>n</u> sah<u>n</u> luh puh-tee day-zhuh-nay
Is half-pension required?	La demi-pension est obligatoire?	lah duh-mee-pah<u>n</u>-see-oh<u>n</u> ay oh-blee-gah-twar
Complete price?	Tout compris?	too koh<u>n</u>-pree
Is it cheaper if I stay three nights?	C'est moins cher si je reste trois nuits?	say mwa<u>n</u> shehr see zhuh rehst twah nwee
I will stay three nights.	Je vais rester trois nuits.	zhuh vay rehs-tay twah nwee
We will stay three nights.	Nous allons rester trois nuits.	nooz ah-loh<u>n</u> rehs-tay twah nwee

SLEEPING

| Is it cheaper if I pay in cash? | *C'est moins cher si je paie en liquide?* | say mwan shehr see zhuh pay ahn lee-keed |
| What is the cost per week? | *Quel est le prix à la semaine?* | kehl ay luh pree ah lah suh-mehn |

In resort towns, some hotels offer *demi-pension* (half-pension), of two meals per day served at the hotel: breakfast and your choice of lunch or dinner. The price for half-pension is often listed per person rather than per room. Hotels that offer half-pension often require it in summer. The meals are usually good, but if you want more freedom, look for hotels that don't push half-pension.

Choosing a Room

Can I see the room?	*Je peux voir la chambre?*	zhuh puh vwar lah shahn-bruh
Can we see the room?	*Nous pouvons voir la chambre?*	noo poo-vohn vwar lah shahn-bruh
Show me another room?	*Montrez-moi une autre chambre?*	mohn-tray-mwah ewn oh-truh shahn-bruh
Show us another room?	*Montrez-nous une autre chambre?*	mohn-tray-nooz ewn oh-truh shahn-bruh
Do you have something...?	*Avez-vous quelque chose de...?*	ah-vay-voo kehl-kuh shohz duh
...larger / smaller	*...plus grand / moins grand*	plew grahn / mwan grahn
...better / cheaper	*...meilleur / moins cher*	meh-yur / mwan shehr
...brighter	*...plus clair*	plew klair
...in the back	*...derrière*	dehr-yehr
...quieter	*...plus tranquille*	plew trahn-keel
Sorry, it's not right for me.	*Désolé, ça ne me convient pas.*	day-zoh-lay sah nuh muh kohn-vee-ahn pah
Sorry, it's not right for us.	*Désolé, ça ne nous convient pas.*	day-zoh-lay sah nuh noo kohn-vee-ahn pah
I'll take it.	*Je la prends.*	zhuh lah prahn
We'll take it.	*Nous la prenons.*	noo lah prahn-nohn
The key, please.	*La clef, s'il vous plaît.*	lah klay see voo play

SLEEPING

Breakfast

Breakfast is rarely included, but at least coffee refills are free.

How much is breakfast?	*Combien coûte petit déjeuner?*	kohn-bee-an koot puh-tee day-zhuh-nay
Is breakfast included?	*Petit déjeuner compris?*	puh-tee day-zhuh-nay kohn-pree
When does breakfast start?	*Le petit déjeuner commence à quelle heure?*	luh puh-tee day-zhuh-nay koh-mahns ah kehl ur
When does breakfast end?	*Le petit déjeuner termine à quelle heure?*	luh puh-tee day-zhuh-nay tehr-meen ah kehl ur
Where is breakfast served?	*Le petit déjeuner est servi où?*	luh puh-tee day-zhuh-nay ay sehr-vee oo

Hotel Help

I'd like...	*Je voudrais...*	zhuh voo-dray
We'd like...	*Nous voudrions...*	noo voo-dree-ohn
...a / another	*...un / un autre*	uhn / uhn oh-truh
...towel.	*...serviette de bain.*	sehrv-yeht duh ban
...clean towel.	*...serviette propre.*	sehrv-yeht proh-puh
...pillow.	*...oreiller.*	oh-reh-yay
...fluffy pillow.	*...coussin.*	koo-san
...clean sheets.	*...draps propres.*	drah proh-pruh
...blanket.	*...couverture.*	koo-vehr-tewr
...glass.	*...verre.*	vehr
...sink stopper.	*...bouchon pour le lavabo.*	boo-shohn poor luh lah-vah-boh
...soap.	*...savon.*	sah-vohn
...toilet paper.	*...papier hygiénique.*	pahp-yay ee-zhay-neek
...electrical adapter.	*...adaptateur électrique.*	ah-dahp-tah-tewr ay-lehk-treek
...brighter light bulb.	*...ampoule plus forte.*	ahn-pool plew fort
...lamp.	*...lampe.*	lahmp
...chair.	*...chaise.*	shehz

SLEEPING

English	French	Pronunciation
...roll-away bed.	...lit pliant.	lee plee-ah<u>n</u>
...table.	...table.	tah-bluh
...modem.	...modem.	moh-dehm
...Internet access.	...accès internet.	ahk-sehs a<u>n</u>-tehr-neht
...different room.	...autre chambre.	oh-truh shah<u>n</u>-bruh
...silence.	...le calme.	luh kahlm
...to speak to the manager.	...parler à la direction.	par-lay ah lah dee-rehk-see-oh<u>n</u>
I've fallen and I can't get up.	Je suis tombé et je ne peux pas me lever.	zhuh swee toh<u>n</u>-bay ay zhuh nuh puh pah muh lay-vay
How can I make the room warmer / cooler?	Comment rendre la chambre plus chaude / plus fraiche?	koh-mah<u>n</u> rah<u>n</u>-druh lah shah<u>n</u>-bruh plew shohd / plew frehsh
Where can I wash / hang my laundry?	Où puis-je faire / étendre ma lessive?	oo pwee-zhuh fair / ay-tah<u>n</u>-druh mah luh-seev
Is a... nearby?	Il y a une... près d'ici?	eel-yah ewn... preh dee-see
...self-service laundry	...laverie automatique	lah-vah-ree oh-toh-mah-teek
...full service laundry	...blanchisserie	blah<u>n</u>-shee-suh-ree
I'd like / We'd like...	Je voudrais / Nous voudrions...	zhuh voo-dray / noo voo-dree-oh<u>n</u>
...to stay another night.	...rester encore une nuit.	rehs-tay ah<u>n</u>-kor ewn nwee
Where can I park?	Je peux me garer où?	zhuh puh muh gah-ray oo
What time do you lock up?	Vous fermez à quelle heure?	voo fehr-may ah kehl ur
Please wake me at 7:00.	Réveillez-moi à sept heures, s'il vous plaît.	ray-veh-yay-mwah ah seht ur see voo play
Where do you go for lunch / dinner / coffee?	Vous allez où pour déjeuner / dîner / un café?	vooz ah-lay oo poor day-zhuh-nay / dee-nay / uh<u>n</u> kah-fay

If you'd rather not struggle all night with a log-style French pillow, check in the closet to see if there's a fluffier American-style pillow, or ask for a *"coussin."*

SLEEPING

Chill Out

Many hotel rooms in the Mediterranean part of Europe come with air-conditioning that you control—often with a stick (like a TV remote). Various sticks have basically the same features:
• fan icon (click to toggle through the wind power from light to gale)
• louver icon (click to choose: steady air flow or waves)
• snowflakes and sunshine icons (heat or cold, generally just one or the other is possible: cool air in summer, heat in winter)
• two clock settings (to determine how many hours the air-conditioning will stay on before turning off, or stay off before turning on).
• temperature control (20° or 21° is a comfortable temperature in Celsius). See the thermometer on page 190.

Hotel Hassles

Come with me.	*Venez avec moi.*	vuh-nayz ah-vehk mwah
I have a problem	*J'ai un problème*	zhay uhn proh-blehm
in the room.	*dans la chambre.*	dahn lah shahn-bruh
It smells bad.	*Elle sent mauvaise.*	ehl sahn moh-vehz
bugs	*insectes*	an-sehkt
mice	*souris*	soo-ree
cockroaches	*cafards*	kah-far
prostitutes	*prostituées*	proh-stee-tew-ay
I'm covered with	*Je suis couvert de*	zhuh swee koo-vehr duh
bug bites.	*piqures d'insectes.*	pee-kewr dan-sehkt
The bed is too	*Le lit est trop*	luh lee eh troh
soft / hard.	*mou / dur.*	moo / dewr
I can't sleep.	*Je ne peux pas*	zhuh nuh puh pah
	dormir.	dor-meer
The room is too...	*La chambre est trop...*	lah shahn-bruh ay troh
...hot / cold.	*...chaude / froide.*	shohd / frwahd
...noisy / dirty.	*...bruyante / sale.*	brew-yahnt / sahl

SLEEPING

I can't	*Je ne peux pas*	zhuh nuh puh pah
open / shut...	*ouvrir / fermer...*	oov-reer / fehr-may
...the door /	*...la porte /*	lah port /
the window.	*la fenêtre.*	lah fuh-neh-truh
Air conditioner...	*Climatisation...*	klee-mah-tee-zah-see-ohn
Lamp...	*Lampe...*	lahmp
Lightbulb...	*Ampoule...*	ahn-pool
Electrical outlet...	*Prise...*	preez
Key...	*Clef...*	klay
Lock...	*Serrure...*	suh-roor
Window...	*Fenêtre...*	fuh-neh-truh
Faucet...	*Robinet...*	roh-bee-nay
Sink...	*Lavabo...*	lah-vah-boh
Toilet...	*Toilette...*	twah-leht
Shower...	*Douche...*	doosh
...doesn't work.	*...ne marche pas.*	nuh marsh pah
There is no	*Il n'y a pas*	eel nee yah pah
hot water.	*d'eau chaude.*	doh shohd
When is the	*L'eau sera chaude*	loh suh-rah shohd
water hot?	*à quelle heure?*	ah kehl ur

Checking Out

When is check-out	*A quelle heure on*	ah kehl ur ohn
time?	*doit libérer*	dwah lee-bay-ray
	la chambre?	lah shahn-bruh
I'll leave...	*Je pars...*	zhuh par
We'll leave...	*Nous partons...*	noo par-tohn
...today /	*...aujourd'hui /*	oh-zhoor-dwee /
tomorrow.	*demain.*	duh-man
...very early.	*...très tôt.*	treh toh
Can I / Can we...?	*Je peux /*	zhuh puh /
	Nous pouvons...?	noo poo-vohn
...pay now	*...régler la note*	ray-glay lah noht
	maintenant	man-tuh-nahn
The bill, please.	*La note, s'il vous plaît.*	lah noht see voo play
Credit card O.K.?	*Carte de crédit O.K.?*	kart duh kray-dee "O.K."

Everything was great.	C'était super.	say-tay sew-pehr
I slept like a baby.	J'ai dormi comme un enfant.	zhay dor-mee kohm uhn ahn-fahn
Will you call my next hotel...?	Pourriez-vous appeler mon prochain hotel...?	poor-yay-vooz ah-puh-lay mohn proh-shahn oh-tehl
...for tonight	...pour ce soir	poor suh swar
...to make a reservation	...pour faire une réservation	poor fair ewn ray-zehr-vah-see-ohn
...to confirm a reservation	...pour confirmer une réservation	poor kohn-feer-may ewn ray-zehr-vah-see-ohn
I will pay for the call	Je paierai l'appel.	zhuh pay-uh-ray lah-pehl
Can I / Can we...?	Je peux / Nous pouvons...?	zhuh puh / noo poo-vohn
...leave baggage here until ___	...laisser les baggages ici jusqu'à ___	lay-say lay bah-gahzh ee-see zhews-kah

I never tip beyond the included service charges in hotels or for hotel services.

Camping

camping	camping	kahn-peeng
campsite	emplacement	ahn-plahs-mahn
tent	tente	tahnt
The nearest campground?	Le camping le plus proche?	luh kahn-peeng luh plew prohsh
Can I / Can we...?	Je peux / Nous pouvons...?	zhuh puh / noo poo-vohn
...camp here for one night	...camper ici pour une nuit	kahn-pay ee-see poor ewn nwee
Are showers included?	Les douches sont comprises?	lay doosh sohn kohn-preez
shower token	jeton	zhuh-tohn

In some French campgrounds and hostels, you need to buy a *jeton* (token) to activate a hot shower. To avoid a sudden cold rinse, buy two *jetons* before getting undressed.

EATING

Restaurants

Types of Restaurants and Cuisine

Diners around the world recognize French food as a work of art. French cuisine is sightseeing for your tastebuds.

Styles of cooking include *haute cuisine* (classic, elaborately prepared, multi-course meals); *cuisine bourgeoise* (the finest-quality home cooking); *cuisine des provinces* (traditional dishes of specific regions, using the best ingredients); and *nouvelle cuisine* (the "new style" from the 1970s, which breaks from tradition with a focus on small portions and close attention to the texture and color of the ingredients).

Here are the types of restaurants you're likely to encounter:

Restaurant—Generally elegant, expensive eatery serving *haute cuisine*

Brasserie—Large café with quick, simple food and drink

Bistro—Small, usually informal neighborhood restaurant offering mainly *cuisine bourgeoise*

Auberge, Hostellerie, or *Relais*—Country inn serving high-quality traditional food

Routier—Truck stop dishing up basic, decent food

Crêperie—Street stand or café specializing in crêpes (thin pancakes, usually served with sweet fillings such as chocolate, Nutella, jam, or butter and sugar)

Salon de thé—Tea and coffee house offering pastries, desserts, and sometimes light meals

Buffet-express or *snack bar*—Cafeteria, usually near a train or bus station

Cabaret—Supper club featuring entertainment

Finding a Restaurant

Where's a good...	*Où se trouve un*	oo suh troov uh<u>n</u>
restaurant nearby?	*bon restaurant...*	boh<u>n</u> rehs-toh-rah<u>n</u>
	près d'ici?	preh dee-see
...cheap	*...bon marché*	boh<u>n</u> mar-shay
...local-style	*...cuisine*	kwee-zeen
	régionale	ray-zhee-oh-nahl
...untouristy	*...pas touristique*	pah too-ree-steek
...vegetarian	*...végétarien*	vay-zhay-tah-ree-a<u>n</u>
...fast food	*...service rapide*	sehr-vees rah-peed
...self-service buffet	*...buffet de libre*	boo-fay duh lee-bruh
	service	sehr-vees
...Chinese	*...chinois*	sheen-wah
with terrace	*avec terrace*	ah-vehk tehr-rahs
with a salad bar	*avec un buffet*	ah-vehk uh<u>n</u> boo-fay
	salade	sah-lahd
with candles	*avec bougies*	ah-vehk boo-zhee
romantic	*romantique*	roh-mah<u>n</u>-teek
moderate price	*prix modéré*	pree moh-day-ray
splurge	*faire une folie*	fair ewn foh-lee
Is it better than	*C'est mieux que*	say mee-uh kuh
McDonald's?	*Mac Do?*	mahk doh

EATING

Restaurants normally serve from 12:00 p.m. to 2:00 p.m., and from 7:00 p.m. until about 10:00 p.m. Cafés are generally open throughout the day. The menu is posted right on the front door or window, and "window shopping" for your meal is a fun, important part of the experience. While the slick self-service restaurants are easy to use, you'll often eat better for the same money in a good little family bistro.

Getting a Table

At what time does this open / close?	À quelle heure c'est ouvert / fermé?	ah kehl ur say oo-vehr / fehr-may
Are you open...?	Vous êtes ouvert...?	vooz eht oo-vehr...
...today / tomorrow	...aujourd'hui / demain	oh-zhoor-dwee / duh-man
...for lunch / dinner	...pour déjeuner / dîner	poor day-zhuh-nay / dee-nay
Are reservations recommended?	Les réservations sont conseillé?	lay ray-zehr-vah-see-ohn sohn kohn-seh-yay

---

KEY PHRASES: RESTAURANTS

Where's a good restaurant nearby?	Où se trouve un bon restaurant près d'ici?	oo suh troov uhn bohn rehs-toh-rahn preh dee-see
I'd like...	Je voudrais...	zhuh voo-dray
We'd like...	Nous voudrions...	noo voo-dree-ohn
...a table for one / two.	...une table pour un / deux.	ewn tah-bluh poor uhn / duh
Non-smoking (if possible).	Non fumeur (si possible).	nohn few-mur (see poh-see-bluh)
Is this seat free?	C'est libre?	say lee-bruh
The menu (in English), please.	La carte (en anglais), s'il vous plaît.	lah kart (ahn ahn-glay) see voo play
The bill, please.	L'addition, s'il vous plaît.	lah-dee-see-ohn see voo play
Credit card O.K.?	Carte de crédit O.K.?	kart duh kray-dee "O.K."

EATING

I'd like...	*Je voudrais...*	zhuh voo-dray
We'd like...	*Nous voudrions...*	noo voo-dree-oh<u>n</u>
...a table for one / two.	*...une table pour un / deux.*	ewn tah-bluh poor uh<u>n</u> / duh
...to reserve a table for two people...	*...réserver une table pour deux personnes...*	ray-zehr-vay ewn tah-bluh poor duh pehr-suhn
...for today / tomorrow	*...pour aujourd'hui / demain*	poor oh-zhoor-dwee / duh-ma<u>n</u>
...at 8 p.m.	*...à huit heures du soir*	ah weet ur duh swar
My name is ___.	*Je m'appelle ___.*	zhuh mah-pehl
I have a reservation for ___ people.	*J'ai une réservation pour ___ personnes.*	zhay ewn ray-zehr-vah-see-oh<u>n</u> poor ___ pehr-suhn
I'd like to sit...	*J'aimerais s'asseoir...*	zhehm-uh-ray sah-swar
We'd like to sit...	*Nous aimerions nous asseoir...*	nooz ehm-uh-roh<u>n</u> nooz ah-swar
...inside / outside.	*...à l'intérieur / dehors.*	ah la<u>n</u>-tay-ree-yoor / duh-or
...by the window.	*...à côté de la fenêtre.*	ah koh-tay duh lah fuh-neh-truh
non-smoking (if possible).	*non fumeur (si possible).*	noh<u>n</u> few-mur (see poh-see-bluh)
...with a view.	*...avec une vue.*	ah-vehk ewn vew
...where it's quiet.	*...dans un coin tranquille.*	dah<u>n</u>z uh<u>n</u> kwa<u>n</u> trah<u>n</u>-keel
Is this table free?	*Cette table est libre?*	seht tah-bluh ay lee-bruh
Can I sit here?	*Je peux s'asseoir ici?*	zhuh puh sah-swar ee-see
Can we sit here?	*Nous pouvons nous asseoir ici?*	noo poo-voh<u>n</u> nooz ah-swar ee-see

Better restaurants routinely take telephone reservations. Guidebooks include phone numbers and the process is simple. If you want to eat at a normal French dinner-time (later than 7:30 p.m.), it's smart to call and reserve a table. Many of my favorite restaurants are filled with

Americans at 7:30 p.m. and can feel like tourist traps.
But if you drop in at (or reserve ahead for) 8:30 or 9:00
p.m., when the French are eating, the restaurants feel
completely local.

The Menu

menu	carte	kart
special of the day	plat du jour	plah dew zhoor
specialty of the house	spécialité de la maison	spay-see-ah-lee-tay duh lah may-zoh**n**
fast service special	formule rapide	for-mewl rah-peed
fixed-price meal	menu, prix fixe	muh-new, pree feeks
breakfast	petit déjeuner	puh-tee day-zhuh-nay
lunch	déjeuner	day-zhuh-nay
dinner	dîner	dee-nay
appetizers	hors-d'oeuvre	or-duh-vruh
sandwiches	sandwiches	sah**n**d-weech
bread	pain	pa**n**
salad	salade	sah-lahd
soup	soupe	soop
first course	entrée	ah**n**-tray
main course	plat principal	plah pra**n**-see-pahl
meat	viande	vee-ah**n**d
poultry	volaille	voh-ligh
fish	poisson	pwah-soh**n**
seafood	fruits de mer	frwee duh mehr
children's plate	assiette d'enfant	ahs-yeht dah**n**-fah**n**
vegetables	légumes	lay-gewm
cheese	fromage	froh-mahzh
dessert	dessert	duh-sehr
munchies (mouth amusements)	amuse bouche	ah-mewz boosh
drink menu	carte des consommation	kart day koh**n**-soh-mah-see-oh**n**
beverages	boissons	bwah-soh**n**
beer	bière	bee-ehr
wine	vin	va**n**

service included	*service compris*	sehr-vees koh<u>n</u>-pree
service not included	*service non compris*	sehr-vees noh<u>n</u> koh<u>n</u>-pree
hot / cold	*chaud / froid*	shoh / frwah
with / and /	*avec / et / ou / sans*	ah-vehk / ay / oo / sah<u>n</u>
or / without		

In France, a menu is a *carte*, and a fixed-price meal
is a *menu* (also called *menu touristique*). So, if you ask
for a *menu* (instead of the *carte*), you'll get this fixed-
price meal, which includes your choice of an appetizer,
entrée, and dessert for one set price. The *menu* is usually a good value, though most locals prefer to order à la
carte (from the *carte*, what we would call the menu).
Service compris (s.c.) means the tip is included. For a
complete culinary language guide, travel with the excellent *Marling Menu-Master* for France.

Ordering

waiter	*Monsieur*	muhs-yur
waitress	*Mademoiselle,*	mahd-mwah-zehl,
	Madame	mah-dahm
I'm / We're ready	*Je suis / Nous sommes*	zhuh swee / noo suhm
to order.	*prêt à commander.*	preh ah koh-mah<u>n</u>-day
I'd like / We'd like...	*Je voudrais /*	zhuh voo-dray /
	Nous voudrions...	noo voo-dree-oh<u>n</u>
...just a	*...une*	ewn
drink.	*consommation*	koh<u>n</u>-soh-mah-see-oh<u>n</u>
	seulement.	suhl-mah<u>n</u>
...a snack.	*...un snack.*	uh<u>n</u> snahk
...just a salad.	*...qu'une salade.*	kewn sah-lahd
...a half portion.	*...une demi-portion.*	ewn duh-mee-por-see-oh<u>n</u>
...the tourist menu.	*...le menu touristique.*	luh muh-new
(fixed-price meal)		too-ree-steek
...to see the menu.	*...voir la carte.*	vwar lah kart
...to order.	*...commander.*	koh-mah<u>n</u>-day
...to pay.	*...payer.*	pay-yay
...to throw up.	*...vomir.*	voh-meer

EATING

Do you have...?	*Avez-vous...?*	ah-vay-voo
...an English menu	*...une carte en anglais*	ewn kart ah<u>n</u> ah<u>n</u>-glay
...a lunch special	*...un plat du jour*	uh<u>n</u> plah dew zhoor
What do you recommend?	*Qu'est-ce que vous recommandez?*	kehs kuh voo ruh-koh-mah<u>n</u>-day
What's your favorite dish?	*Quel est votre plat favori?*	kehl eh voh-truh plah fah-voh-ree
Is it...?	*C'est...?*	say
...good	*...bon*	boh<u>n</u>
...expensive	*...cher*	shehr
...light	*...léger*	lay-zhay
...filling	*...copieux*	kohp-yuh
What is...?	*Qu'est-ce...?*	kehs
...that	*...que c'est*	kuh say
...local	*...que vous avez de la région*	kuh vooz ah-vay duh lah ray-zhee-oh<u>n</u>
...fresh	*...qu'il y a de frais*	keel yah duh fray
...cheap and filling	*...qu'il y a de bon marché et de copieux*	keel yah duh boh<u>n</u> mar-shay ay duh kohp-yuh
...fast (already prepared)	*...qui est déjà préparé*	kee ay day-zhah pray-pah-ray
Can we split this and have an extra plate?	*Nous pouvons partager et avoir une assiette de plus?*	noo poo-voh<u>n</u> par-tah-zhay ay ah-vwar ewn ahs-yeht duh plew
I've changed my mind.	*J'ai changé d'avis.*	zhay shah<u>n</u>-zhay dah-vee
Nothing with eyeballs.	*Rien avec des yeux.*	ree-a<u>n</u> ah-vehk dayz yuh
Can I substitute (something) for ___?	*Je peux substituer (quelque chose) pour ___?*	zhuh puh soob-stee-too-ay (kehl-kuh shohz) poor
Can I / Can we get it "to go"?	*Je peux / Nous pouvons prendre ça "à emporter"?*	zhuh puh / noo poo-voh<u>n</u> prah<u>n</u>-druh sah ah ah<u>n</u>-por-tay
"To go"?	*"À emporter"?*	ah ah<u>n</u>-por-tay

Once you're seated, the table is yours for the entire lunch or dinner period. The waiter or waitress is there to serve you, but only when you're ready. To get his or her attention, simply ask, *"S'il vous plaît?"* ("Please?").

This is the sequence of a typical restaurant experience: The waiter will give you a menu (*carte*) and then ask what you'd like to drink (*Vous voulez quelque choses à boire?*), if you're ready to order (*Vous êtes prets à commander?*) or what you'd like to eat (*Qu'est ce que je vous sers?*), if everything is okay (*Tout va bien?*), if you'd like dessert (*Vous voulez un dessert?*), and if you're finished (*Vous avez terminer?*). You ask for the bill (*L'addition, s'il vous plaît*).

Tableware and Condiments

plate	*assiette*	ahs-yeht
extra plate	*une assiette de plus*	ewn ahs-yeht duh plew
napkin	*serviette*	sehrv-yeht
silverware	*couverts*	koo-vehr
knife	*couteau*	koo-toh
fork	*fourchette*	foor-sheht
spoon	*cuillère*	kwee-yehr
cup	*tasse*	tahs
glass	*verre*	vehr
carafe	*carafe*	kah-rahf
water	*l'eau*	loh
bread	*pain*	pa<u>n</u>
butter	*beurre*	bur
margarine	*margarine*	mar-gah-reen
salt / pepper	*sel / poivre*	sehl / pwah-vruh
sugar	*sucre*	sew-kruh
artificial sweetener	*édulcorant*	ay-dewl-koh-rah<u>n</u>
honey	*miel*	mee-ehl
mustard	*moutarde*	moo-tard
ketchup	*ketchup*	"ketchup"
mayonnaise	*mayonnaise*	mah-yuh-nehz
toothpick	*cure-dent*	kewr-dah<u>n</u>

EATING

The Food Arrives

Is it included with the meal?	C'est inclus avec le repas?	say an-klew ah-vehk luh ruh-pah
I did not order this.	Je n'ai pas commandé ça.	zhuh nay pah koh-mahn-day sah
We did not order this.	Nous n'avons pas commandé ça.	noo nah-vohn pah koh-mahn-day sah
Heat this up?	Vous pouvez réchauffer ça?	voo poo-vay ray-shoh-fay sah
A little.	Un peu.	uhn puh
More. / Another.	Plus. / Un autre.	plew / uhn oh-truh
One more please.	Encore un s'il vous plaît.	ahn-kor uhn see voo play
The same.	La même chose.	lah mehm shohz
Enough.	Assez.	ah-say
Finished.	Terminé.	tehr-mee-nay

After bringing your meal, your server might wish you a cheery "*Bon appétit!*" (pronounced bohn ah-pay-tee).

Complaints

This is...	C'est...	say
...dirty.	...sale.	sahl
...greasy.	...graisseux.	gray-suh
...salty.	...salé.	sah-lay
...undercooked.	...pas assez cuit.	pah ah-say kwee
...overcooked.	...trop cuit.	troh kwee
...inedible.	...immangeable.	an-mahn-zhah-bluh
...cold.	...froid.	frwah
Do any of your customers return?	Avez-vous des clients qui reviennent?	ah-vay-voo day klee-ahn kee ruh-vee-an
Yuck!	Pouah!	pwah

EATING

Compliments to the Chef

Yummy!	*Miam-miam!*	myahm-myahm
Delicious!	*Délicieux!*	day-lee-see-uh
Magnificent!	*Magnifique!*	mahn-yee-feek
Very tasty!	*Très bon!*	treh boh<u>n</u>
I love French food / this food.	*J'aime la cuisine française / cette cuisine.*	zhehm lah kwee-zeen frah<u>n</u>-sehz / seht kwee-zeen
Better than my mom's cooking.	*Meilleur que la cuisine de ma mère.*	meh-yur kuh lah kwee-zeen duh mah mehr
My compliments to the chef!	*Mes compliments au chef!*	may koh<u>n</u>-plee-mah<u>n</u> oh shehf

Paying for Your Meal

The bill, please.	*L'addition, s'il vous plaît.*	lah-dee-see-oh<u>n</u> see voo play
Together.	*Ensemble.*	ah<u>n</u>-sah<u>n</u>-bluh
Separate checks.	*Notes séparées.*	noht say-pah-ray
Credit card O.K.?	*Carte de crédit O.K.?*	kart duh kray-dee "O.K."
This is not correct.	*Ce n'est pas exact.*	suh nay pah ehg-zahkt
Explain this?	*Expliquez ça?*	ehk-splee-kay sah
Can you explain / itemize the bill?	*Vous pouvez expliquer / détailler cette note?*	voo poo-vay ehk-splee-kay / day-tay-yay seht noht
What if I wash the dishes?	*Et si je lave la vaisselle?*	ay see zhuh lahv lah veh-sehl
Is tipping expected?	*Je dois laisser un pourboire?*	zhuh dwah lay-say uh<u>n</u> poor-bwar
What percent?	*Quel pourcentage?*	kehl poor-sah<u>n</u>-tahzh
tip	*pourboire*	poor-bwar
Keep the change.	*Gardez la monnaie.*	gar-day lah moh-nay
This is for you.	*C'est pour vous.*	say poor voo
May I have a receipt, please?	*Je peux avoir une fiche, s'il vous plaît?*	zhuh puh ah-vwar ewn feesh see voo play

In France, slow service is good service (fast service would rush the diners). Out of courtesy, your waiter will not bring your bill until you ask for it. While a service charge is included in the bill, this only brings the waiter's pay up to the minimum wage. It's polite to tip an additional 10 to 15 percent if the service was good, helpful, and friendly. If you ordered just a drink, tip by rounding up to the next euro. When you're uncertain whether to tip, ask another customer if tipping is expected (*Je dois laisser un pourboire?*).

Special Concerns

In a Hurry

I'm / We're in a hurry.	*Je suis / Nous sommes pressé.*	zhuh swee / noo suhm preh-say
I need / We need...	*J'ai besoin / Nous avons besoin...*	zhay buh-swan / nooz ah-vohn buh-swan
...to be served quickly.	*...d'être servi vite.*	deh-truh sehr-vee veet
Is that possible?	*C'est possible?*	say poh-see-bluh
I must / We must...	*Je dois / Nous devons...*	zhuh dwah / noo duh-vohn
...leave in 30 minutes / one hour.	*...partir dans trente minutes / une heure.*	par-teer dahn trahnt mee-newt / ewn ur
Will the food be ready soon?	*Ce sera prêt bientôt?*	suh suh-rah preh bee-an-toh

If you are in a rush, seek out a brasserie or restaurant that offers *service rapide* (fast food).

Dietary Restrictions

I'm allergic to...	*Je suis allergique à...*	zhuh sweez ah-lehr-zheek ah
I cannot eat...	*Je ne peux pas manger de...*	zhuh nuh puh pah mah<u>n</u>-zhay duh
He / She cannot eat...	*Il / Elle ne peut pas manger de...*	eel / ehl nuh puh pah mah<u>n</u>-zhay duh
...dairy products.	*...produits laitiers.*	proh-dwee lay-tee-yay
...wheat.	*...blé.*	blay
...meat / pork.	*...viande / porc.*	vee-ah<u>n</u>d / por
...salt / sugar.	*...sel / sucre.*	sehl / sew-kruh
...shellfish.	*...crustacés.*	krew-stah-say
...spicy foods.	*...nourriture épicée.*	noo-ree-tewr ay-pee-say
...nuts.	*...noix.*	nwah
I'm a diabetic.	*Je suis diabétique.*	zhuh swee dee-ah-bay-teek
I'd like / We'd like...	*Je voudrais / Nous voudrions...*	zhuh voo-dray / noo voo-dree-oh<u>n</u>
...a kosher meal.	*...repas kasher.*	ruh-pah kah-shay
...a low-fat meal.	*...repas allege en matières grasses.*	ruh-pah ah-lehzh ah<u>n</u> mah-tee-yehr grahs
I eat only insects.	*Je ne mange que les insectes.*	zhuh nuh mah<u>n</u>zh kuh layz a<u>n</u>-sehkt
No salt.	*Sans sel.*	sah<u>n</u> sehl
No sugar.	*Sans sucre.*	sah<u>n</u> sew-kruh
No fat.	*Sans matière grasse.*	sah<u>n</u> mah-tee-yehr grahs
Minimal fat.	*Léger en matière grasse.*	lay-zhay ah<u>n</u> mah-tee-yehr grahs
Low cholesterol.	*Allégé.*	ah-lay-zhay
No caffeine.	*Décaféiné.*	day-kah-fay-nay
No alcohol.	*Sans alcool.*	sah<u>n</u>z ahl-kohl
Organic.	*Biologique.*	bee-oh-loh-zheek
I'm a...	*Je suis...*	zhuh swee
...vegetarian. (male)	*...végétarien.*	vay-zhay-tah-ree-a<u>n</u>

EATING

...vegetarian. (female)	...végétarienne.	vay-zhay-tah-ree-ehn
...strict vegetarian.	...strict végétarien.	streekt vay-zhay-tah-ree-an
...carnivore.	...carnivore.	kar-nee-vor
...big eater.	...gourmand.	goor-mahn
Is any meat or animal fat used in this?	Il y a des produits ou dérivés animaux dans ça?	eel yah dayz proh-dwee oo day-ree-vay ah-nee-moh dahn sah

Children

Do you have...?	Vous avez...?	vooz ah-vay
...a children's portion	...une assiette enfant	ewn ahs-yeht ahn-fahn
...a half portion	...une demi-portion	ewn duh-mee-por-see-ohn
a high chair / a booster seat	une chaise enfant / un réhausseur	oon shehz ahn-fahn / uhn ray-oh-sur
plain noodles / plain rice	pâtes natures / riz nature	paht nah-toor / ree nah-toor
with butter	avec beurre	ah-vehk bur
no sauce	pas de sauce	pah duh sohs
sauce or dressing on the side	sauce à part	sohs ah par
pizza	pizza	"pizza"
...cheese only	...juste fromage	zhoost froh-mahzh
...pepperoni and cheese	...chorizo et fromage	shoh-ree-zoh ay froh-mahzh
toasted cheese sandwich	croque monsieur	krohk muhs-yur
hot dog and fries	saucisse-frites	soh-sees-freet
hamburger	hamburger	ahm-boor-gehr
cheeseburger	cheeseburger	sheez-boor-gehr
French fries	frites	freet
ketchup	ketchup	ketchup
crackers	crackers	krah-kehr
Nothing spicy.	Rien d'épicé.	ree-an day-pee-say

EATING

English	French	Pronunciation
Not too hot.	*Pas trop chaud.*	pah troh shoh
Don't let the food mix together on the plate.	*Merci d'eviter que la nourriture se mêle sur l'assiette.*	mehr-see duh-vee-tay kuh lah noo-ree-tewr suh mehl sewr lahs-yeht
He will / She will / They will...	*Il va / Elle va / Ils vont...*	eel vah / ehl vah / eel vohn
...share our meal.	*...partager notre repas.*	par-tah-zhay noh-truh ruh-pah
We need our food quickly, please.	*Nous avons besoin de notre repas très vite, s'il vous plaît.*	nooz ah-vohn buh-swan duh noh-truh ruh-pah tray veet see voo play
Can I / Can we have an extra...?	*Je peux / Nous pouvons avoir une... de plus?*	zhuh puh / noo poo-vohn ah-vwar ewn... duh plew
...plate	*...assiette*	ahs-yeht
...cup	*...tasse*	tahs
...spoon / fork	*...cuillère / fourchette*	kwee-yehr / foor-sheht
Can I / Can we have two extra...?	*Je peux / Nous pouvons deux... de plus?*	zhuh puh / noo poo-vohn duh... duh plew
...plates	*...assiettes*	ahs-yeht
...cups	*...tasses*	tahs
...spoons / forks	*...cuillères / fourchettes*	kwee-yehr / foor-sheht
Milk (in a plastic cup).	*Du lait (dans une verre plastique).*	doo lay (dahnz oon vehr plah-steek)
Straw(s).	*Paille(s)*	pī-yee
More napkins, please.	*Des serviettes, s'il vous plaît.*	day sehrv-yeht see voo play
Sorry for the mess.	*Désolé pour le désordre.*	day-zoh-lay poor luh day-zor-druh

What's Cooking

Breakfast

breakfast	petit déjeuner	puh-tee day-zhuh-nay
bread	pain	pa<u>n</u>
roll	petit pain	puh-tee pa<u>n</u>
little loaf of bread	baguette	bah-geht
toast	toast	tohst
butter	beurre	bur
jelly	confiture	koh<u>n</u>-fee-tewr
pastry	pâtisserie	pah-tee-suh-ree
croissant	croissant	kwah-sah<u>n</u>
cheese	fromage	froh-mahzh
yogurt	yaourt	yah-oort
cereal	céréale	say-ray-ahl
milk	lait	lay
hot chocolate	chocolat chaud	shoh-koh-lah shoh
fruit juice	jus de fruit	zhew duh frwee
orange juice	jus d'orange	zhew doh-rah<u>n</u>zh
(fresh)	(pressé)	(preh-say)
coffee / tea	café / thé	kah-fay / tay
Is breakfast included?	Le petit déjeuner est compris?	luh puh-tee day-zhuh-nay ay koh<u>n</u>-pree

What's Probably Not for Breakfast

omelet	omelette	oh-muh-leht
eggs	des oeufs	dayz uh
fried eggs	oeufs au plat	uh oh plah

EATING

scrambled eggs	oeufs brouillés	uh broo-yay
boiled egg...	oeuf à la coque...	uhf ah lah kohk
...soft / hard	...mollet / dur	moh-lay / dewr
ham	jambon	zhah<u>n</u>-boh<u>n</u>

French hotel breakfasts are small, expensive, and often optional. They normally include coffee and a fresh *croissant* or a chunk of *baguette* with butter and jelly. Being a juice and cheese man, I keep a liter box of O.J. in my rooms for a morning eye-opener and a wedge of "Laughing Cow" cheese in my bag for a moo-vable feast. You can also save money by breakfasting at a *bar* or *café*, where it's acceptable to bring in a *croissant* from the neighboring *boulangerie* (bakery). You can get an *omelette* almost any time of day at a café.

Snacks and Quick Lunches

crêpe	crêpe	krehp
buckwheat crêpe	galette	gah-leht
omelet	omelette	oh-muh-leht
quiche...	quiche...	keesh
...with cheese	...au fromage	oh froh-mahzh
...with ham	...au jambon	oh zhah<u>n</u>-boh<u>n</u>
...with mushrooms	...aux champignons	oh shah<u>n</u>-peen-yoh<u>n</u>
...with bacon, cheese, and onions	...lorraine	lor-rehn
paté	pâté	pah-tay
onion tart	tarte à l'oignon	tart ah loh-yoh<u>n</u>
cheese tart	tarte au fromage	tart oh froh-mahzh

Light meals are quick and easy at *cafés* and *bars* throughout France. A *salade, crêpe, quiche,* or *omelette* is a fairly cheap way to fill up, even in Paris. Each can be made with various extras like ham, cheese, mushrooms, and so on. *Crêpes* come in dinner or dessert varieties.

EATING

KEY PHRASES: WHAT'S COOKING

food	*nourriture*	noo-ree-tewr
breakfast	*petit déjeuner*	puh-tee day-zhuh-nay
lunch	*déjeuner*	day-zhuh-nay
dinner	*dîner*	dee-nay
bread	*pain*	pan
cheese	*fromage*	froh-mahzh
soup	*soupe*	soop
salad	*salade*	sah-lahd
meat	*viande*	vee-ahnd
fish	*poisson*	pwah-sohn
fruit	*fruit*	frwee
vegetables	*légumes*	lay-gewm
dessert	*dessert*	duh-sehr
Delicious!	*Délicieux!*	day-lee-see-uh

Hors d'Oeuvres

hors-d'oeuvres	*or-duh-vruh*	appetizers
escargots	*ehs-kar-goh*	snails baked in the shell w/ garlic butter
pâté de foie gras	*pah-tay duh fwah grah*	goose- or duck-liver spread
huîtres	*wee-truh*	oysters (usually served on the half shell)
terrine	*tehr-reen*	type of paté served in a deep pot—made w/ fish, poultry, game, or pork
crudités	*krew-dee-tay*	raw vegetables served w/ vinaigrette
artichauts à la vinaigrette	*ar-tee-shoh ah lah vee-nay-greht*	artichokes in a vinaigrette dressing
quenelles	*kehn-ehl*	dumplings w/meat or fish in white sauce
bouchée à la reine	*boo-shay ah lah rehn*	pastry shell filled with creamed veal brains and mushrooms

EATING

| soufflé | *soo-flay* | fluffy eggs baked w/ savory fillings (cheese, meat, and vegetables) |
| tapenade | *tah-puh-nahd* | paste made from olives, anchovies, lemon, and olive oil |

Sandwiches

I'd like a sandwich.	*Je voudrais un sandwich.*	zhuh voo-dray uhn sahnd-weech
We'd like two sandwiches.	*Nous voudrions deux sandwichs.*	noo voo-dree-ohn duh sahnd-weech
toasted	*grillé*	gree-yay
toasted ham and cheese sandwich	*croque monsieur*	krohk muhs-yur
toasted ham, cheese, and fried egg sandwich	*croque madame*	krohk mah-dahm
cheese	*fromage*	froh-mahzh
tuna	*thon*	tohn
fish	*poisson*	pwah-sohn
chicken	*poulet*	poo-lay
turkey	*dinde, dindon*	dand, dan-dohn
ham	*jambon*	zhahn-bohn
salami	*salami*	sah-lah-mee
boiled egg	*oeuf à la coque*	uhf ah lah kohk
garnished with veggies	*crudités*	krew-dee-tay
lettuce	*laitue*	lay-too
tomato	*tomate*	toh-maht
onions	*oignons*	oh-yohn
mustard	*moutarde*	moo-tard
mayonnaise	*mayonnaise*	mah-yuh-nehz
peanut butter	*beurre de cacahuètes*	bur duh kah-kah-weet
jelly	*confiture*	kohn-fee-tewr

EATING

pork sandwich	sandwich au porc	sah<u>n</u>d-weech oh por
Does this come	C'est servi froid	say sehr-vee frwah
cold or warm?	ou chaud?	oo shoh
Heated, please.	Réchauffé,	ray-shoh-fay
	s'il vous plaît.	see voo play

Sandwiches, as well as small quiches, often come ready-made at *boulangeries* (bakeries).

If You Knead Bread

bread	pain	pa<u>n</u>
thin, long loaf	baguette	bah-geht
sweet, soft bun	brioche	bree-osh
crescent roll	croissant	kwah-sah<u>n</u>
lace-like bread (Riviera)	fougasse	foo-gahs
dark-grain bread	pain bisse, pain de seigle	pa<u>n</u> bees, pa<u>n</u> duh seh-gluh
onion and anchovy pizza	pissaladière	pees-ah-lah-dee-yehr
cheese pastry	croûte au fromage	kroot oh froh-mahzh

Say Cheese

cheese...	fromage...	froh-mahzh
...mild	...doux	doo
...sharp	...fort	for
...goat	...chèvre	sheh-vruh
...bleu	...bleu	bluh
...with herbs	...aux herbes	oh ehrb
...cream	...à la crème	ah lah krehm
...of the region	...de la région	duh lah ray-zhee-oh<u>n</u>
Swiss cheese	gruyère, emmenthal	grew-yehr, eh-mehn-tahl
Laughing Cow	La vache qui rit	lah vahsh kee ree
cheese platter	le plâteau de fromages	luh plah-toh duh froh-mahzh
May I taste a little?	Je peux goûter un peu?	zhuh puh goo-tay uh<u>n</u> puh

EATING

In France, the cheese course is served just before (or instead of) dessert. It not only helps with digestion, it gives you a great opportunity to sample the tasty regional cheeses. There are over 500 different French cheeses to try. You've heard of *Camembert* and *Brie*. *Port Salut* comes in a sweet, soft wedge, and *Roquefort* is strong and blue-veined. *Boursin* is a soft cheese with herbs. Some cheeses are named after the city they come from (*pont l'éveque*—flavorful and smooth; *liverot*—strong fragrance and a rich, creamy taste). *Fromage aux cindres* (cheese with cinders) is ash-ually better than it sounds. Visit a *fromagerie* (cheese shop) and experiment. Ask for a *fromage de la région* (of the region), and specify mild, sharp, goat, or bleu (see list above).

Soups and Salads

soup (of the day)	*soupe (du jour)*	soop (dew zhoor)
broth	*bouillon*	boo-yoh<u>n</u>
...chicken	*...de poulet*	duh poo-lay
...beef	*...de boeuf*	duh buhf
...with noodles	*...aux nouilles*	oh noo-ee
...with rice	*...au riz*	oh ree
thick vegetable soup	*potage de légumes*	poh-tahzh duh lay-gewm
Provençal vegetable soup	*soupe au pistou*	soop oh pees-too
onion soup	*soupe à l'oignon*	soop ah lohn-yoh<u>n</u>
cream of asparagus soup	*crème d'asperges*	krehm dah-spehrzh
potato and leek soup	*vichyssoise*	vee-shee-swah
shellfish chowder	*bisque*	beesk
seafood stew	*bouillabaisse*	boo-yah-behs
meat and vegetable stew	*pot au feu*	poht oh fuh
salad...	*salade...*	sah-lahd
...green / mixed	*...verte / mixte*	vehrt / meekst
...with goat cheese	*...au chèvre chaud*	oh sheh-vruh shoh

...chef's	*...composée*	kohn-poh-zay
...seafood	*...océane*	oh-shay-ahn
...tuna	*...de thon*	duh tohn
...veggie	*...crudités*	krew-dee-tay
...with ham /	*...avec jambon /*	ah-vehk zhahn-bohn /
cheese / egg	*fromage / oeuf*	froh-mahzh / uh
lettuce	*laitue*	lay-too
tomatoes	*tomates*	toh-maht
onions	*oignons*	ohn-yohn
cucumber	*concombre*	kohn-kohn-bruh
oil / vinegar	*huile / vinaigre*	weel / vee-nay-gruh
dressing on the side	*sauce à part*	sohs ah par
What is in	*Qu'est-ce qu'il ya*	kehs keel yah
this salad?	*dans cette salade?*	dahn seht sah-lahd

Salads are usually served with a vinaigrette dressing and often eaten after the main course.

Seafood

seafood	*fruits de mer*	frwee duh mehr
assorted seafood	*assiette de fruits*	ahs-yeht duh frwee
	de mer	duh mehr
fish	*poisson*	pwah-sohn
anchovies	*anchois*	ahn-shwah
clams	*palourdes*	pah-loord
cod	*cabillaud*	kah-bee-yoh
crab	*crabe*	krahb
herring	*hareng*	ah-rahn
lobster	*homard*	oh-mar
mussels	*moules*	mool
oysters	*huîtres*	wee-truh
prawns	*scampi*	skahn-pee
salmon	*saumon*	soh-mohn
salty cod	*morue*	moh-rew
sardines	*sardines*	sar-deen
scallops	*coquilles*	koh-keel
shrimp	*crevettes*	kruh-veht

squid	*calamar*	kahl-mar
trout	*truite*	trweet
tuna	*thon*	toh<u>n</u>
What's fresh today?	*Qu'est-ce frais aujourd'hui?*	kehs kay fray oh-joord-wee
Do you eat this part?	*Ça se mange?*	sah suh mah<u>nzh</u>
Just the head, please.	*Seulement la tête, s'il vous plaît.*	suhl-mah<u>n</u> lah teht see voo play

Poultry

poultry	*volaille*	voh-lī
chicken	*poulet*	poo-lay
duck	*canard*	kah-nar
turkey	*dinde, dindon*	dand, da<u>n</u>-dohn
How long has this been dead?	*Il est mort depuis longtemps?*	eel ay mor duh-pwee loh<u>n</u>-tah<u>n</u>

Meat

meat	*viande*	vee-ah<u>n</u>d
beef	*boeuf*	buhf
beef steak	*bifteck*	beef-tehk
flank steak	*faux-filet*	foh-fee-lay
ribsteak	*entrecôte*	ah<u>n</u>-truh-koht
bunny	*lapin*	lah-pa<u>n</u>
cutlet	*côtelette*	koh-tuh-leht
frog's legs	*cuisses de grenouilles*	kwees duh greh-noo-ee
ham	*jambon*	zhah<u>n</u>-boh<u>n</u>
lamb	*agneau*	ahn-yoh
meat stew	*ragoût*	rah-goo
mixed grill	*grillades*	gree-yahd
pork	*porc*	por
roast beef	*rosbif*	rohs-beef
sausage	*saucisse*	soh-sees
snails	*escargots*	ehs-kar-goh
veal	*veau*	voh

EATING

AVOIDING MIS-STEAKS

By American standards, the French undercook meats. In France, rare (*saignant*) is nearly raw, medium (*à point*) is rare, and well-done (*bien cuit*) is medium.

tenderloin	*médaillon*	may-dī-yohn
T-bone	*côte de boeuf*	koht duh buhf
tenderloin of T-bone	*tournedos*	toor-nah-doh
alive	*vivant*	vee-vahn
raw	*cru*	krew
very rare	*bleu*	bluh
rare	*saignant*	sayn-yahn
medium	*à point*	ah pwan
well-done	*bien cuit*	bee-an kwee
very well-done	*très bien cuit*	treh bee-an kwee

Meat, but...

These are the cheapest items on a menu for good reason.

brains	*cervelle*	sehr-vehl
calf pancreas	*ris de veau*	ree duh voh
horse meat	*viande de cheval*	vee-ahnd duh shuh-vahl
intestines	*andouillette*	ahn-doo-yeht
liver	*foie*	fwah
tongue	*langue*	lahng
tripe	*tripes*	treep

How Food is Prepared

assorted	*assiette, variés*	ahs-yeht, vah-ree-ay
baked	*cuit au four*	kweet oh foor
boiled	*bouilli*	boo-yee
braised	*braisé*	breh-zay
cold	*froid*	frwah
cooked	*cuit*	kwee
deep-fried	*frit*	free
fillet	*filet*	fee-lay

EATING

fresh	*frais*	fray
fried	*frit*	free
grilled, broiled	*grillé*	gree-yay
homemade	*fait à la maison*	fay ah lah may-zoh<u>n</u>
hot	*chaud*	shoh
in cream sauce	*en crème*	ah<u>n</u> krehm
medium	*moyen*	moh-yah<u>n</u>
microwave	*four à micro-ondes*	foor ah mee-kroh-oh<u>n</u>d
mild	*doux*	doo
mixed	*mixte*	meekst
poached	*poché*	poh-shay
rare	*saignant*	sayn-yah<u>n</u>
raw	*cru*	krew
roasted	*rôti*	roh-tee
sautéed	*sauté*	soh-tay
smoked	*fumé*	few-may
sour	*aigre*	ay-gruh
spicy hot	*piquant*	pee-kah<u>n</u>
steamed	*à la vapeur*	ah lah vah-pur
stuffed	*farci*	far-see
sweet	*doux*	doo
topped with cheese	*gratinée*	grah-tee-nay
well-done	*bien cuit*	bee-a<u>n</u> kwee
with rice	*avec du riz*	ah-vehk dew ree

FRENCH REGIONAL SPECIALTIES

Each region is followed by the name of a local city (in parentheses) and the region's specialties.

Alps (Chamonix): Try *raclette* (melted cheese over potatoes and meats) and *fondue Savoyarde* (cheese fondue).

Alsace (Colmar): Flavored by German heritage, Alsace is known for *choucroute* (sauerkraut and sausage), *tarte à l'oignon* (onion tart), *tarte flambée* (thin quiche), and *baeckeanoffe* (stew of onions, meat, and potatoes).

–continues–

EATING

FRENCH REGIONAL SPECIALTIES –continued

Burgundy (Beaune): This wine region excels in *coq au vin* (chicken with wine sauce), *boeuf bourgignon* (beef stew cooked with wine, bacon, onions, and mushrooms), *oeufs en meurette* (eggs poached in red wine), *escargots* (snails), and *jambon persillé* (ham with garlic and parsley).

Languedoc (Carcassonne): Try the hearty *cassoulet* (white bean, duck, and sausage stew), *canard* (duck), and *cargolade* (snail, lamb, and sausage stew).

Loire Valley (Amboise): Savor the fresh *truite* (trout), *veau* (veal), *rillettes* (cold minced pork paté), *fromage du chèvre* (goat cheese), *aspèrges* (asparagus), and *champignons* (mushrooms).

Normandy (Bayeux): Munch some *moules* (mussels) and *escalope Normande* (veal in cream sauce). Swallow some *cidre* (apple cider) or *calvados* (apple brandy).

Périgord (Sarlat): The food is ducky. Try the *confit de canard* (duck cooked in its own juice), *pâté de foie gras* (goose liver paté), *salade périgourdine* (mixed green salad with foie gras, gizzards, and various duck parts), *pommes sarladaise* (potatoes fried in duck fat), *truffes* (truffles, earthy mushrooms), and anything with *noix* (walnuts).

Provence (Avignon): Sample the *soupe au pistou* (vegetable soup with garlic, cheese, and basil), *ratatouille* (casserole of eggplant, zucchini, tomatoes, onions, and green peppers), *brandade* (salted cod in garlic cream), and *tapenade* (a spread of pureed olives, garlic, and anchovies).

Riviera (Nice): Dive into *bouillabaisse* (seafood stew), *bourride* (creamy fish soup), *salade niçoise* (salad with potatoes, tomatoes, olives, tuna, and anchovies), and *pan bagna* (a salade niçoise on a bun).

EATING

Veggies

vegetables	*légumes*	lay-gewm
mixed vegetables	*légumes variés*	lay-gewm vah-ree-ay
with vegetables	*garni*	gar-nee
artichoke	*artichaut*	ar-tee-shoh
asparagus	*asperges*	ah-spehrzh
beans	*haricots*	ah-ree-koh
beets	*betterave*	beh-teh-rahv
broccoli	*brocoli*	broh-koh-lee
cabbage	*chou*	shoo
carrots	*carottes*	kah-roht
cauliflower	*chou-fleur*	shoo-flur
corn	*maïs*	mah-ees
cucumber	*concombre*	koh<u>n</u>-koh<u>n</u>-bruh
eggplant	*aubergine*	oh-behr-zheen
garlic	*ail*	ah-ee
green beans	*haricots verts*	ah-ree-koh vehr
leeks	*poireaux*	pwah-roh
lentils	*lentilles*	lah<u>n</u>-teel
mushrooms	*champignons*	shah<u>n</u>-peen-yoh<u>n</u>
olives	*olives*	oh-leev
onions	*oignons*	oh<u>n</u>-yoh<u>n</u>
peas	*pois*	pwah
pepper...	*poivron...*	pwah-vroh<u>n</u>
...green / red / yellow	*...vert / rouge / jaune*	vehr / roozh / zhohn
pickles	*cornichons*	kor-nee-shoh<u>n</u>
potato	*pomme de terre*	pohm duh tehr
radish	*radis*	rah-dee
rice	*riz*	ree
spaghetti	*spaghetti*	spah-geh-tee
spinach	*épinards*	ay-pee-nar
tomatoes	*tomates*	toh-maht
truffles	*truffes*	trewf
zucchini	*courgette*	koor-zheht

FRENCH COOKING STYLES AND SAUCES

aïoli	ah-ee-oh-lee	garlic mayonnaise
à l'anglaise	ah lahn-glehz	boiled
au jus	oh zhew	in its natural juices
Béarnaise	bayr-nehz	sauce of egg yolks, butter, tarragon, white wine, and shallots
beurre blanc	bur blahn	sauce of butter, white wine, and shallots
Bourguignon	boor-geen-yohn	cooked in red wine
confit	kohn-fee	any meat cooked in its own fat
fines herbes	feen ehrb	with chopped fresh herbs
forestière	foh-rehs-tee-yehr	with mushrooms
gratinée	grah-tee-nay	topped with cheese, then broiled
Hollandaise	oh-lahn-dayz	sauce of butter and egg yolks
jardinière	zhar-dan-yehr	with vegetables
meunière	muhn-yehr	coated with flour and fried in butter
mornay	mor-nay	white sauce with grated gruyère cheese
Normande	nor-mahnd	cream sauce
nouvelle cuisine	noo-vehl kwee-zeen	fresh ingredients: appealing, low in fat, and expensive
Provençale	proh-vahn-sahl	with tomatoes, garlic, olive oil, and herbs

Fruits

apple	*pomme*	pohm
apricot	*abricot*	ah-bree-koh
banana	*banane*	bah-nahn
berries	*baies*	bay
cherry	*cerise*	suh-reez

date	datte	daht
fig	figue	feeg
fruit	fruit	frwee
grapefruit	pamplemousse	pahn-pluh-moos
grapes	raisins	ray-zan
lemon	citron	see-trohn
melon	melon	muh-lohn
orange	orange	oh-rahnzh
peach	pêche	pehsh
pear	poire	pwar
pineapple	ananas	ah-nah-nah
plum	prune	prewn
prune	pruneau	prew-noh
raspberry	framboise	frahn-bwahz
strawberry	fraise	frehz
tangerine	mandarine	mahn-dah-reen
watermelon	pastèque	pah-stehk

Nuts

almond	amande	ah-mahnd
chestnut	marron, chataîgne	mah-rohn, shah-tayn
coconut	noix de coco	nwah duh koh-koh
hazelnut	noisette	nwah-zeht
peanut	cacahuète	kah-kah-weet
pistachio	pistache	pee-stahsh
walnut	noix	nwah

Just Desserts

dessert	dessert	duh-sehr
cake	gâteau	gah-toh
ice cream...	glace...	glahs
...scoop	...boule	bool
...cone	...cornet	kor-nay
...cup	...bol	bohl
...vanilla	...vanille	vah-nee
...chocolate	...chocolat	shoh-koh-lah
...strawberry	...fraise	frehz

sherbet	sorbet	sor-bay
fruit cup	salade de fruits	sah-lahd duh frwee
tart	tartelette	tar-tuh-leht
pie	tarte	tart
whipped cream	crème chantilly	krehm shahn-tee-yee
pastry	pâtisserie	pah-tee-suh-ree
fruit pastry	chausson	shoh-sohn
chocolate-filled pastry	pain au chocolat	pan oh shoh-koh-lah
buttery cake	madeleine	mah-duh-lehn
crêpes	crêpes	krehp
sweet crêpes	crêpes sucrées	krehp sew-kray
cookies	petits gâteaux	puh-tee gah-toh
candy	bonbon	bohn-bohn
low calorie	bas en calories	bah ahn kah-loh-ree
homemade	fait à la maison	fay ah lah may-zohn
We'll split one.	Nous le partageons.	noo luh par-tah-zhohn
Two forks / spoons, please.	Deux fourchettes / cuillères, s'il vous plaît.	duh foor-sheht / kwee-yehr see voo play
I shouldn't, but...	Je ne devrais pas, mais...	zhuh nuh duh-vray pah may
Exquisite!	Exquis!	ehk-skee
It's heavenly!	C'est divin!	say dee-van
Death by pleasure.	C'est à mourir de plaisir.	say ah moo-reer duh play-zeer
Orgasmic.	Orgasmique.	or-gahz-meek
A moment on the lips, forever on the hips.	Un moment sur les lèvres et pour toujours sur les hanches.	uhn moh-mahn sewr lay lehv-ruh ay poor too-zhoor sewr lay ahnsh

Crème de la Crème

beignets	*bahn-yay*	fritters made with fruit (usually apples)
crème brulée	*krehm brew-lay*	rich caramelized custard
crème caramel	*krehm ka-ra-mehl*	custard with caramel sauce
crêpes suzette	*krehp soo-zeht*	crepes flambéed with an orange brandy sauce
fromage blanc	*froh-mahzh blah<u>n</u>*	fresh white cheese eaten with sugar
gâteau	*gah-toh*	decorated sponge cake layered w/ pastry cream
île flottante	*eel floh-tah<u>n</u>t*	meringues floating in cream sauce
mille feuille (literally "thousand sheets")	*meel foy-ee*	light pastry
mousse au chocolat	*moos oh shoh-koh-lah*	ultra-light chocolate pudding
poires au vin rouge	*pwar oh va<u>n</u> roozh*	pears poached in red wine and spices
profitterolle	*proh-fee-tuh-rohl*	cream puff filled with ice cream
soufflé au chocolat	*soo-flay oh shoh-koh-lah*	chocolate soufflé
tarte tatin	*tart tah-ta<u>n</u>*	upside-down apple pie
tourteau fromager	*toor-toh froh-mah-zhay*	goat-cheese cake

EATING

Drinking

Water, Milk, and Juice

mineral water...	*eau minérale...*	oh mee-nay-rahl
...carbonated	*...gazeuse*	gah-zuhz
...not carbonated	*...non gazeuse*	nohn gah-zuhz
tap water	*l'eau du robinet*	loh dew roh-bee-nay
whole milk	*lait entier*	lay ah<u>n</u>t-yay
skim milk	*lait écrémé*	lay ay-kray-may
fresh milk	*lait frais*	lay fray
chocolate milk	*lait au chocolat*	lay oh shoh-koh-lah
hot chocolate	*chocolat chaud*	shoh-koh-lah shoh
fruit juice	*jus de fruit*	zhew duh frwee
100% juice	*cent pour cent jus*	sah<u>n</u> poor sah<u>n</u> zhew
orange juice	*jus d'orange*	zhew doh-rah<u>n</u>zh
freshly squeezed	*pressé*	preh-say
apple juice	*jus de pomme*	zhew duh pohm
grapefruit juice	*jus de pamplemouse*	zhew duh pah<u>n</u>-pluh-moos
iced tea	*thé glacé*	tay glah-say
with / without...	*avec / sans...*	ah-vehk / sah<u>n</u>
...sugar	*...sucre*	sew-kruh
...ice	*...glaçons*	glah-soh<u>n</u>
glass / cup	*verre / tasse*	vehr / tahs
small / large	*petite / grande*	puh-teet / grah<u>n</u>d
bottle	*bouteille*	boo-teh-ee
Is the water safe to drink?	*L'eau est potable?*	loh ay poh-tah-bluh

To get free tap water at a restaurant, say, "*L'eau du robinet, s'il vous plaît.*" The French typically order mineral water (and wine) with their meals. The half-liter plastic water bottles with screw tops are light and sturdy—great to pack along and re-use as you travel.

KEY PHRASES: DRINKING

drink	*verre*	vehr
(mineral) water	*eau (minérale)*	oh (mee-nay-rahl)
tap water	*l'eau du robinet*	loh dew roh-bee-nay
milk	*lait*	lay
juice	*jus*	zhew
coffee	*café*	kah-fay
tea	*thé*	tay
wine	*vin*	va<u>n</u>
beer	*bière*	bee-ehr
Cheers!	*Santé!*	sah<u>n</u>-tay

Coffee and Tea

coffee...	*café...*	kah-fay
...black	*...noir*	nwar
...with milk	*...crème*	krehm
...with lots of milk	*...au lait*	oh lay
...American-style	*...américain*	ah-may-ree-ka<u>n</u>
espresso	*express*	"express"
espresso with a touch of brandy	*café-calva*	kah-fay-kahl-vah
espresso with a touch of milk	*noisette*	nwah-zeht
instant coffee	*Nescafé*	"Nescafé"
decaffeinated / decaf	*décaféiné / déca*	day-kah-fay-nay / day-kah
sugar	*sucre*	sew-kruh
hot water	*l'eau chaude*	loh shohd
tea / lemon	*thé / citron*	tay / see-troh<u>n</u>
tea bag	*sachet de thé*	sah-shay duh tay
herbal tea	*tisane*	tee-zahn
lemon tea / orange tea	*thé au citron / thé à l'orange*	tay oh see-troh<u>n</u> / tay ah loh-rah<u>n</u>zh
peppermint tea / fruit tea	*thé à la menthe / thé de fruit*	tay ah lah mehnt / tay duh frwee
small / big	*petit / grand*	puh-tee / grah<u>n</u>

EATING

Another cup.	*Encore une tasse.*	ah<u>n</u>-kor ewn tahs
Is it the same price	*C'est le même prix au*	say luh mehm pree oh
if I sit or stand?	*bar ou dans la salle?*	bar oo dah<u>n</u> lah sahl

Every **café** or **bar** has a complete price list posted. In bigger cities, prices go up when you sit down. It's cheapest to stand at the bar (**au bar** or **au comptoir**), more expensive to sit in the dining room (**la salle**), and most expensive to sit outside (**la terrasse**). Refills aren't free.

Wine

I would like...	*Je voudrais...*	zhuh voo-dray
We would like...	*Nous voudrions...*	noo voo-dree-oh<u>n</u>
...a glass...	*...un verre...*	uh<u>n</u> vehr
...a carafe..	*...une carafe...*	ewn kah-rahf
...a half bottle..	*...une demi-bouteille...*	ewn duh-mee-boo-teh-ee
...a bottle..	*...une bouteille...*	ewn boo-teh-ee
...a 5-liter jug..	*...un bidon de*	uh<u>n</u> bee-doh<u>n</u> duh
	cinq litres...	sa<u>n</u>k lee-truh
...a barrel..	*...un tonneau...*	uh<u>n</u> toh-noh
...a vat..	*...un fût...*	uh<u>n</u> foewt
...of red wine	*...de vin rouge*	duh va<u>n</u> roozh
...of white wine	*...de vin blanc*	duh va<u>n</u> blah<u>n</u>
...of the region.	*...de la région.*	duh lah ray-zhee-oh<u>n</u>
...the wine list.	*...la carte des vins.*	lah kart day va<u>n</u>

In France, wine is a work of art. Each wine-growing region and each vintage has its own distinct personality. I prefer drinking wine from the region I'm in. Ask for **vin de la région,** available at reasonable prices. As you explore France, look for the **dégustation** signs welcoming you in for a wine tasting. It's normally free or very cheap. To get a decent table wine in a region that doesn't produce wine (Normandy, Brittany, Paris / Ile de France), ask for **un Côtes du Rhône.**

Look for these regional specialties. **Alsace** specializes in white wines—try the *Reisling*, *Tokay*, and *Slyvaner*. **Bordeaux** offers elegant, expensive red wines, along with *Sauternes* (a sweet dessert wine) and *Graves* (a fine white).

Burgundy has the best *Chardonnay* in France. Its reds are mostly *Pinot Noir*—to save money, try a *Gamay*. The people of **Brittany** are proud of their *Muscadet* (excellent with seafood). In **Périgord**, try the full-bodied red *Cahors*. The **Loire Valley** produces dry whites (*Sancerre* and *Pouilly Fumé*) and the sweet white *Vouvray* wines. Fruity reds rule **Provence**—look for *Côtes du Rhône* and *Chateauneuf du Pape*. Hilly **Champagne** pops the cork on the finest *champagne* in the world.

Wine Words

wine	*vin*	va<u>n</u>
table wine	*vin de table*	va<u>n</u> duh tah-bluh
house wine (cheapest)	*vin ordinaire*	va<u>n</u> or-dee-nair
local	*du coin*	dew kwa<u>n</u>
of the region	*de la région*	duh lah ray-zhee-oh<u>n</u>
red	*rouge*	roozh
white	*blanc*	blah<u>n</u>
rosé	*rosé*	roh-zay
sparkling	*mousseux*	moo-suh
sweet	*doux*	doo
semi-dry	*demi-sec*	duh-mee-sehk
dry	*sec*	sehk
very dry	*brut*	brewt
full-bodied	*robuste*	roh-boost
fruity	*fruité*	frwee-tay
light	*léger*	lay-zhay
mature	*prêt à boire*	preh ah bwar
cork	*bouchon*	boo-shoh<u>n</u>
corkscrew	*tire-bouchon*	teer-boo-shoh<u>n</u>
vineyard	*vignoble*	veen-yoh-bluh
harvest	*vendange*	vah<u>n</u>-dah<u>n</u>zh

EATING

| What is a good vintage? | *Quelles est un bon millésime?* | kehl ay uh<u>n</u> boh<u>n</u> mee-lay-zeem |
| What do you recommend? | *Qu'est-ce que vous recommandez?* | kehs kuh voo ruh-koh-mah<u>n</u>-day |

Wine Labels

The information on a French wine label can give you a lot of details about the wine. Listed below are several terms to help you identify and choose a specific wine.

AOC (appellation d'origine contrôlée)	meets nationwide laws for production of the highest-quality French wines
VDQS (vin délimité de qualité supérieure)	quality standards for specific regional wines
vin de pays	local wine (medium quality)
vin de table	table wine (quality varies)
millésime	vintage
mis en bouteilles dans nos caves	bottled in our cellars
cru	superior growth
cépage	grape variety

Beer

beer	*bière*	bee-ehr
from the tap	*pression*	preh-see-oh<u>n</u>
bottle	*bouteille*	boo-teh-ee
light / dark	*blonde / brune*	bloh<u>n</u>d / brewn
local / imported	*régionale / importée*	ray-zhee-oh-nahl / a<u>n</u>-por-tay
a small beer	*un demi*	uh<u>n</u> duh-mee
a large beer	*une chope*	ewn shohp
low-calorie beer (hard to find)	*biere "light"*	bee-ehr "light"
alcohol-free	*sans alcool*	sah<u>n</u>z ahl-kohl
hard apple cider	*cidre*	see-druh
cold	*fraîche*	fraysh
colder	*plus fraîche*	plew fraysh

Bar Talk

Would you like to go out for a drink?	Voulez-vous prendre un verre?	voo-lay-vooz prah<u>n</u>-druh uh<u>n</u> vehr
I'll buy you a drink.	Je vous offre un verre.	zhuh voo oh-fruh uh<u>n</u> vehr
It's on me.	C'est moi qui paie.	say mwah kee pay
The next one's on me.	Le suivant est sur moi.	luh see-vah<u>n</u> ay sewr mwhah
What would you like?	Qu'est-ce que vous prenez?	kehs kuh voo pruh-nay
I'll have a...	Je prends un...	zhuh prah<u>n</u> uh<u>n</u>
I don't drink alcohol.	Je ne bois pas d'alcool.	zhuh nuh bwah pah dahl-kohl
alcohol-free	sans alcool	sah<u>n</u>z ahl-kohl
What is the local specialty?	Quelle est la spécialité régionale?	kehl ay lah spay-see-ah-lee-tay ray-zhee-oh-nahl
What is a good drink for a man / a woman?	Quelle est une bonne boisson pour un homme / une dame?	kehl ay ewn buhn bwah-soh<u>n</u> poor uh<u>n</u> ohm / ewn dahm
Straight.	Sec.	sehk
With / Without...	Avec / Sans...	ah-vehk / sah<u>n</u>
...alcohol.	...alcool.	ahl-kohl
...ice.	...glaçons.	glah-soh<u>n</u>
One more.	Encore une.	ah<u>n</u>-kor ewn
Cheers!	Santé!	sah<u>n</u>-tay
To your health!	À votre santé!	ah voh-truh sah<u>n</u>-tay
Long live France!	Vive la France!	veev lah frah<u>n</u>s
I'm feeling...	Je me sens...	zhuh muh sah<u>n</u>
...tipsy.	...éméché.	ay-may-shay
...a little drunk.	...un peu ivre.	uh<u>n</u> puh ee-vruh
...blitzed. (m / f)	...ivre mort / ivre morte.	ee-vruh mor / ee-vruh mort
I'm hung over.	J'ai la gueule de bois.	zhay lah guhl duh bwah

EATING

An *apéritif* is served before dinner, and a *digestif* is served after dinner. Ask what's local.

Typical *apéritifs* are *champagne, bière* (beer), *kir* (white wine and black currant liqueur), *kir royal* (champagne with cassis), *pastis* (anise-flavored—Pernod and Ricard are popular brands), *pineau* (cognac and grape juice), and *port.*

Common *digestifs* (for after the meal) are *cognac* (wine-distilled brandy from the Charentes region—well-known brands are Rémy Martin, Hennessy, and Martel), *armagnac* (cognac from a different region), *calvados* (apple brandy from Normandy), *eaux de vie* (fruit brandy, literally "waters of life"—Framboise, Poire William, and Kirsch are best known), and liqueurs such as *Cointreau* (orange-based), *Chartreuse* and *Benedictine* (two distinct, herb-based liqueurs, made by monks with secret formulas), *Grand Marnier* (orange brandy), *B&B* (brandy and Benedictine), *crème de menthe,* and *Chambord* (raspberry).

Picnicking

At the Grocery

Is it self-service?	*C'est libre service?*	say lee-bruh sehr-vees
Ripe for today?	*Pour manger aujourd'hui?*	poor mahn-zhay oh-joord-wee
Does it need to be cooked?	*Il faut le faire cuire?*	eel foh luh fair kweer
Can I taste it?	*Je peux goûter?*	zhuh puh goo-tay
Fifty grams.	*Cinquante grammes.*	san-kahnt grahm
One hundred grams.	*Cent grammes.*	sahn grahm
More. / Less.	*Plus. / Moins.*	plew / mwan
A piece.	*Un morceau.*	uhn mor-soh
A slice.	*Une tranche.*	ewn trahnsh
Four slices.	*Quatre tranches.*	kah-truh trahnsh
Sliced.	*Tranché.*	trahn-shay
Half.	*La moitié.*	lah mwaht-yay
A few.	*Quelques.*	kehl-kuh
A handful.	*Une poignée.*	ewn pwahn-yay
A small bag.	*Un petit sachet.*	uhn puh-tee sah-shay
A bag, please.	*Un sachet, s'il vous plaît.*	uhn sah-shay see voo play
Can you make me...?	*Vous pouvez me faire...?*	voo poo-vay muh fair
Can you make us...?	*Vous pouvez nous faire...?*	voo poo-vay noo fair
...a sandwich	*...un sandwich*	uhn sahnd-weech
...two sandwiches	*...deux sandwiches*	duh sahnd-weech
To take out.	*Pour emporter.*	poor ahn-por-tay
Can I / Can we use...?	*Je peux / Nous pouvons utiliser...?*	zhuh puh / noo poo-vohn oo-tee-lee-zay
...the microwave	*...le micro-onde*	luh mee-kroh-ohnd
May I borrow a...?	*Je peux emprunter...?*	zhuh puh ahn-pruhn-tay
Do you have a...?	*Vous avez...?*	vooz ah-vay

EATING

Where can I buy / find a...?	*Où puis-je acheter / trouver un...?*	oo pwee-zhuh ah-shuh-tay / troo-vay uh<u>n</u>
...corkscrew	*...tire-bouchon*	teer-boo-shoh<u>n</u>
...can opener	*...ouvre boîte*	oo-vruh bwaht
Is there a park nearby?	*Il y a un parc près d'ici?*	eel yah uh<u>n</u> park preh dee-see
Where is a good place to picnic?	*Il y a un coin sympa pour pique-niquer?*	eel yah uh<u>n</u> kwa<u>n</u> sah<u>n</u>-pah poor peek-nee-kay
Is picnicking allowed here?	*On peut pique-niquer ici?*	oh<u>n</u> puh peek-nee-kay ee-see

Ask if there's a *marché* (open air market) nearby. These lively markets offer the best selection and ambience.

Tasty Picnic Words

open air market	*marché*	mar-shay
grocery store	*épicerie*	ay-pee-suh-ree
supermarket	*supermarché*	sew-pehr-mar-shay
super-duper market	*hypermarché*	ee-pehr-mar-shay
delicatessen	*charcuterie- traiteur*	shar-koo-tuh-ree- tray-tur
bakery	*boulangerie*	boo-lah<u>n</u>-zhuh-ree
pastry shop	*patisserie*	pah-tee-suh-ree
sweets shop	*confiserie*	koh<u>n</u>-fee-suh-ree
cheese shop	*fromagerie*	froh-mah-zhuh-ree
picnic	*pique-nique*	peek-neek
sandwich	*sandwich*	sah<u>n</u>d-weech
bread	*pain*	pa<u>n</u>
roll	*petit pain*	puh-tee pa<u>n</u>
ham	*jambon*	zhah<u>n</u>-boh<u>n</u>
sausage	*saucisse*	soh-sees
cheese	*fromage*	froh-mahzh
mustard...	*moutarde...*	moo-tard

EATING

mayonnaise...	*mayonnaise...*	mah-yuh-nehz
...in a tube	*...en tube*	ah<u>n</u> tewb
yogurt	*yaourt*	yah-oort
fruit	*fruit*	frwee
juice	*jus*	zhew
cold drinks	*boissons fraîches*	bwah-soh<u>n</u> frehsh
spoon / fork...	*cuillère / fourchette...*	kwee-yehr / foor-sheht
...made of plastic	*...en plastique*	ah<u>n</u> plah-steek
cup / plate...	*gobelet / assiette...*	gob-leh / ahs-yeht
...made of paper	*...en papier*	ah<u>n</u> pahp-yay

For convenience, you can assemble your picnic at a *supermarché* (supermarket)—but smaller shops or a *marché* (open-air market) are more fun. Get bread for your sandwich at a **boulangerie** and order meat and cheese by the gram at an *épicerie.* One hundred grams is about a quarter pound, enough for two sandwiches. To weigh and price your produce at more modern stores, put it on the scale, push the photo or number (keyed to the bin it came from), and then stick your sticker on the food. To get real juice, look for *100%* or *sans sucre* on the label.

MENU
DECODER

French/English

This handy decoder won't list every word on the menu, but it'll help you get *riz et veau* (rice and veal) instead of *ris de veau* (calf pancreas).

à l'anglaise	boiled
à la carte	side dishes
à la vapeur	steamed
à point	medium (meat)
abricot	apricot
agneau	lamb
ail	garlic
aïoli	garlic mayonnaise
alcool	alcohol
amande	almond
amuse bouche	munchies
ananas	pineapple
anchois	anchovies
artichaut	artichoke
asperges	asparagus
assiette	plate
assiette d'enfant	children's plate

au jus	in its natural juices
auberge	country inn
aubergine	eggplant
avec	with
baguette	long loaf of bread
baies	berries
banane	banana
Béarnaise	sauce of egg and wine
beignets	fritters with fruit
betterave	beets
beurre	butter
beurre blanc	sauce of butter, white wine, and shallots
beurre de cacahuètes	peanut butter
bien cuit	well-done (meat)
bière	beer
bifteck	beef steak
biologique	organic
bisque	shellfish chowder
bistro	small, informal restaurant
blanc	white
bleu	blue (cheese); very rare (meat)
blonde	light
boeuf	beef
boissons	beverages
bon	good
bonbon	candy
bouchée à la reine	pastry shell with creamed sweetbreads
bouillabaisse	seafood stew
bouilli	boiled
bouillon	broth
boulangerie	bakery
boule	scoop
Bourguignon	cooked in red wine
bouteille	bottle
braisé	braised

brasserie	large café with simple food
brioche	sweet, flaky roll
brocoli	broccoli
brouillés	scrambled
brune	dark
brut	very dry (wine)
cabillaud	cod
cacahuète	peanut
café	coffee
café américain	American-style coffee
café au lait	coffee with lots of milk
café crème	coffee with milk
café noir	black coffee
café-calva	espresso with a touch of brandy
calamar	squid
canard	duck
carafe	carafe
carottes	carrots
carte	menu
carte des consommation	drink menu
carte des vins	wine list
cassoulet	bean and meat stew
cerise	cherry
cervelle	brains
champignons	mushrooms
charcuterie	delicatessen
chataîgne	chestnut
chaud	hot
chausson	fruit pastry
cheval	horse
chèvre	goat
chinois	Chinese
chocolat	chocolate
chope	large beer
chorizo	pepperoni
chou	cabbage
chou-fleur	cauliflower

cidre	hard apple cider
citron	lemon
complet	whole, full
compris	included
concombre	cucumber
confiserie	sweets shop
confit	cooked in its own fat
confiture	jelly
consommé	broth
copieux	filling
coq	rooster
coquilles	scallops
cornichon	pickle
costaud	full-bodied (wine)
côte de boeuf	T-bone
côtelette	cutlet
courgette	zucchini
couvert	cover charge
crabe	crab
crème	cream
crème (velouté) d'asperges	cream of asparagus soup
crème brulée	caramelized custard
crème caramel	custard with caramel sauce
crème chantilly	whipped cream
crêpe	crepe
crêpes froment	buckwheat crepes
crêpes sucrées	sweet crepes
crêpes suzette	crepes flambéed with orange brandy sauce
crevettes	shrimp
croissant	crescent roll
croque madame	ham, cheese, and egg sandwich
croque monsieur	ham and cheese sandwich
crôute au fromage	cheese pastry
cru	raw
crudités	raw vegetables
cuisses de grenouilles	frog legs

cuit	cooked
cuit au four	baked
cure-dent	toothpick
datte	date
déjeuner	lunch
demi	half, small beer
demi-bouteille	half bottle
demi-sec	medium, semi-dry (wine)
dinde	turkey
dîner	dinner
doux	mild, sweet (wine)
eau	water
édulcorant	artificial sweetener
emmenthal	Swiss cheese
entier	whole
entrecôte	rib steak
entrée	first course
épicée	spicy
épinards	spinach
escargots	snails
et	and
express	espresso
fait à la maison	homemade
farci	stuffed
faux-filet	flank steak
figue	fig
filet	fillet
fines herbes	with chopped fresh herbs
flambée	flaming
foie	liver
forestière	with mushrooms
fort	sharp (cheese)
fougasse	lace-like bread
frais	fresh
fraise	strawberry
framboise	raspberry
frit	fried

froid	cold
fromage	cheese
fromage à la crème	cream cheese
fromage aux herbes	cheese with herbs
fromage blanc	fresh white cheese eaten with sugar
fromage bleu	bleu cheese
fromage chèvre	goat cheese
fromage de la région	cheese of the region
fromage doux	mild cheese
fromage fort	sharp cheese
fromagerie	cheese shop
froment	wheat
fruit	fruit
fruité	fruity (wine)
fruits de mer	seafood
fumé	smoked
galette	buckwheat crepe
garni	with vegetables
gâteau	cake
gazeuse	carbonated
glace	ice cream
glaçons	ice
grand	large
gras	fat
gratinée	topped with cheese
grenouille	frog
grillades	mixed grill
grillé	grilled
gruyère	Swiss cheese
hareng	herring
haricots	beans
Hollandaise	sauce of egg and butter
homard	lobster
hors d'oeuvre	appetizers
huile	oil
huîtres	oysters

île flottante	meringues floating in cream sauce
importée	imported
jambon	ham
jardinière	with vegetables
jus	juice
kasher	kosher
La vache qui rit	Laughing Cow (brand of cheese)
lait	milk
laitue	lettuce
langue	tongue
lapin	rabbit
léger	light
légumes	vegetables
lentilles	lentils
light	light
madeleine	buttery cake
maïs	corn
maison	house
mandarine	tangerine
marron	chestnut
médaillon	tenderloin
melon	canteloupe
menu du jour	menu of the day
meunière	fried in butter
micro-onde	microwave
miel	honey
mille feuille	light pastry
millésime	vintage date (wine)
mixte	mixed
morceau	piece
mornay	white sauce with gruyère
morue	salty cod
moules	mussels
mousseux	sparkling
moutarde	mustard
Nescafé	instant coffee

noir	black
noisette	hazelnut
noix	walnut
noix de coco	coconut
Normande	cream sauce
nouvelle	new
oeufs	eggs
oeufs à la coque	boiled eggs
(mollet / dur)	(soft / hard)
oeufs au plat	fried eggs
oeufs brouillés	scrambled eggs
oignon	onion
olives	olives
onglet	steak
orange	orange
ou	or
pain	bread
pain bisse	dark-grain bread
pain complet	whole-grain bread
pain de seigle	dark bread
palourdes	clams
pamplemousse	grapefruit
pas	not
pastèque	watermelon
pâté	paté
pâtes	pasta
pâtisserie	pastry, pastry shop
pêche	peach
petit	small
petit déjeuner	breakfast
petits gâteaux	cookies
petits pois	peas
piquant	spicy hot
pissaladière	onion and anchovy pizza
pistache	pistachio
plat du jour	special of the day
plat principal	main course

plâteau	platter
plâteau de fromages	cheese platter
poché	poached
poire	pear
poireaux	leeks
poires au vin rouge	pears poached in red wine and spices
pois	peas
poisson	fish
poivre	pepper
poivron	bell pepper
pomme	apple
pomme de terre	potato
pommes frites	French fries
porc	pork
potage	soup
potage de légumes	thick vegetable soup
poulet	chicken
pour emporter	to go
pression	draft (beer)
prix fixe	fixed price
profitterole	cream puff with ice cream
Provençale	with garlic and tomatoes
prune	plum
pruneau	prune
quenelles	meat or fish dumplings
quiche	quiche
quiche au fromage	quiche with cheese
quiche au jambon	quiche with ham
quiche aux champignons	quiche with mushrooms
quiche lorraine	quiche with bacon, cheese, and onions
radis	radish
ragoût	meat stew
raisins	grapes
ratatouille	eggplant casserole
régionale	local

rillettes	cold, minced pork
ris de veau	sweetbreads
riz	rice
robuste	full-bodied (wine)
rosbif	roast beef
rosé	rosé (wine)
rôti	roasted
rouge	red
routier	truck stop with simple food
saignant	rare (meat)
salade	salad
sans	without
sauce	sauce
saucisse	sausage
saucisse-frites	hot dog and fries
saumon	salmon
scampi	prawns
sec	dry
sel	salt
service compris	service included
service non compris	service not included
sorbet	sherbet
soufflé	soufflé (light, fluffy eggs baked with savory fillings)
soufflé au chocolat	chocolate soufflé
soupe	soup
soupe à l'oignon	onion soup
soupe au pistou	Provençal vegetable soup
spécialité	specialty
steak tartare	raw hamburger
sucre	sugar
tapenade	olive, anchovy paste
tartare	raw
tarte	pie
tarte à l'oignon	onion tart
tarte au fromage	cheese tart
tarte tatin	upside-down apple pie

tartelette	tart
tasse	cup
terrine	paté
thé	tea
thon	tuna
tire-bouchon	corkscrew
tisane	herbal tea
tournedos	tenderloin of T-bone
tourteau fromager	goat cheese cake
tranche	slice
tranché	sliced
très bien cuit	very well-done (meat)
tripes	tripe
truffes	truffles (earthy mushrooms)
truite	trout
vapeur	steamed
variées	assorted
veau	veal
végétarien	vegetarian
vendange	harvest (wine)
verre	glass
vert	green
viande	meat
vichyssoise	potato, leek soup
vignoble	vineyard
vin	wine
vin de table	table wine
vin ordinaire	house wine
vinaigre	vinegar
volaille	poultry
yaourt	yogurt

English/French

alcohol	alcool
almond	amande
anchovies	anchois
and	et
appetizers	hors d'oeuvre
apple	pomme
apple cider, hard	cidre
apple pie, upside-down	tarte tatin
apricot	abricot
artichoke	artichaut
artificial sweetener	édulcorant
asparagus	asperges
assorted	variées
baked	cuit au four
bakery	boulangerie
banana	banane
beans	haricots
beef	boeuf
beef steak	bifteck
beer	bière
beer, draft	pression
beer, large	chope
beer, small (half)	demi
beets	betterave
bell pepper	poivron
berries	baies
beverages	boissons
black	noir
blue cheese	fromage bleu
boiled	à l'anglaise, bouilli
boiled egg	oeuf à la coque
(soft / hard)	(mollet / dur)
bottle	bouteille
brains	cervelle

braised	braisé
bread	pain, baguette
bread, dark-grain	pain bisse, pain de seigle
bread, lace-like	fougasse
bread, whole-grain	pain complet
breakfast	petit déjeuner
broccoli	brocoli
broth	bouillon, consommé
buckwheat crêpe	galette, crepe froment
butter	beurre
cabbage	chou
cake	gateau
candy	bonbon
canteloupe	melon
carafe	carafe
caramelized custard	crème brulée
carbonated	gazeuse
carrots	carottes
cauliflower	chou-fleur
cheese	fromage
cheese of the region	fromage de la région
cheese pastry	croute au fromage
cheese platter	plateau de fromages
cheese shop	fromagerie
cheese tart	tarte au fromage
cheese with herbs	fromage aux herbes
cheese, blue	fromage bleu
cheese, cream	fromage à la crème
cheese, Laughing Cow	La vache qui rit
cheese, Swiss	gruyère, emmenthal
cheese, topped with	gratinée
cheese, white	fromage blanc
cherry	cerise
chestnut	chataigne, marron
chicken	poulet
children's plate	assiette d'enfant
Chinese	chinois

chocolate	chocolat
chocolate soufflé	soufflé au chocolat
clams	palourdes
coconut	noix de coco
cod	cabillaud
cod, salty	morue
coffee	café
coffee, American-style	café américain
coffee, black	café noir
coffee, instant	Nescafé
coffee with lots of milk	café au lait
coffee with some milk	café crème
cold	froid
cooked	cuit
cooked in its own fat	confit
cooked in red wine	Bourguignon
cookies	petits gateaux
corkscrew	tire-bouchon
corn	maïs
country inn	auberge
course, first	entrée
course, main	plat principal
cover charge	couvert
crab	crabe
cream	crème
cream cheese	fromage à la crème
cream puff (with ice cream)	profitterole
cream sauce	Normande
crêpe	crepe
crêpe, buckwheat	galette, crepe froment
crêpes flambéed with orange brandy sauce	crepes suzette
crêpes, sweet	creepes sucrées
crescent roll	croissant
cucumber	concombre
cup	tasse
custard with caramel sauce	crème caramel

custard, caramelized	crème brulée
cutlet	cotelette
dark	brune
dark-grain bread	pain bisse, pain de seigle
date	datte
delicatessen	charcuterie
dinner	diner
draft (beer)	pression
drink menu	carte des consommation
dry	sec
dry, very (wine)	brut
duck	canard
dumplings, meat or fish	quenelles
eggplant	aubergine
eggplant casserole	ratatouille
eggs	oeufs
eggs, boiled	oeuf à la coque
(soft / hard)	(mollet / dur)
eggs, fried	oeufs au plat
eggs, scrambled	oeufs brouillés
espresso	express
espresso with brandy	café-calva
fat	gras
fig	figue
fillet	filet
filling	copieux
first course	entrée
fish	poisson
fixed price	prix fixe
flaming	flambée
flank steak	faux-filet
French fries	pommes frites
fresh	frais
fried	frit
fried eggs	oeufs au plat
fried in butter	meunière
fritters	beignets

frog	grenouille
frog legs	cuisses de grenouilles
fruit	fruit
fruit pastry	chausson
fruity (wine)	fruité
full-bodied (wine)	robuste, costaud
garlic	ail
garlic and tomatoes, with	Provençale
garlic mayonnaise	aïoli
glass	verre
goat	chèvre
goat cheese	fromage chèvre
good	bon
grapefruit	pamplemousse
grapes	raisins
green	vert
grill, mixed	grillades
grilled	grillé
half bottle	demi-bouteille
half, small beer	demi
ham	jambon
ham and cheese sandwich	croque monsieur
ham and egg sandwich	croque madame
hard apple cider	cidre
harvest (wine)	vendange
hazelnut	noisette
herbal tea	tisane
herring	hareng
homemade	fait à la maison
honey	miel
horse	cheval
hot	chaud
hot dog and fries	saucisse-frites
house	maison
house wine	vin ordinaire
ice	glaçons
ice cream	glace

imported	importée
included	compris
jelly	confiture
juice	jus
kosher	kasher
lamb	agneau
large	grand
large beer	chope
Laughing Cow cheese	La vache qui rit
leeks	poireaux
lemon	citron
lentils	lentilles
lettuce	laitue
light	blonde
light	léger
liver	foie
lobster	homard
local	régionale
lunch	déjeuner
main course	plat principal
mayonnaise, garlic	aïoli
meat	viande
meat stew	ragout
medium (meat)	à point
medium (wine)	demi-sec
menu	carte
menu of the day	menu du jour
menu, drink	carte des consommation
menu, wine	carte des vins
microwave	micro-onde
mild (cheese)	doux
mild, sweet (wine)	doux
milk	lait
mixed	mixte
mixed grill	grillades
munchies	amuse bouche
mushrooms	champignons

mushrooms, with	forestière
mussels	moules
mustard	moutarde
new	nouvelle
not	pas
oil	huile
olives	olives
onion	oignon
onion tart	tarte à l'oignon
or	ou
orange	orange
organic	biologique
oysters	huitres
pasta	pates
pastry shop	patisserie
pâté	paté, terrine
peach	peche
peanut	cacahuète
peanut butter	beurre de cacahuètes
pear	poire
peas	pois
pepper	poivre
pepper (bell)	poivron
pepperoni	chorizo
pickle	cornichon
pie	tarte
piece	morceau
pineapple	ananas
pistachio	pistache
plate	assiette
platter	plateau
plum	prune
poached	poché
pork	porc
potato	pomme de terre
poultry	volaille
prawns	scampi

prune	pruneau
quiche	quiche
quiche with bacon, cheese, and onions	quiche lorraine
quiche with cheese	quiche au fromage
quiche with ham	quiche au jambon
quiche with mushrooms	quiche aux champignons
rabbit	lapin
radish	radis
rare (meat)	saignant
rare, very (meat)	bleu
raspberry	framboise
raw	cru, tartare
raw hamburger	steak tartare
raw vegetables	crudités
red	rouge
rib steak	entrecote
rice	riz
roast beef	rosbif
roasted	roti
rooster	coq
rosé (wine)	rosé
salad	salade
salmon	saumon
salt	sel
sandwich, ham and cheese	croque monsieur
sandwich, ham and egg	croque madame
sauce	sauce
sauce of butter, white wine, and shallots	beurre blanc
sauce of egg and butter	Hollandaise
sauce of egg and wine	Béarnaise
sauce, cream	Normande
sauce, white, with gruyère	mornay
sausage	saucisse
scallops	coquilles
scoop	boule

scrambled	brouillés
scrambled eggs	oeufs brouillés
seafood	fruits de mer
seafood stew	bouillabaisse
semi-dry (wine)	demi-sec
service included	service compris
service not included	service non compris
sharp (cheese)	fort
shellfish chowder	bisque
sherbet	sorbet
shrimp	crevettes
side dishes	à la carte
slice	tranche
sliced	tranché
small	petit
smoked	fumé
snacks	amuse bouche
snails	escargots
soufflé	soufflé
soufflé, chocolate	soufflé au chocolat
soup	soupe, potage
soup, cream of asparagus	crème (velouté) d'asperges
soup, onion	soupe à l'oignon
soup, potato and leek	vichyssoise
soup, Provençal vegetable	soupe au pistou
soup, thick vegetable	potage de légumes
sparkling	mousseux
special of the day	plat du jour
specialty	spécialité
spicy	épicée, piquant
spinach	épinards
squid	calamar
steak	onglet
steak, beef	bifteck
steamed	à la vapeur
stew, bean and meat	cassoulet
stew, seafood	bouillabaisse

strawberry	fraise
stuffed	farci
sugar	sucre
sweet, mild (wine)	doux
sweetbreads	ris de veau
sweetener, artificial	édulcorant
sweets shop	confiserie
Swiss cheese	gruyère, emmenthal
table wine	vin de table
tangerine	mandarine
tart	tartelette
tart, cheese	tarte au fromage
tart, onion	tarte à l'oignon
T-bone	cote de boeuf
tea	thé
tenderloin	médaillon, tournedos
to go	pour emporter
tomatoes and garlic, with	Provençale
tongue	langue
toothpick	cure-dent
tripe	tripes
trout	truite
truffles	truffes
tuna	thon
turkey	dinde
veal	veau
vegetables	légumes
vegetables, raw	crudités
vegetables, with	jardinière, garni
vegetarian	végétarien
very dry (wine)	brut
very rare (meat)	bleu
very well-done (meat)	très bien cuit
vinegar	vinaigre
vineyard	vignoble
vintage date (wine)	millésime
walnut	noix

water	eau
watermelon	pastèque
well-done (meat)	bien cuit
well-done, very (meat)	très bien cuit
wheat	froment
whipped cream	crème chantilly
white	blanc
whole (entire)	entier
whole (full)	complet
whole-grain bread	pain complet
wine	vin
wine, dry	sec
wine, fruity	fruité
wine, full-bodied	robuste, costaud
wine, medium dry	demi-sec
wine, mild, sweet	doux
wine, semi-dry	demi-sec
wine, very dry	brut
wine list	carte des vins
wine, house	vin ordinaire
wine, table	vin de table
with	avec
without	sans
yogurt	yaourt
zucchini	courgette

ACTIVITIES

Sightseeing

Where?

Where is...?	*Où est...?*	oo ay
...the tourist information office	...*l'office du tourisme*	loh-fees dew too-reez-muh
...the best view	...*la meilleure vue*	lah meh-yur vew
...the main square	...*la place principale*	lah plahs pra<u>n</u>-see-pahl
...the old town center	...*la vieille ville*	lah vee-yay-ee veel
...the museum	...*le musée*	luh mew-zay
...the castle	...*le château*	luh shah-toh
...the palace	...*le palais*	luh pah-lay
...an amusement park	...*un parc d'amusement*	uh<u>n</u> park dah-mooz-mah<u>n</u>
...the entrance / exit	...*l'entrée / la sortie*	lah<u>n</u>-tray / lah sor-tee
Where are...?	*Où sont...?*	oo soh<u>n</u>
...the toilets	...*les toilettes*	lay twah-leht
...the ruins	...*les ruines*	lay rween
Is there a festival nearby?	*Il y a un festival dans la région?*	eel yah uh<u>n</u> fehs-tee-vahl dah<u>n</u> lah ray-zhee-oh<u>n</u>

132

At the Sight

Do you have...?	*Vous avez...?*	vooz ah-vay
...information	*...des renseignements*	day rahn-sehn-yuh-mahn
...a guidebook	*...un guide*	ewn geed
...in English	*...en anglais*	ahn ahn-glay
Is it free?	*C'est gratuit?*	say grah-twee
How much is it?	*C'est combien?*	say kohn-bee-an
Is the ticket good all day?	*Le billet est valable toute la journée?*	luh bee-yay ay vah-lah-bluh toot lah zhoor-nay
Can I get back in?	*Je peux rentrer?*	zhuh puh rahn-tray
At what time does this open / close?	*À quelle heuere c'est ouvert / fermé?*	ah kehl ur say oo-vehr / fehr-may
What time is the last entry?	*La dernière entrée est à quelle heure?*	lah dehrn-yehr ahn-tray ay ah kehl ur

Please

PLEASE let me in.	*S'IL VOUS PLAÎT, laissez-moi entrer.*	see voo play lay-say-mwah ahn-tray
PLEASE let us in.	*S'IL VOUS PLAÎT, laissez-nous entrer.*	see voo play lay-say-nooz ahn-tray
I've traveled all the way from ___.	*Je suis venu de ___.*	zhuh swee vuh-new duh

---

KEY PHRASES: SIGHTSEEING

Where is...?	*Où est...?*	oo ay
How much is it?	*C'est combien?*	say kohn-bee-an
At what time does this open / close?	*À quelle heuere c'est ouvert / fermé?*	ah kehl ur say oo-vehr / fehr-may
Do you have a guided tour?	*Vous avez une visite guidée?*	vooz ah-vay ewn vee-zeet gwee-day
When is the next tour in English?	*La prochaine visite en anglais est à quelle heure?*	lah proh-shehn vee-zeet ahn ahn-glay ay ah kehl ur

We've traveled all the way from ___.	Nous sommes venus de ___.	noo suhm vuh-new duh
I must leave tomorrow.	Je dois partir demain.	zhuh dwah par-teer duh-man
We must leave tomorrow.	Nous devons partir demain.	noo duh-vohn par-teer duh-man
I promise I'll be fast.	Je promets d'aller vite.	zhuh proh-may dah-lay veet
We promise we'll be fast.	Nous promettons d'aller vite.	noo proh-meh-tohn dah-lay veet
It was my mother's dying wish that I see this.	C'était le dernier souhait de ma mère que je voies ça.	say-tay luh dehrn-yay soo-ay duh mah mehr kuh zhuh vwah sah
I've always wanted to see this.	J'ai toujours voulu voir ça.	zhay too-zhoor voo-lew vwar sah

Tours

Do you have...?	Vous avez...?	vooz ah-vay
...an audioguide	...un guide audio	uhn gweed oh-dee-oh
...a guided tour	...une visite guidée	ewn vee-zeet gwee-day
...a city walking tour	...une promenade guidée de la ville	ewn proh-muh-nahd gwee-day duh lah veel
...in English	...en anglais	ahn ahn-glay
When is the next tour in English?	La prochaine visite en anglais est à quelle heure?	lah proh-shehn vee-zeet ahn ahn-glay ay ah kehl ur
Is it free?	C'est gratuit?	say grah-twee
How much is it?	C'est combien?	say kohn-bee-an
How long does it last?	Ça dure combien de temps?	sah door kohn-bee-an duh tahn
Can I / Can we join a tour in progress?	Je peux / Nous pouvons joindre une visite qui a commencé?	zhuh puh / noo poo-vohn zhwahn-druh ewn vee-zeet kee ah koh-mahn-say

Entrance Signs

adultes	the price you'll pay
dernière entrée	last admission before sight closes
exposition	special exhibit
ticket global	combination ticket with another sight
visite guidée	guided tour
vous êtes ici	you are here (on map)

Discounts

You may be eligible for a discount at tourist sights, hotels, or on buses and trains—ask.

Is there a discount for...?	*Il y a une réduction pour...?*	eel yah ewn ray-dewk-see-ohn poor
...youth	*...les jeunes*	lay juh-nehs
...students	*...les étudiants*	layz ay-tew-dee-ahn
...families	*...les familles*	lay fah-meel
...seniors	*...les gens âgés*	lay zhahn ah-zhay
...groups	*...les groupes*	lay groop
I am...	*J'ai...*	zhay
He / She is...	*Il / Elle a...*	eel / ehl ah
...___ years old.	*...___ans.*	___ahn
...extremely old.	*...très âgé.*	treh ah-zhay

In the Museum

Where is...?	*Où est...?*	oo ay
I'd like to see...	*Je voudrais voir...*	zhuh voo-dray vwar
We'd like to see...	*Nous voudrions voir...*	noo voo-dree-ohn vwar
Photo / Video O.K.?	*Photo / Vidéo O.K.?*	foh-toh / vee-day-oh "O.K."
No flash / tripod.	*Pas de flash / trépied.*	pah duh flahsh / tray-pee-yay

I like it.	Ça me plaît.	sah muh play
It's so...	C'est si...	say see
...beautiful.	...beau.	boh
...ugly.	...laid.	lay
...strange.	...bizarre.	bee-zar
...boring.	...ennuyeux.	ahn-new-yuh
...interesting.	...intéressant.	an-tay-reh-sahn
...pretentious.	...prétentieux.	pray-tahn-see-uh
...thought-provoking.	...provocateur.	proh-voh-kah-tur
...B.S.	...con.	kohn
I don't get it.	Je n'y comprends rien.	zhuhn yuh kohn-prahn ree-an
Is it upside down?	C'est à l'envers?	say ah lahn-vehr
Who did this?	Qui a fait ça?	kee ah fay sah
How old is this?	C'est vieux?	say vee-uh
Wow!	Sensass!	sahn-sahs
My feet hurt!	J'ai mal aux pieds!	zhay mahl oh pee-yay
I'm exhausted!	Je suis épuisé!	zhuh sweez ay-pwee-zay
We're exhausted!	Nous sommes épuisé!	noo suhm ay-pwee-zay

France's national museums close on Tuesdays. For efficient sightseeing in Paris, buy a Museum Pass. It'll save you money and time (because you're entitled to slip right into museums, bypassing the notorious lines).

Art and Architecture

art	art	ar
artist	artiste	ar-teest
painting	tableau	tah-bloh
self-portrait	autoportrait	oh-toh-por-tray
sculptor	sculpteur	skewlp-tur
sculpture	sculpture	skewlp-tewr
architect	architecte	ar-shee-tehkt
architecture	architecture	ar-shee-tehk-tewr
original	original	oh-ree-zhee-nahl
restored	restauré	rehs-toh-ray

B.C.	*avant J.-C.*	ah-vah<u>n</u> zhay-zew-kree
A.D.	*après J.-C.*	ah-preh zhay-zew-kree
century	*siècle*	see-eh-kluh
style	*style*	steel
after the style of ___	*de l'époque ___*	duh lay-pohk
copy by ___	*reproduction de ___*	ray-proh-dook-see-oh<u>n</u> duh
from the school of ___	*de l'école de ___*	duh lay-kohl duh
abstract	*abstrait*	ahb-stray
ancient	*ancien*	ah<u>n</u>-see-a<u>n</u>
Art Nouveau	*art nouveau*	ar noo-voh
Baroque	*baroque*	bah-rohk
classical	*classique*	klahs-seek
Gothic	*gothique*	goh-teek
Impressionist	*impressionniste*	a<u>n</u>-preh-see-uh-neest
medieval	*médiéval*	mayd-yay-vahl
modern	*moderne*	moh-dehrn
neoclassical	*néoclassique*	nay-oh-klah-seek
Renaissance	*renaissance*	ruh-nay-sah<u>n</u>s
Romanesque	*romanesque*	roh-mah-nehsk
Romantic	*romantique*	roh-mah<u>n</u>-teek

Castles and Palaces

castle	*château*	shah-toh
fortified castle	*château-fort*	shah-toh-for
palace	*palais*	pah-lay
hall	*grande salle*	grah<u>n</u>d sahl
kitchen	*cuisine*	kwee-zeen
cellar	*cave*	kahv
dungeon	*cachot*	kah-shoh
castle keep	*donjon*	doh<u>n</u>-zhoh<u>n</u>
moat	*fossé*	foh-say
fortified walls	*remparts*	rah<u>n</u>-par
tower	*tour*	toor
fountain	*fontaine*	foh<u>n</u>-tehn

garden	*jardin*	zhar-da<u>n</u>
king	*roi*	rwah
queen	*reine*	rehn
knights	*chevaliers*	shuh-vahl-yay

Religious Words

cathedral	*cathédrale*	kah-tay-drahl
church	*église*	ay-gleez
monastery	*monastère*	moh-nah-stehr
mosque	*mosquée*	mohs-kay
synagogue	*synagogue*	see-nah-gohg
chapel	*chapelle*	shah-pehl
altar	*autel*	oh-tehl
bells	*cloches*	klohsh
choir	*choeur*	kur
cloister	*cloître*	klwah-truh
cross	*croix*	krwah
crypt	*crypte*	kreept
dome	*dôme*	dohm
organ	*orgue*	org
pulpit	*chaire*	shair
relic	*relique*	ruh-leek
treasury	*trésorerie*	tray-zoh-ree
saint (m /f)	*saint / sainte*	sah<u>n</u> / sah<u>nt</u>
God	*Dieu*	dee-uh
Christian	*chrétien*	kray-tee-a<u>n</u>
Protestant	*protestant*	proh-tehs-tah<u>n</u>
Catholic	*catholique*	kah-toh-leek
Jew	*juif*	zhweef
Muslim	*musulman*	mew-zewl-mah<u>n</u>
agnostic	*agnostique*	ahn-yoh-steek
atheist	*athée*	ah-tay
When is the service?	*La messe est quand?*	lah mehs ay kah<u>n</u>
Are there church concerts?	*Il y a des concerts à l'église?*	eel yah day koh<u>n</u>-sehr ah lay-gleez

Shopping

French Shops

Where is a...?	*Où est un...?*	oo ay uh<u>n</u>
antique shop	*magasin d'antiquités*	mah-gah-za<u>n</u> dah<u>n</u>-tee-kee-tay
art gallery	*gallerie d'art*	gah-luh-ree dar
bakery	*boulangerie*	boo-lah<u>n</u>-zhuh-ree
barber shop	*coiffeur*	kwah-fur
beauty salon	*coiffeur pour dames*	kwah-fur poor dahm
book shop	*librairie*	lee-bray-ree
camera shop	*magasin de photo*	mah-gah-za<u>n</u> duh foh-toh
cell phone shop	*magasin de portables*	mah-gah-za<u>n</u> duh por-tah-bluh
cheese shop	*fromagerie*	froh-mah-zhuh-ree
clothing boutique	*boutique, magasin de vêtements*	boo-teek, mah-gah-za<u>n</u> duh veht-mah<u>n</u>
coffee shop	*café*	kah-fay
delicatessen	*charcuterie-traiteur*	shar-koo-tuh-ree-tray-tur

KEY PHRASES: SHOPPING

Where can I buy...?	*Où puis-je acheter...?*	oo pwee-zhuh ah-shuh-tay
Where is...?	*Où est...?*	oo ay
...a grocery store	*...une épicerie*	ewn ay-pee-suh-ree
...a department store	*...un grand magasin*	uh<u>n</u> grah<u>n</u> mah-gah-za<u>n</u>
...an Internet café	*...un café internet*	uh<u>n</u> kah-fay a<u>n</u>-tehr-neht
...a launderette	*...une laverie*	ewn lah-vuh-ree
...a pharmacy	*...une pharmacie*	ewn far-mah-see
How much is it?	*C'est combien?*	say koh<u>n</u>-bee-a<u>n</u>
I'm just browsing.	*Je regarde.*	zhuh ruh-gard

department store	grand magasin	grahn mah-gah-zan
flea market	marché aux puces	mar-shay oh pews
flower market	marché aux fleurs	mar-shay oh flur
grocery store	épicerie	ay-pee-suh-ree
hardware store	quincaillerie	kan-kay-yay-ree
Internet café	café internet	kah-fay an-tehr-neht
jewelry shop	bijouterie	bee-zhoo-tuh-ree
launderette	laverie	lah-vuh-ree
newsstand	maison de la presse	meh-zohn duh lah prehs
office supplies	papeterie	pah-pay-tuh-ree
open-air market	marché en plein air	mar-shay ahn plan air
optician	opticien	ohp-tee-see-an
pastry shop	patisserie	pah-tee-suh-ree
pharmacy	pharmacie	far-mah-see
photocopy shop	magasin de photocopie	mah-gah-zan duh foh-toh-koh-pee
shopping mall	centre commercial	sahn-truh koh-mehr-see-ahl
souvenir shop	boutique de souvenirs	boo-teek duh soo-vuh-neer
supermarket	supermarché	sew-pehr-mar-shay
sweets shop	confiserie	kohn-fee-suh-ree
toy store	magasin de jouets	mah-gah-zan duh zhway
travel agency	agence de voyages	ah-zhahns duh voy-yahzh
used bookstore...	boutique de livres d'occasion...	boo-teek duh lee-vruh doh-kah-zee-ohn
...with books in English	...avec des livres en anglais	ah-vehk day lee-vruh ahn ahn-glay
wine shop	marchand de vin	mar-shahn duh van

In France, most shops close for a long lunch (noon until about 2:00 p.m.), and all day on Sundays and Mondays. Grocery stores are often open on Sunday mornings.

Shop Till You Drop

opening hours	*les heures d'ouverture*	layz ur doo-vehr-tewr
sale	*solde*	sohld
I'd like...	*Je voudrais...*	zhuh voo-dray
We'd like...	*Nous voudrions...*	noo voo-dree-oh<u>n</u>
Where can I buy...?	*Où puis-je acheter...?*	oo pwee-zhuh ah-shuh-tay
Where can we buy...?	*Où pouvons-nous acheter...?*	oo poo-voh<u>n</u>-noo ah-shuh-tay
How much is it?	*C'est combien?*	say koh<u>n</u>-bee-a<u>n</u>
I'm just browsing.	*Je regarde.*	zhuh ruh-gard
We're just browsing.	*Nous regardons.*	noo ruh-gar-doh<u>n</u>
Do you have...?	*Vous avez...?*	vooz ah-vay
...more	*...plus*	plew
...something cheaper	*...quelque chose de moins cher*	kehl-kuh shohz duh mwa<u>n</u> shehr
Better quality, please.	*De meilleure qualité, s'il vous plaît.*	duh meh-yur kah-lee-tay, see voo play
genuine / imitation	*authentique / imitation*	oh-tah<u>n</u>-teek / ee-mee-tah-see-oh<u>n</u>
Can I / Can we see more?	*Je peux / Nous pouvons en voir d'autres?*	zhuh puh / noo poo-voh<u>n</u> ah<u>n</u> vwar doh-truh
This one.	*Celui ci.*	suh-lwee see
Can I try it on?	*Je peux l'essayer?*	zhuh puh leh-say-yay
A mirror?	*Un miroir?*	uh<u>n</u> meer-war
Too...	*Trop...*	troh
...big.	*...grand.*	grah<u>n</u>
...small.	*...petit.*	puh-tee
...expensive.	*...cher.*	shehr
It's too...	*C'est trop...*	say troh
...short / long.	*...court / long.*	koor / loh<u>n</u>
...tight / loose.	*...serré / grand.*	suh-ray / grah<u>n</u>
...dark / light.	*...foncé / clair.*	foh<u>n</u>-say / klair
What is it made out of?	*De quoi c'est fait?*	duh kwah say fay

Is it machine washable?	C'est lavable en machine?	say lah-vah-bluh ahn mah-sheen
Will it shrink?	Ça va rétrécir?	sah vah ray-tray-seer
Will it fade in the wash?	Ça va déteindre au lavage?	sah vah day-tan-druh oh lah-vahzh
Credit card O.K.?	Carte de crédit O.K.?	kart duh kray-dee "O.K."
Can you ship this?	Vous pouvez l'envoyer?	voo poo-vay lahn-voy-ay
Tax-free?	Hors taxe?	or tahks
I'll think about it.	Je vais y penser.	zhuh vay ee pahn-say
What time do you close?	Vous fermez à quelle heure?	voo fehr-may ah kehl ur
What time do you open tomorrow?	Vous allez ouvrir à quelle heure demain?	vooz ah-lay oo-vreer ah kehl ur duh-man

The French definition of customer service is different from ours. At department stores, be prepared to be treated as if you're intruding on the clerk's privacy. Exchanges are possible with receipts. Refunds are difficult. Buy to keep.

Street Markets

Did you make this?	C'est vous qui l'avez fait?	say voo kee lah-vay fay
Is that your lowest price?	C'est votre prix le plus bas?	say voh-truh pree luh plew bah
Cheaper?	Moins cher?	mwan shehr
My last offer.	Ma dernière offre.	mah dehrn-yehr oh-fruh
Good price.	C'est bon marché.	say bohn mar-shay
I'll take it.	Je le prends.	zhuh luh prahn
We'll take it.	Nous le prenons.	noo luh prahn-nohn
I'm nearly broke.	Je suis presque fauché.	zhuh swee prehsk foh-shay
We're nearly broke.	Nous sommes presque fauché.	noo suhm prehsk foh-shay
My friend...	Mon ami...	mohn ah-mee
My husband...	Mon mari...	mohn mah-ree
My wife...	Ma femme...	mah fahm...
...has the money.	...a l'argent.	ah lar-zhahn

Clothes

For...	Pour...	poor
...a male baby	...un bébé garçon /	uhn bay-bay gar-sohn /
a female baby.	un bébé fille.	uhn bay-bay fee-ee
...a male child.	...un petit garçon /	uhn puh-tee gar-sohn /
a female child.	une petite fille.	ewn puh-tee fee-ee
...a male teenager	...un adolescent /	uhn ah-doh-luh-sahn /
a female teenager.	une adolescente.	ewn ah-doh-luh-sahnt
...a man.	...un homme.	uhn ohm
...a woman.	...une femme.	ewn fahm
bathrobe	peignoir de bain	peh-nwar duh ban
bib	bavoir	bah-vwar
belt	ceinture	san-tewr
bra	soutien gorge	soo-tee-an gorzh
clothing	vêtement	veht-mahn
dress	robe	rohb
flip-flops	tongues	tohn-guh
gloves	gants	gahn
hat	chapeau	shah-poh
jacket	veste	vehst
jeans	jeans	"jeans"
nightgown	chemise de nuit	shuh-meez duh nwee
nylons	collants	koh-lahn
pajamas	pyjama	pee-zhah-mah
pants	pantalons	pahn-tah-lohn
raincoat	imperméable	an-pehr-may-ah-bluh
sandals	sandales	sahn-dahl
scarf	foulard	foo-lar
shirt...	chemise...	shuh-meez
...long-sleeved	...à manches longues	ah mahnsh lohn-guh
...short-sleeved	...à manches courtes	ah mahnsh koort
...sleeveless	...sans manche	sahn mahnsh
shoelaces	lacets	lah-say
shoes	chaussures	shoh-sewr
shorts	shorts	short

skirt	jupe	zhoop
slip	jupon	zhoo-pohn
slippers	chaussons	shoh-sohn
socks	chaussettes	shoh-seht
sweater	pull	pool
swimsuit	maillot de bain	mī-yoh duh ban
tennis shoes	baskettes	bahs-keht
T-shirt	T-shirt	"T-shirt"
underwear	sous vêtements	soo veht-mahn
vest	gilet sans manche	gee-lay sahn mahnsh

Colors

black	noir	nwar
blue	bleu	bluh
brown	marron	mah-rohn
gray	gris	gree
green	vert	vehr
orange	orange	oh-rahnzh
pink	rose	rohz
purple	violet	vee-oh-lay
red	rouge	roozh
white	blanc	blahn
yellow	jaune	zhohn
dark / light	foncé / clair	fohn-say / klair
A shade...	Un teint...	uhn tan
...lighter.	...plus clair.	plew klair
...brighter.	...plus coloré.	plew koh-loh-ray
...darker.	...plus foncé.	plew fohn-say

Materials

brass	cuivre jaune	kwee-vruh zhohn
bronze	bronze	brohnz
ceramic	céramique	say-rah-meek
copper	cuivre	kwee-vruh

cotton	*cotton*	koh-toh<u>n</u>
glass	*verre*	vehr
gold	*or*	or
lace	*dentelle*	dah<u>n</u>-tehl
leather	*cuir*	kweer
linen	*lin*	leen
marble	*marbre*	mar-bruh
metal	*métal*	may-tahl
nylon	*nylon*	nee-loh<u>n</u>
paper	*papier*	pahp-yay
pewter	*laiton*	lay-toh<u>n</u>
plastic	*plastique*	plah-steek
polyester	*polyester*	poh-lee-ehs-tehr
porcelain	*porcelaine*	por-suh-lehn
silk	*soie*	swah
silver	*argent*	ar-zhah<u>n</u>
velvet	*velours*	veh-loor
wood	*bois*	bwah
wool	*laine*	lehn

Jewelry

bracelet	*bracelet*	brah-suh-lay
brooch	*broche*	brohsh
earrings	*boucles d'oreille*	boo-kluh doh-ray
jewelry	*bijoux*	bee-zhoo
necklace	*collier*	kohl-yay
ring	*bague*	bahg
Is this...?	*C'est...?*	say
...sterling silver	*...de l'argent*	duh lar-zhah<u>n</u>
...real gold	*...de l'or véritable*	duh lor vay-ree-tah-bluh
...stolen	*...volé*	voh-lay

Sports

Bicycling

bicycle / bike	*bicyclette / vélo*	bee-see-kleht / vay-loh
mountain bike	*VTT*	vay-tay-tay
I'd like to rent a bike.	*Je voudrais louer un vélo.*	zhuh voo-dray loo-ay uhn vay-loh
We'd like to rent two bikes.	*Nous voudrions louer deux vélos.*	noo voo-dree-ohn loo-ay duh vay-loh
How much per...?	*C'est combien par...?*	say kohn-bee-an par
...hour	*...heure*	ur
...half day	*...demie-journée*	duh-mee-zhoor-nay
...day	*...jour*	zhoor
Is a deposit required?	*Une caution est obligatoire?*	ewn koh-see-ohn ay oh-blee-gah-twar
deposit	*caution*	koh-see-ohn
helmet	*casque*	kahsk
lock	*antivol*	ahn-tee-vohl
air / no air	*air / pas d'air*	air / pah dair
tire	*pneu*	puh-nuh
pump	*pompe*	pohmp
map	*carte*	kart
How many gears?	*Combien vitesses?*	kohn-bee-an vee-tehs
What is a...	*Quel est un...*	kehl ay uhn...
route of about ___ kilometers?	*circuit de ___ kilometers?*	seer-kwee duh ___ kee-loh-meh-truh
...good	*...bon*	bohn
...scenic	*...panoramique, beau*	pah-noh-rah-meek, boh
...interesting	*...intéressante*	an-tay-reh-sahn
...easy	*...facile*	fah-seel
How many minutes / hours by bicycle?	*Combien de minutes / d'heures à vélo?*	kohn-bee-an duh mee-newt / dur ah vay-loh
I like hills.	*J'aime les côtes.*	zhehm lay koht

| I don't like hills. | *Je n'aime pas les côtes.* | zhuh nehm pah lay koht |
| I brake for bakeries. | *Je m'arrête à chaque boulangerie.* | zhuh mah-reht ah shahk boo-lahn-zhuh-ree |

Swimming and Boating

Where can I / can we rent a...?	*Où puis-je / pouvons-nous louer...?*	oo pwee-zhuh / poo-vohn-noo loo-ay
...paddleboat	*...pédalo*	pay-dah-loh
...rowboat	*...barque*	bark
...boat	*...bâteau*	bah-toh
...sailboat	*...voilier*	vwah-lee-ay
How much per...?	*C'est combien par...?*	say kohn-bee-an par
...hour	*...heure*	ur
...half day	*...demie-journée*	duh-mee-zhoor-nay
...day	*...jour*	zhoor
beach	*plage*	plahg
nude beach (topless)	*plage naturiste (monokini)*	plahg nah-toor-eest (moh-noh-kee-nee)
Where's a good beach?	*Où est une belle plage?*	oo ay ewn behl plahg
Is it safe for swimming?	*On peut nager en sécurité?*	ohn puh nah-zhay ahn say-kew-ree-tay
flip-flops	*tongues*	tohn-guh
pool	*piscine*	pee-seen
snorkel and mask	*tuba et masque*	too-bah ay mahsk
sunglasses	*lunettes de soleil*	loo-neht duh soh-lay
sunscreen	*crème solaire*	krehm soh-lair
surfboard	*planche de surf*	plahnsh duh surf
surfer	*surfeur*	surf-ur
swimsuit	*maillot de bain*	mī-yoh duh ban
towel	*serviette*	sehrv-yeht
waterskiing	*ski nautique*	skee noh-teek
windsurfing	*planche à voile*	plahnsh ah vwahl

In France, nearly any beach is topless. For a nude beach, look for a *naturiste plage.*

Sports Talk

sports	sport	spor
game	match	"match"
championship	championnat	shah-pee-oh-nah
soccer	football	foot-bahl
basketball	basket	bah-skeht
hockey	hockey	oh-kay
American football	football américain	foot-bahl ah-may-ree-ka<u>n</u>
baseball	baseball	bahz-bahl
tennis	tennis	teh-nees
golf	golf	"golf"
skiing	ski	"ski"
gymnastics	gymnastique	zheem-nah-steek
jogging	jogging	zhoh-geeng
Olympics	Olympiques	oh-leem-peek
medal...	médaille	meh-dī
...gold / silver /	d'or / d'argent /	dor / dar-zhah<u>n</u> /
bronze	du bronze	duh brohnz
What sport /	Quel sport /	kehl spor /
athlete / team	jouer / équipe	zhoo-ay / ay-keep
is your favorite?	est votre préferé?	ay voh-truh pray-fuh-ray
Where can I	Où puis-je voir	oo pwee-zhuh vwar
see a game?	un match?	uh<u>n</u> "match"
Where's a good	Où puis-je faire	oo pwee-zhuh fair
place to jog?	du jogging?	duh zhoh-geeng

Entertainment

What's happening tonight?	Qu'est-ce qui ce passe ce soir?	kehs kee suh pahs suh swar
What do you recommend?	Qu'est-ce que vous recommandez?	kehs kuh voo ruh-koh-mahn-day
Where is it?	C'est où?	say oo
How to get there?	Comment le trouver?	koh-mahn luh troo-vay
Is it free?	C'est gratuit?	say grah-twee
Are there seats available?	Il y a des places disponible?	eel yah day plahs dee-spoh-nee-bluh
Where can I buy a ticket?	Où puis-je acheter un billet?	oo pwee-zhuh ah-shuh-tay uhn bee-yay
Do you have tickets for today / tonight?	Avez-vous des billets pour aujourd'hui / ce soir?	ah-vay-voo day bee-yay poor oh-zhoor-dwee / suh swar
When does it start?	Ça commence à quelle heure?	sah koh-mahns ah kehl ur
When does it end?	Ça se termine à quelle heure?	sah suh tehr-meen ah kehl ur
The best place to dance nearby?	Le meilleur dancing dans le coin?	luh meh-yur dahn-seeng dahn luh kwan
Where do people stroll?	Les gens se balladent où?	lay zhahn suh bah-lah-dahn oo

Entertaining Words

movie...	film...	feelm
...original version	...version originale (V.O.)	vehr-see-ohn oh-ree-zhee-nahl
...in English	...en anglais	ahn ahn-glay
...with subtitles	...avec sous-titres	ah-vehk soo-tee-truh
...dubbed	...doublé	doo-blay
music...	musique...	mew-zeek
...live	...en directe	ahn dee-rehkt

ACTIVITIES

...classical	...classique	klahs-seek
...folk	...folklorique	fohk-loh-reek
...opera	...d'opéra	doh-pay-rah
...symphony	...symphonique	seem-foh-neek
...choir	...de choeur	duh koh-ur
...traditional	...traditionnelle	trah-dee-see-oh-nehl
rock / jazz / blues	rock / jazz / blues	rohk / zhahz / "blues"
male singer	chanteur	shahn-tur
female singer	chanteuse	shahn-tuhz
concert	concert	kohn-sehr
show	spectacle	spehk-tahk-luh
sound and light show	son et lumière	sohn ay lew-mee-ehr
dancing	danse	dahns
folk dancing	danse folklorique	dahns fohk-loh-reek
disco	disco	dee-skoh
bar with live music	bar avec un groupe musical	bar ah-vehk uhn groop mew-zee-kahl
nightclub	boîte	bwaht
(no) cover charge	(pas de) admission	(pah duh) ahd-mee-see-ohn
sold out	complet	kohn-play

For concerts and special events, ask at the local tourist office. Cafés, very much a part of the French social scene, are places for friends to spend the evening together. To meet new friends, the French look for *pubs* or *bars américains.*

Paris has a great cinema scene, especially on the Champs-Élysées. Pick up a *Pariscope,* the periodical entertainment guide, and choose from hundreds of films (often discounted on Mondays). Those listed V.O. (rather than V.F.) are in their original language.

CONNECT

Phoning

I'd like to buy a...	Je voudrais acheter une...	zhuh voo-dray ah-shuh-tay oon
...telephone card.	...carte téléphonique.	kart tay-lay-foh-neek
...cheap international telephone card.	...carte téléphonique à code internationale.	kart tay-lay-foh-neek ah kohd an-tehr-nah-see-oh-nahl
The nearest phone?	Le téléphone le plus proche?	luh tay-lay-fohn luh plew prohsh
It doesn't work.	Ça ne marche pas.	sah nuh marsh pah
May I use your phone?	Je peux téléphoner?	zhuh puh tay-lay-foh-nay
Can you talk for me?	Vous pouvez parler pour moi?	voo poo-vay par-lay poor mwah
It's busy.	C'est occupé.	say oh-kew-pay
Will you try again?	Essayez de nouveau?	eh-say-yay duh noo-voh
Hello. (on the phone)	Âllo.	ah-loh
My name is ___.	Je m'appelle ___.	zhuh mah-pehl
Sorry, I speak only a little French.	Désolé, je parle seulement un petit peu de français.	day-zoh-lay zhuh parl suhl-mahn uhn puh-tee puh duh frahn-say

151

Speak slowly	*Parlez lentement*	par-lay lah<u>n</u>-tuh-mah<u>n</u>
and clearly.	*et clairement.*	ay klair-mah<u>n</u>
Wait a moment.	*Un moment.*	uh<u>n</u> moh-mah<u>n</u>

In this book, you'll find phrases to reserve a hotel room (page 54) or a table at a restaurant (page 72). To spell your name on the phone, refer to the code alphabet (page 56).

Make your calls using a handy phone card (*carte télé-phonique*), sold at post offices, train stations, and tobacco (*tabac*) shops. There are two kinds of phone cards: an insertable card that you slide into a phone in a phone booth, and a cheaper-per-minute international telephone card (with a scratch-off PIN code) that you can use from any phone, even your hotel room. Post offices often have easy-to-use metered phones.

At phone booths, you'll encounter these words: *inser-er votre carte* (insert your card) and *composer votre numéro* (dial your number); it will also tell you how many *unités* are left on your card. If the number you're calling is out of service, you'll hear the dreaded recording: "*Le numéro que vous demandez n'est pas attribué.*" For more tips, see "Let's Talk Telephones" in the Appendix (page 262).

Telephone Words

telephone	*téléphone*	tay-lay-fohn
telephone card	*carte téléphonique*	kart tay-lay-foh-neek
cheap international	*carte téléphonique*	kart tay-lay-foh-neek
telephone card	*à code*	ah kohd
	internationale	a<u>n</u>-tehr-nah-see-oh-nahl
PIN code	*code*	kohd
phone booth	*cabine téléphonique*	kah-been tay-lay-foh-neek
out of service	*hors service*	or sehr-vees
post office	*Poste*	pohst
operator	*standardiste*	stah<u>n</u>-dar-deest
international	*renseignements*	rah<u>n</u>-sehn-yuh-mah<u>n</u>
assistance	*internationaux*	a<u>n</u>-tehr-nah-see-oh-noh
international call	*appel*	ah-pehl
	international	a<u>n</u>-tehr-nah-see-oh-nahl

collect call	*appel en PCV*	ah-pehl ahn pay-say-vay
credit card call	*appel avec une carte de crédit.*	ah-pehl ah-vehk ewn kart duh kray-dee
toll-free	*gratuit*	grah-twee
fax	*fax*	fahks
country code	*code international*	kohd an-tehr-nah-see-oh-nahl
area code	*code régional*	kohd ray-zhee-oh-nahl
extension	*poste*	pohst
telephone book	*bottin, annuaire*	boh-tan, ahn-new-air
yellow pages	*pages jaunes*	pahzh zhohn

CONNECT

Cell Phones

Where is a cell phone shop?	*Où est un magasin de portables?*	oo ay uhn mah-gah-zan duh por-tah-bluh
I'd like...	*Je voudrais...*	zhuh voo-dray
We'd like...	*Nous voudrions...*	noo voo-dree-ohn
...a cell phone.	*...un portable.*	uhn por-tah-bluh
...a chip.	*...une puce.*	ewn pews
...to buy more time.	*...acheter plus de temps.*	ah-shuh-tay plew duh tahn
How do you...?	*Comment vous...?*	koh-mahn voo
...make calls	*...appelez*	ah-puh-lay
...receive calls	*...recevez les appels*	ruh-suh-vay layz ah-pehl
Will this work outside this country?	*Ça marche en dehors de ce pays?*	sah marsh ahn duh-or duh suh peh-ee
Where can I buy more time for this phone?	*Où puis-je acheter une recharge pour ce portable?*	oo pwee-zhuh ah-shuh-tay ewn reh-sharzh poor suh por-tah-bluh

Many travelers now buy cell phones in Europe to make both local and international calls. You'll pay under $100 for a "locked" phone that works only in the country you buy it in (includes about $20 worth of calls). You can buy additional time at a newsstand or cell phone shop. An "unlocked" phone is more expensive (over $100), but it works all over Europe: when you cross a border, buy a SIM card at a cell phone shop and insert the pop-out chip, which comes with a new phone number. Pricier tri-band phones (*tribande*) also work in North America.

E-Mail and the Web

E-Mail

My e-mail address is ___.	*Mon adresse e-mail est ___.*	mohn ah-drehs ee-mayl ay
What's your e-mail address?	*Quelle est votre adresse e-mail?*	kehl ay voh-truh ah-drehs ee-mayl
Can I use this computer to check my e-mail?	*Je peux utiliser cet ordinateur pour regarder mon e-mail?*	zhuh puh oo-tee-lee-zay seht or-dee-nah-tur poor ruh-gar-day mohn ee-mayl
Where can I get get access to the Internet?	*Où est-ce que je peux accéder à l'internet?*	oo ehs kuh zhuh puh ahk-say-day ah lan-tehr-neht
Where is an Internet café?	*Où se trouve un café internet?*	oo suh troov uhn kah-fay an-tehr-neht
How much for... minutes?	*C'est combien pour... minutes?*	say kohn-bee-an poor... mee-newt
...10	*...dix*	dees
...15	*...quinze*	kanz
...30	*...trente*	trahnt
...60	*...soixante*	swah-sahnt
Help me, please.	*Aidez-moi, s'il vous plaît.*	ay-day-mwah, see voo play
How...	*Comment...*	koh-mahn
...do I start this?	*... je démarre ça?*	zhuh day-mar sah
...do I send a file?	*...j'envoie un fichier?*	zhahn-vwah uhn fee-shee-ay

CONNECT

...do I print out a file?	...j'imprime le fichier?	zhan-preem luh fee-shee-ay
...do I make this symbol?	...je fais ce symbole?	zhuh fay suh seem-bohl
...do I type @?	...je tape arobase?	zhuh tahp ah-roh-bahs
This doesn't work.	Ça ne marche pas.	sah nuh marsh pah

Web Words

Web site	site web	seet wehb
Internet	internet	an-tehr-neht
surf the Web	surfer le web	surf-ay luh wehb
download	télécharge	tay-lay-sharzh
@ sign	signe arobase	seen ah-roh-bahs
dot	point	pwan
hyphen (-)	tiret	tee-ray
underscore (_)	souligne	soo-leen
modem	modem	moh-dehm

On Screen

delete	annuler	message	message
send	envoyer	save	sauver
file	fichier	open	ouvrir
print	imprimer		

KEY PHRASES: E-MAIL AND THE WEB

e-mail	e-mail	ee-mayl
Internet	internet	an-tehr-neht
Where is the nearest Internet café?	Où se trouve le café internet le plus prôche?	oo suh troov luh kah-fay an-tehr-neht luh plew prohsh
I'd like to check my e-mail.	Je voudrais regarder mon e-mail.	zhuh voo-dray ruh-gar-day mohn ee-mayl

Mailing

Where is the post office?	*Où est la Poste?*	oo ay lah pohst
Which window for...?	*Quel guichet pour...?*	kehl gee-shay poor
Is this the line for...?	*C'est la file pour...?*	say lah feel poor
...stamps	*...les timbres*	lay tan-bruh
...packages	*...les colis*	lay koh-lee
To the United States...	*Aux Etats-Unis...*	ohz ay-tah-zew-nee
...by air mail.	*...par avion.*	par ah-vee-ohn
...by surface mail.	*...par surface.*	par sewr-fahs
How much is it?	*C'est combien?*	say kohn-bee-an
How much to send a letter / postcard to ___?	*Combien pour envoyer une lettre / carte postale pour __?*	kohn-bee-an poor ahn-voh-yay ewn leht-ruh / kart poh-stahl poor
I need stamps for ___ postcards to...	*J'ai besoin de timbres pour ___ cartes postales pour...*	zhay buh-swan duh tan-bruh poor ___ kart poh-stahl poor
...America / Canada.	*...l'Amérique / le Canada.*	lah-may-reek / luh kah-nah-dah
Pretty stamps, please.	*De jolis timbres, s'il vous plaît.*	duh zhoh-lee tan-bruh see voo play
I always choose the slowest line.	*Je choisis toujours la file la plus lente.*	zhuh shwah-see too-zhoor lah feel lah plew lahnt
How many days will it take?	*Ça va prendre combien de jours?*	sah vah prahn-druh kohn-bee-an duh zhoor

You can also buy stamps at *tabac* shops—very handy, so long as you know in advance the amount of postage you need.

Licking the Postal Code

post office	*La Poste*	lah pohst
stamp	*timbre*	tan-bruh
postcard	*carte postale*	kart poh-stahl

letter	*lettre*	leht-ruh
envelope	*enveloppe*	ah<u>n</u>-vuh-lohp
package	*colis*	koh-lee
box	*boîte en carton*	bwaht ah<u>n</u> kar-toh<u>n</u>
string	*ficelle*	fee-sehl
tape	*scotch*	skotch
mailbox	*boîte aux lettres*	bwaht oh leht-truh
air mail	*par avion*	par ah-vee-oh<u>n</u>
express	*par express*	par ehk-sprehs
surface	*surface*	sewr-fahs
(slow and cheap)	*(lent et pas cher)*	(lah<u>n</u> ay pah shehr)
book rate	*tarif-livres*	tah-reef-lee-vruh
weight limit	*poids limite*	pwah lee-meet
registered	*enregistré*	ah<u>n</u>-ruh-zhee-stray
insured	*assuré*	ah-sew-ray
fragile	*fragile*	frah-zheel
contents	*contenu*	koh<u>n</u>-tuh-new
customs	*douane*	doo-ahn
to / from	*à / de*	ah / duh
address	*adresse*	ah-drehs
zip code	*code postal*	kohd poh-stahl
general delivery	*poste restante*	pohst rehs-tah<u>n</u>t

CONNECT

KEY PHRASES: MAILING

post office	*La Poste*	lah pohst
stamp	*timbre*	ta<u>n</u>-bruh
postcard	*carte postale*	kart poh-stahl
letter	*lettre*	leht-ruh
air mail	*par avion*	par ah-vee-oh<u>n</u>
Where is the post office?	*Où est La Poste?*	oo ay lah pohst
I'd like to buy stamps for __ postcards / letters to send to America.	*Je voudrais acheter timbres pour __ cartes postales / lettres d'envoyer pour l'Amérique.*	zhuh voo-dray ah-shuh-tay ta<u>n</u>-bruh poor __ kart poh-stahl / leht-ruh dahn-voh-yay poor lah-may-reek

HELP!

Help!	*Au secours!*	oh suh-koor
Help me!	*À l'aide!*	ah layd
Call a doctor!	*Appelez un docteur!*	ah-puh-lay uhn dohk-tur
Call...	*Appelez...*	ah-puh-lay
...the police.	*...la police.*	lah poh-lees
...an ambulance.	*...une ambulance.*	ewn ahn-bew-lahns
...the fire department.	*...les pompiers.*	lay pohn-pee-yay
I'm lost.	*Je suis perdu.*	zhuh swee pehr-dew
We're lost.	*Nous sommes perdus.*	noo suhm pehr-dew
Thank you for your help.	*Merci pour votre aide.*	mehr-see poor voh-truh ayd
You are very kind.	*Vous êtes très gentil.*	vooz eht treh zhahn-tee

KEY PHRASES: HELP!

accident	*accident*	ahk-see-dahn
emergency	*urgence*	ewr-zhahns
police	*police*	poh-lees
Help!	*Au secours!*	oh suh-koor
Call a doctor / the police!	*Appelez un docteur / la police!*	ah-puh-lay uhn dohk-tur / lah poh-lees
Stop, thief!	*Arrêtez, au voleur!*	ah-reh-tay oh voh-lur

158

France's medical emergency phone number is 15. *SOS médecins* are doctors who make emergency house calls. If you need help, someone will call an *SOS médecin* for you.

Theft and Loss

Stop, thief!	*Arrêtez, au voleur!*	ah-reh-tay oh voh-lur
I have been / We have been robbed.	*On m'a / Nous a volé.*	ohn mah / nooz ah voh-lay
A thief took...	*Un voleur à pris...*	uhn voh-lur ah pree
Thieves took...	*Des voleurs ont pris...*	day voh-lur ohn pree
I've lost...	*J'ai perdu...*	zhay pehr-dew
...my money.	*...mon argent.*	mohn ar-zhahn
...my passport.	*...mon passeport.*	mohn pah-spor
...my ticket.	*...mon billet.*	mohn bee-yay
...my baggage.	*...mes bagages.*	may bah-gahzh
...my purse.	*...mon sac.*	mohn sahk
...my wallet.	*...mon portefeuille.*	mohn por-tuh-fuh-ee
...my faith in humankind.	*...ma foi en l'humanité.*	mah fwah ahn lew-mah-nee-tay
We've lost our...	*Nous avons perdu nos...*	nooz ah-vohn pehr-dew noh
...passports.	*...passeports.*	pah-spor
...tickets.	*...billets.*	bee-yay
...bags.	*...bagages.*	bah-gahzh
I want to contact my embassy.	*Je veux contacter mon ambassade.*	zhuh vuh kohn-tahk-tay mohn ahm-bah-sahd
I need to file a police report for my insurance.	*Je veux porter plainte à la police pour mon assurance.*	zhuh vuh por-tay plant ah lah poh-lees poor mohn ah-sewr-rahns

HELP!

See page 264 in the Appendix for contact information on the U.S. embassies in Paris.

Helpful Words

ambulance	*ambulance*	ah<u>n</u>-bew-lah<u>n</u>s
accident	*accident*	ahk-see-dah<u>n</u>
injured	*blessé*	bleh-say
emergency	*urgence*	ewr-zhah<u>n</u>s
emergency room	*aux urgences*	ohz ewr-zhah<u>n</u>s
fire	*feu*	fuh
police	*police*	poh-lees
smoke	*fumée*	foo-may
thief	*voleur*	voh-lur
pickpocket	*pickpocket*	peek-poh-keht

Help for Women

Leave me alone.	*Laissez-moi tranquille.*	lay-say-mwah trah<u>n</u>-keel
I want to be alone.	*Je veux être seule.*	zhuh vuh eh-truh suhl
I'm not interested.	*Ça ne m'intéresse pas.*	sah nuh ma<u>n</u>-tay-rehs pah
I'm married.	*Je suis mariée.*	zhuh swee mah-ree-ay
I'm a lesbian.	*Je suis lesbienne.*	zhuh swee lehz-bee-ehn
I have a contagious disease.	*J'ai une maladie contagieuse.*	zhay ewn mah-lah-dee koh<u>n</u>-tah-zhuhz
You are bothering me.	*Vous m'embêtez.*	voo mah<u>n</u>-beh-tay
He is bothering me.	*Il m'embête.*	eel mah<u>n</u>-beht
Don't touch me.	*Ne me touchez pas.*	nuh muh too-shay pah
You're disgusting.	*Vous êtes dégoutant.*	vooz eht day-goo-tah<u>n</u>
Stop following me.	*Arrêtez de me suivre.*	ah-reh-tay duh muh swee-vruh
Stop it!	*Arrêtez!*	ah-reh-tay
Enough!	*Ça suffit!*	sah sew-fee
Get lost!	*Dégagez!*	day-gah-zhay
Drop dead!	*Foutez-moi la paix!*	foo-tay-mwah lah pay
I'll call the police.	*J'appelle la police.*	zhah-pehl lah poh-lees

HELP!

SERVICES

Laundry

Is a... nearby?	*Il y a une... près d'ici?*	eel-yah ewn... preh dee-see
...self-service laundry	*...laverie automatique*	lah-vah-ree oh-toh-mah-teek
...full service laundry	*...blanchisserie*	blahn-shee-suh-ree
Help me, please.	*Aidez-moi, s'il vous plaît.*	ay-day-mwah see voo play
How does this work?	*Ça marche comment?*	sah marsh koh-mahn
Where is the soap?	*Où se trouve la lessive?*	oo suh troov lah luh-seev
Are these yours?	*C'est à vous?*	say ah voo
This stinks.	*Ça pue.*	sah pew
This smells like...	*Ça sent comme...*	sah sahn kohm
...spring time.	*...le printemps.*	luh pran-tahn
...a locker room.	*...un vestiare.*	ewn vehs-tee-ar
...cheese.	*...le fromage.*	luh froh-mahzh
I need change.	*J'ai besoin de monnaie.*	zhay buh-swan duh moh-nay
Same-day service?	*Lavé le même jour?*	lah-vay luh mehm zhoor

161

By when do I need to drop off my clothes?	Je dois déposer mon linge quand?	zhuh dwah day-poh-zay mohn lanzh kahn?
When will my clothes be ready?	Mon linge sera prêt quand?	mohn lanzh suh-rah preh kahn
Dried?	Séché?	say-shay
Folded?	Plié?	plee-ay
Ironed?	Repassé?	ray-pah-say
Hey there, what's spinning?	Pardon, qu'est-ce qui tourne?	par-dohn kehs kee toorn

Clean Words

full-service laundry	blanchisserie	blahn-shee-suh-ree
self-service laundry	laverie automatique	lah-vah-ree oh-toh-mah-teek
wash / dry	laver / sécher	lah-vay / say-shay
washer / dryer	machine à laver / machine à sécher	mah-sheen ah lah-vay / mah-sheen ah say-shay
detergent	lessive	luh-seev
token	jeton	zhuh-tohn
whites	blancs	blahn
colors	couleurs	koh-lur
delicates	délicats	day-lee-kah
handwash	laver à la main	lah-vay a lah man

Haircuts

Where is a barber / hair salon?	Où se trouve un salon de coiffure hommes / femmes?	oo suh troov uhn sah-lohn duh kwah-fur ohm / fahm
I'd like...	J'aimerais...	zhehm-uh-ray
...a haircut.	...une coupe.	ewn koop
...a permanent.	...une permanente.	ewn pehr-mah-nahnt
...just a trim.	...juste raffraîchir.	zhoost rah-freh-sheer
Cut about this much off.	Coupez ça à peu près.	koo-pay sah ah puh preh

Cut my bangs here.	*Coupez ma frange ici.*	koo-pay mah frah<u>n</u>zh ee-see
Longer / Shorter here.	*Plus long / Plus court ici.*	plew loh<u>n</u> / plew koort ee-see
I'd like my hair...	*J'aimerais mes cheveux...*	zhehm-uh-ray may shuh-vuh
...short.	*...courts.*	koort
...colored.	*...colorés.*	koh-loh-ray
...shampooed.	*...lavés.*	lah-vay
...blow dried.	*...séchés.*	say-shay
It looks good.	*C'est bien.*	say bee-a<u>n</u>

Repair

These handy lines can apply to any repair, whether it's a ripped rucksack, bad haircut, or crabby camera.

This is broken.	*C'est cassé.*	say kah-say
Can you fix it?	*Vous pouvez le réparer?*	voo poo-vay luh ray-pah-ray
Just do the essentials.	*Ne faites que le minimum.*	nuh fayt kuh luh mee-nee-muhm
How much will it cost?	*Ça coutera combien?*	sah koo-teh-rah koh<u>n</u>-bee-a<u>n</u>
When will it be ready?	*Ce sera prêt quand?*	suh suh-rah preh kah<u>n</u>
I need it by ___.	*Il me le faut avant ___.*	eel muh luh foh ah-vah<u>n</u>
We need it by ___.	*Il nous le faut avant ___.*	eel noo luh foh ah-vah<u>n</u>
Without it, I'm...	*Sans, je suis...*	sah<u>n</u> zhuh swee
...lost.	*...perdu.*	pehr-dew
...toast.	*...grillé.*	gree-yay
...dead in the water. (literally, a shipwreck)	*...une épave.*	ewn ay-pahv

Filling Out Forms

Monsieur	Mr.
Madame	Mrs.
Mademoiselle	Miss
prénom	first name
nom	name
adresse	address
lieu de domicile	address
rue	street
ville	city
état	state
pays	country
nationalité	nationality
originaire de...	origin
destination	destination
âge	age
date de naissance	date of birth
lieu de naissance	place of birth
sexe	sex
mâle / femelle	male / female
marié / célibataire	married / single
profession	profession
adulte	adult
enfant / garçon / fille	child / boy / girl
enfants	children
famille	family
signature	signature

When filling out dates, do it European-style: day/month/year.

HEALTH

I am sick.	*Je suis malade.*	zhuh swee mah-lahd
I feel (very) sick.	*Je me sens (très) malade.*	zhuh muh sah<u>n</u> (treh) mah-lahd
My husband / My wife...	*Mon mari / Ma femme...*	moh<u>n</u> mah-ree / mah fahm
My son / My daughter...	*Mon fils / Ma fille...*	moh<u>n</u> fees / mah fee
My male friend / My female friend...	*Mon ami / Mon amie...*	moh<u>n</u> ah-mee / mah ah-mee
...feels (very) sick.	*...se sent (très) malade.*	suh sah<u>n</u> (treh) mah-lahd
It's urgent.	*C'est urgent.*	say ewr-zhah<u>n</u>
I need a doctor...	*J'ai besoin d'un docteur...*	zhay buh-swa<u>n</u> duh<u>n</u> dohk-tur

KEY PHRASES: HEALTH

doctor	*docteur*	dohk-tur
hospital	*hôpital*	oh-pee-tahl
pharmacy	*pharmacie*	far-mah-see
medicine	*médicament*	may-dee-kah-mah<u>n</u>
I am sick.	*Je suis malade.*	zhuh swee mah-lahd
I need a doctor (who speaks English).	*J'ai besoin d'un docteur (qui parle anglais).*	zhay buh-swa<u>n</u> duh<u>n</u> dohk-tur (kee parl ah<u>n</u>-glay)
It hurts here.	*J'ai mal ici.*	zhay mahl ee-see

We need a doctor...	Nous avons besoin d'un docteur...	nooz ah-vohn buh-swan duhn dohk-tur
...who speaks English.	...qui parle anglais.	kee parl ahn-glay
Please call a doctor.	S'il vous plaît appelez un docteur.	see voo play ah-puh-lay uhn dohk-tur
Could a doctor come here?	Un docteur pourrait venir?	uhn dohk-tur poo-ray vuh-neer
I am...	Je suis...	zhuh swee
He / She is...	Il / Elle est...	eel / ehl ay
...allergic to penicillin / sulfa.	...allergique à la pénicilline / les sulfamides.	ah-lehr-zheek ah lah pay-nee-see-leen / lay sool-fah-meed
I am diabetic.	Je suis diabétique.	zhuh swee dee-ah-bay-teek
I have cancer.	J'ai le cancer.	zhay luh kahn-say
I had a heart attack ___ years ago.	J'ai eu une crise cardiaque il y a ___ ans.	zhay uh ewn kreez kar-dee-ahk eel yah ___ ahn
It hurts here.	J'ai mal ici.	zhay mahl ee-see
I feel faint.	Je me sens faible.	zhuh muh sahn fay-bluh
It hurts to urinate.	Uriner me fait mal.	ew-ree-nay muh fay mahl
I have body odor.	Je sens mauvais.	zhuh sahn moh-vay
I'm going bald.	Je deviens chauve.	zhuh duh-vee-ahn shohv
Is it serious?	C'est sérieux?	say say-ree-uh
Is it contagious?	C'est contagieux?	say kohn-tah-zhee-uh
Aging sucks.	Vieillir c'est la poisse.	ve-yay-yeer say lah pwahs
Take one pill every ___ hours for ___ days before / with meals.	Prendre un comprimé toutes les ___ heures pendant ___ jours avant / durant les repas.	prahn-druh uhn kohn-pree-may toot lay ___ ur pahn-dahn ___ zhoor ah-vahn / doo-rahn lay ruh-pah
I need a receipt for my insurance.	J'ai besoin d'un reçu pour mon assurance.	zhay buh-swan duhn ruh-sew poor mohn ah-sew-rahns

Ailments

I have...	J'ai...	zhay
He / She has...	Il / Elle a...	eel / ehl ah
I need / We need medication for...	J'ai / Nous avons besoin d'un médicament pour...	zhay / nooz ah-vohn buh-swan duhn may-dee-kah-mahn poor
...arthritis.	...l'arthrite.	lar-treet
...asthma.	...l'asthme.	lahz-muh
...athlete's foot (fungus).	...la mycose.	lah mee-kohz
...bad breath.	...mauvaise haleine.	moh-vehz ah-leen
...blisters.	...des ampoules.	dayz ahm-pool
...bug bites.	...des piqures d'insectes.	day peek-ruh dan-sehkt
...a burn.	...une brûlure.	ewn brew-lewr
...chest pains.	...maux de poitrine.	mahl duh pwah-treen
...chills.	...des frissons.	day free-sohn
...a cold.	...un rhume.	uhn rewm
...congestion.	...la congestion.	lah kohn-zhehs-tee-ohn
...constipation.	...la constipation.	lah kohn-stee-pah-see-ohn
...a cough.	...la toux.	lah too
...cramps.	...des crampes.	day krahmp
...diabetes.	...du diabète.	doo dee-ah-beht
...diarrhea.	...la diarrhée.	lah dee-ah-ray
...dizziness.	...le vertige.	luh vehr-teezh
...earache.	...mal aux oreilles.	mahl ohz oh-ray
...epilepsy.	...l'épilepsie.	lay-pee-lehp-see
...a fever.	...une fièvre.	ewn fee-eh-vruh
...the flu.	...la grippe.	lah greep
...food poisoning.	...empoisonement alimentaire.	ahn-pwah-zuh-mahnt ah-lee-mahn-tair
...the giggles.	...le fou rire.	luh foo reer
...hay fever.	...le rhume des foins.	luh rewm day fwan
...a headache.	...mal à la tête.	mahl ah lah teht
...a heart condition.	...problème cardiaque.	proh-blehm kar-dee-ak
...hemorrhoids.	...hémorroïdes.	ay-mor-wahd

HEALTH

...high blood pressure.	...de l'hypertension.	duh lee-pehr-tah<u>n</u>-see-oh<u>n</u>
...indigestion.	...une indigestion.	ewn a<u>n</u>-dee-zhuh-stee-oh<u>n</u>
...an infection.	...une infection.	ewn a<u>n</u>-fehk-see-oh<u>n</u>
...inflammation.	...une inflation.	ewn a<u>n</u>-flah-see-oh<u>n</u>
...a migraine.	...une migraine.	ewn mee-grayn
...nausea.	...la nausée.	lah noh-zay
...pneumonia.	...la pneumonie.	lah puh-noo-moh-nee
...a rash.	...des boutons.	day boo-toh<u>n</u>
...sinus problems.	...problèmes de sinus.	proh-blehm duh see-noo
...a sore throat.	...mal à la gorge.	mahl ah lah gorzh
...a stomach ache.	...mal à l'estomac.	mahl ah luh-stoh-mah
...sunburn.	...un coup de soleil.	uh<u>n</u> koo duh soh-lay
...a swelling.	...une enflure.	ewn ah<u>n</u>-flewr
...a toothache.	...mal aux dents.	mahl oh dah<u>n</u>
...a urinary infection.	...une infection urinarire.	ewn a<u>n</u>-fehk-see-oh<u>n</u> ew-ree-nah-reer
...a venereal disease.	...une maladie vénérienne.	ewn mah-lah-dee vay-nay-ree-eh<u>n</u>
...vicious sunburn.	...un méchant coup de soleil.	uh<u>n</u> may-shah<u>n</u> koo duh soh-lay
...vomiting.	...le vomissement.	luh voh-mee-suh-mah<u>n</u>
...worms.	...des vers.	day vehr

Women's Health

menstruation	menstruation	mah<u>n</u>-stroo-ah-see-oh<u>n</u>
menstrual cramps	crampes de menstruation	krahmp duh mah<u>n</u>-stroo-ah-see-oh<u>n</u>
period	les règles	lay reh-gluh
pregnancy (test)	(test de) grossesse	(tehst duh) groh-sehs
miscarriage	fausse couche	fohs koosh
abortion	avortement	ah-vor-tuh-mah<u>n</u>
birth control pill	la pilule	lah pee-lewl
diaphragm	diaphragme	dee-ah-frahm
I'd like to see a female...	Je voudrais voir une femme-...	zhuh voo-dray vwar ewn fahm-
...doctor.	...docteur.	dohk-tur

...gynecologist.	...gynécologue.	zhee-nay-koh-lohg
I've missed a period.	J'ai du retard dans mes règles.	zhay dew ruh-tar dahn may reh-gluh
My last period started on ___.	Mes dernières règles étaient le ___.	may dehrn-yehr reh-gluh ay-tan luh
I am / She is... pregnant.	Je suis / Elle est enceinte...	zhuh swee / ehl ay ahn-sant
...___ months	...de ___ mois.	duh ___ mwah

Parts of the Body

ankle	cheville	shuh-veel
arm	bras	brah
back	dos	doh
bladder	vessie	veh-see
breast	seins	san
buttocks	fesses	feh-say
chest	poitrine	pwah-treen
ear	oreille	oh-ray
elbow	coude	kood
eye / eyes	oeil / yeux	oy / yuh
face	visage	vee-sahzh
finger	doigt	dwat
foot	pied	pee-ay
hair	cheveux	shuh-vuh
hand	main	man
head	tête	teht
heart	coeur	koor
hip	hanche	ahnsh
intestines	intestins	an-tehs-tan
knee	genou	zhuh-noo
leg	jambe	zhahmb
lung	poumon	poo-mohn
mouth	bouche	boosh
neck	cou	koo
nose	nez	nay
penis	pénis	pay-nee
rectum	rectum	rehk-toom

HEALTH

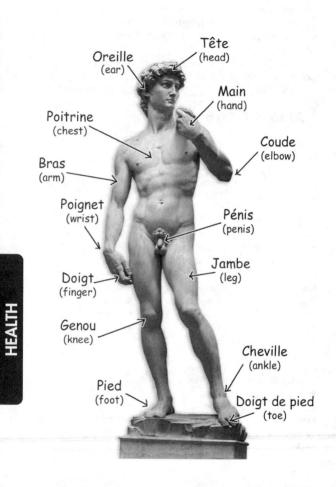

Tête
(head)

Oreille
(ear)

Main
(hand)

Poitrine
(chest)

Coude
(elbow)

Bras
(arm)

Poignet
(wrist)

Pénis
(penis)

Jambe
(leg)

Doigt
(finger)

Genou
(knee)

Cheville
(ankle)

Pied
(foot)

Doigt de pied
(toe)

HEALTH

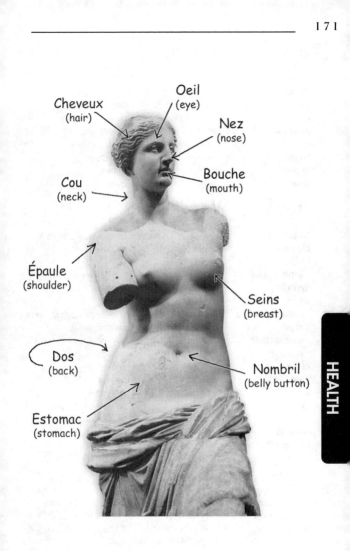

Cheveux
(hair)

Oeil
(eye)

Nez
(nose)

Bouche
(mouth)

Cou
(neck)

Épaule
(shoulder)

Seins
(breast)

Dos
(back)

Nombril
(belly button)

Estomac
(stomach)

HEALTH

shoulder	*épaule*	ay-pohl
stomach	*estomac*	ay-stoh-mah
teeth	*dents*	dah<u>n</u>
testicles	*testicules*	tehs-tee-kool
throat	*gorge*	gorzh
toe	*doigt de pied*	dwat duh pee-ay
urethra	*urèthre*	ew-reh-truh
uterus	*utérus*	ew-tay-rew
vagina	*vagin*	vah-zheen
waist	*taille*	tah-ee
wrist	*poignet*	pwah<u>n</u>-yay

Healthy Words

24-hour pharmacy	*pharmacie de garde*	far-mah-see duh gard
bleeding	*saignement*	seh<u>n</u>-yah-mahn
blood	*sang*	sa<u>n</u>
contraceptive	*contraceptif*	koh<u>n</u>-trah-sehp-teef
dentist	*dentiste*	dah<u>n</u>-teest
doctor	*docteur*	dohk-tur
health insurance	*assurance maladie*	ah-sew-rah<u>n</u>s mah-lah-dee
hospital	*hôpital*	oh-pee-tahl
medical clinic	*clinique médicale*	klee-neek may-dee-kal
medicine	*médicament*	may-dee-kah-mah<u>n</u>
nurse	*infirmière*	ah<u>n</u>-fehrm-yay
pain	*douleur*	doo-lur
pharmacy	*pharmacie*	far-mah-see
pill	*pilule, comprimé*	pee-lewl, koh<u>n</u>-pree-may
prescription	*ordonnance*	or-duh-nah<u>n</u>s
refill (v)	*remplir de nouveau*	rah<u>n</u>-pleer duh noo-voh
unconscious	*inconscient*	a<u>n</u>-koh<u>n</u>-see-ah<u>n</u>
x-ray	*radio*	rah-dee-oh

After 7:00 p.m., most pharmacies are closed, but you'll find the name, address, and phone number on their front door of the after-hours *pharmacie de garde.* In an emergency, go to the police station, which will call ahead to the pharmacist. At the pharmacy, ring the doorbell and the pharmacist will open the door. *Voilà.*

First-Aid Kit

antacid	*anti-acide*	ah<u>n</u>-tee-ah-seed
antibiotic	*antibiotique*	ah<u>n</u>-tee-bee-oh-teek
aspirin	*aspirine*	ah-spee-reen
non-aspirin substitute	*Tylenol*	tee-luh-nohl
bandage	*bandage*	bah<u>n</u>-dahzh
Band-Aids	*pansements*	pah<u>n</u>-suh-mah<u>n</u>
cold medicine	*remède contre le rhume*	ruh-mehd koh<u>n</u>-truh luh rewm
cough drops	*pastilles pour la toux*	pah-steel poor lah too
decongestant	*décongestant*	day-koh<u>n</u>-zhehs-tah<u>n</u>
disinfectant	*désinfectant*	day-za<u>n</u>-fehk-tah<u>n</u>

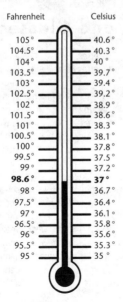

Fahrenheit	Celsius
105°	40.6°
104.5°	40.3°
104°	40°
103.5°	39.7°
103°	39.4°
102.5°	39.2°
102°	38.9°
101.5°	38.6°
101°	38.3°
100.5°	38.1°
100°	37.8°
99.5°	37.5°
99°	37.2°
98.6°	**37°**
98°	36.7°
97.5°	36.4°
97°	36.1°
96.5°	35.8°
96°	35.6°
95.5°	35.3°
95°	35°

HEALTH

first-aid cream	crème antiseptique	krehm ahn-tee-sehp-teek
gauze / tape	gaze / sparadra	gahz / spah-rah-drah
laxative	laxatif	lahk-sah-teef
medicine for diarrhea	médicament pour la diarrhée	may-dee-kah-mahn poor lah dee-ah-ray
moleskin	grain de beauté	gran duh boh-tay
pain killer	calmant	kahl-mahn
Preparation H	Préparation H (no kidding)	pray-pah-rah-see-ohn ahsh
support bandage	pansement élastique	pahn-suh-mahn ay-lah-steek
thermometer	thermomètre	tehr-moh-meh-truh
Vaseline	Vaseline	vah-zuh-leen
vitamins	vitamines	vee-tah-meen

Contacts and Glasses

glasses	lunettes	lew-neht
sunglasses	lunettes de soleil	lew-neht duh soh-lay
prescription	ordonnance	or-duh-nahns
contact lenses...	lentilles de contact...	lahn-tee duh kohn-tahkt
...soft	...souples	soop-luh
...hard	...dures	dewr
cleaning solution	solution nettoyante	soh-lew-see-ohn neh-toy-yahnt
soaking solution	solution à trempage	soh-lew-see-ohn ah trahn-pahzh
all-purpose solution (for cleaning and soaking)	solution pour tout (pour nettoyer et tremper)	soh-lew-see-ohn poor too (poor neh-toy-ay ay trahn-pay)
20/20 vision	vision vingt sur vingt	veez-yohn van sewr van
I've... a contact lens.	J'ai... une de mes lentilles de contact.	zhay... ewn duh may lahn-tee duh kohn-tahkt
...lost	...perdu	pehr-dew
...swallowed	...avalé	ah-vah-lay

Toiletries

comb	*peigne*	pehn-yuh
conditioner for hair	*après-shampoing*	ah-preh-shahn-pwan
condoms	*préservatifs*	pray-zehr-vah-teef
dental floss	*fil dentaire*	feel dahn-tair
deodorant	*déodorant*	day-oh-doh-rahn
facial tissue	*kleenex*	klay-nehks
hairbrush	*brosse*	brohs
hand lotion	*crème pour les mains*	krehm poor lay man
lip salve	*beaume pour les lèvres*	bohm poor lay leh-vruh
mirror	*mirroir*	meer-war
nail clipper	*clip-ongles*	kleep-ohn-gluh
razor	*rasoir*	rah-zwahr
sanitary napkins	*serviettes hygiéniques*	sehrv-yeht ee-zhay-neek
scissors	*ciseaux*	see-zoh
shampoo	*shampoing*	shahn-pwan
shaving cream	*mousse à raser*	moos ah rah-zehr
soap	*savon*	sah-vohn
sunscreen / suntan lotion	*crème solaire*	krehm soh-layr
tampons	*tampons*	tahn-pohn
tissues	*mouchoirs en papier*	moosh-wahr ahn pahp-yay
toilet paper	*papier hygiénique*	pahp-yay ee-zhay-neek
toothbrush	*brosse à dents*	brohs ah dahn
toothpaste	*dentifrice*	dahn-tee-frees
tweezers	*pince à épiler*	pans ah ay-pee-lay

HEALTH

Makeup

blush	*blush, rouge à joues*	bloosh, roozh ah zhoo
eye shadow	*ombre à paupières*	ohm-bruh ah pohp-yehr
eyeliner	*eyeliner, crayon pour les yeux*	"eyeliner," kray-oh<u>n</u> poor layz yuh
face cleanser	*lait nettoyant*	lay neh-toy-ah<u>n</u>
face powder	*fond de teint compact*	foh<u>n</u> duh ta<u>n</u> koh<u>n</u>-pahkt
foundation	*fond de teint*	fohnd duh ta<u>n</u>t
lipstick	*rouge à lèvres*	roozh ah leh-vruh
makeup	*maquillage*	mah-kee-ahzh
makeup remover	*lait démaquillant*	lay day-mah-kee-ah<u>n</u>
mascara	*mascara*	mas-kah-rah
moisturizer...	*crème hydratante...*	krehm ee-drah-tah<u>n</u>t
...with sun block	*...avec protection solaire*	ah-vehk proh-tehk-see-oh<u>n</u> soh-lair
nail polish	*vernis à ongles*	vehr-nee ah oh<u>n</u>-gluh
nail polish remover	*dissolvant*	dee-sohl-vah<u>n</u>
perfume	*parfum*	par-foom

For Babies

baby	*bébé*	bay-bay
baby food	*nourriture pour bébé*	noo-ree-tewr poor bay-bay
bib	*bavoir*	bah-vwar
bottle	*biberon*	bee-behr-oh<u>n</u>
diaper...	*couche...*	koosh
...wipes	*...lingettes*	la<u>n</u>-yeht
...ointment	*...pommade*	poh-mahd
diapers	*couches*	koosh
formula...	*lait pour bébé...*	lay poor bay-bay
...powdered	*...en poudre*	ah<u>n</u> poo-druh
...liquid	*...liquide*	lee-keed
...soy	*...soja*	soh-zhah

medication for...	médicament pour...	may-dee-kah-mahn poor
...diaper rash	...l'érythème fessier	lay-ree-tehm fuh-see-ay
...teething	...la poussée	lah poo-say
	des dents	day dahn
nipple	tétine	tay-teen
pacifier	sucette	soo-seht
Will you refrigerate this?	Vous pouvez mettre ça au frigo?	voo poo-vay meh-truh sah oh free-goh
Will you warm... for a baby?	Vous pouvez réchauffer...pour un bébé?	voo poo-vay ray-shoh-fay... poor uhn bay-bay
...this	...ça	sah
...some milk	...un peu de lait	uhn puh duh lay
...some water	...un peu d'eau	uhn puh doh
Not too hot, please.	Pas trop chaud, s'il vous plaît.	pah troh shoh see voo play

More Baby Things

backpack to carry baby	porte-bébé	port-bay-bay
booster seat	réhausseur	ray-oh-sur
car seat	siège voiture	see-ehzh vwah-tewr
high chair	chaise haute	shehz oht
playpen	parc	park
stroller	poussette	poo-seht

CHATTING

English	French	Pronunciation
My name is ___.	Je m'appelle ___.	zhuh mah-pehl
What's your name?	Quel est votre nom?	kehl ay voh-truh nohn
Pleased to meet you.	Enchanté.	ahn-shahn-tay
This is ___.	C'est ___.	say
How are you?	Comment allez-vous?	koh-mahnt ah-lay-voo
Very well, thanks.	Très bien, merci.	treh bee-an mehr-see
Where are you from?	D'où venez-vous?	doo vuh-nay-voo
What city?	Quelle ville?	kehl veel
What country?	Quel pays?	kehl pay-ee
What planet?	Quelle planète?	kehl plah-neht
I am...	Je suis...	zhuh swee
...a male American.	...américain.	zah-may-ree-kan
...a female American.	...américaine.	zah-may-ree-kehn
...a male Canadian.	...canadien.	kah-nah-dee-an
...a female Canadian.	...canadienne.	kah-nah-dee-ehn
...a pest.	...une peste.	ewn pehst
Where are you going?	Où allez-vous?	oo ah-lay-voo
I'm going to ___.	Je vais à ___.	zhuh vay ah
We're going to ___.	Nous allons à ___.	nooz ah-lohnz ah
Will you take my / our photo?	Vous pouvez prendre ma / notre photo?	voo-poo-vay prahn-druh mah / noh-truh foh-toh

KEY PHRASES: CHATTING

My name is ___.	*Je m'appelle ___.*	zhuh mah-pehl
What's your name?	*Quel est votre nom?*	kehl ay voh-truh noh<u>n</u>
Pleased to meet you.	*Enchanté.*	ah<u>n</u>-shah<u>n</u>-tay
Where are you from?	*D'où venez-vous?*	doo vuh-nay-voo
I'm from ___.	*Je viens de ___.*	zhuh vee-ah<u>n</u> duh
Where are you going?	*Où allez-vous?*	oo ah-lay-voo
I'm going to ___.	*Je vais à ___.*	zhuh vay ah
I like...	*J'aime...*	zhehm
Do you like...?	*Vous aimez...?*	vooz eh-may
Thank you very much.	*Merci beaucoup.*	mehr-see boh-koo
Have a good trip!	*Bon voyage!*	boh<u>n</u> voy-yahzh

Can I take a photo of you?	*Je peux prendre votre photo?*	zhuh puh prah<u>n</u>-druh noh-truh foh-toh
Smile!	*Souriez!*	soo-ree-ay

Nothing More than Feelings...

I am / You are...	*Je suis / Vous êtes...*	zhuh swee / vooz eht
He / She is...	*Il / Elle est...*	eel / ehl ay
...happy. (m / f)	*...content / contente.*	koh<u>n</u>-tah<u>n</u> / koh<u>n</u>-tah<u>n</u>t
...sad.	*...triste.*	treest
...tired.	*...fatigué.*	fah-tee-gay
I am / You are...	*J'ai / Vous avez...*	zhay / vooz ah-vay
He / She is...	*Il / Elle a...*	eel / ehl ah
...hungry.	*...faim.*	fa<u>n</u>
...thirsty.	*...soif.*	swahf
...lucky.	*...de la chance.*	duh lah shah<u>n</u>s
...homesick.	*...le mal du pays.*	luh mahl dew pay-ee
...cold.	*...froid.*	frwah
...hot.	*...trop chaud.*	troh shoh

CHATTING

Who's Who

This is my friend.	*C'est mon ami.*	say moh<u>n</u> ah-mee
This is my... (m / f)	*C'est mon / ma...*	say moh<u>n</u> / mah
...boyfriend /	*...petit ami /*	puh-teet ah-mee /
girlfriend.	*petite amie.*	puh-teet ah-mee
...husband / wife.	*...mari / femme.*	mah-ree / fahm
...son / daughter.	*...fils / fille.*	fees / fee
...brother / sister.	*...frère / soeur.*	frehr / sur
...father / mother.	*...père / mère.*	pehr / mehr
...uncle / aunt.	*...oncle / tante.*	oh<u>n</u>-kluh / tah<u>n</u>t
...nephew / niece.	*...neveu / nièce.*	nuh-vuh / nees
...male / female cousin.	*...cousin / cousine.*	koo-za<u>n</u> / koo-zeen
...grandfather / grandmother.	*...grand-père / grand-mère.*	grah<u>n</u>-pehr / grah<u>n</u>-mehr
...grandson / granddaughter.	*...petit-fils / petite-fille.*	puh-tee-fees / puh-teet-fee

Family

Are you married?	*Vous êtes marié?*	vooz eht mah-ree-ay
Do you have children?	*Vous avez des enfants?*	vooz ah-vay dayz ah<u>n</u>-fah<u>n</u>
How many boys / girls?	*Combien de garçons / filles?*	koh<u>n</u>-bee-a<u>n</u> duh gar-soh<u>n</u> / feel
Do you have photos?	*Vous avez des photos?*	vooz ah-vay day foh-toh
How old is your child?	*Quel âge à votre enfant?*	kehl ahzh ah voh-truh ah<u>n</u>-fah<u>n</u>
Beautiful child!	*Quel bel enfant!*	kehl behl ah<u>n</u>-fah<u>n</u>
Beautiful children!	*Quels beaux enfants!*	kehl bohz ah<u>n</u>-fah<u>n</u>

Work

What is your occupation?	*Quel est votre métier?*	kehl eh voh-truh may-tee-yay

CHATING

Do you like your work?	*Aimez-vous votre métier?*	eh-may-voo voh-truh may-tee-yay
I'm a...	*Je suis...*	zhuh swee
...male student.	*...étudiant.*	zay-tew-dee-ahn
...female student.	*...étudiante.*	zay-tew-dee-ahnt
I work in...	*Je travaille dans...*	zhuh trah-vay-ee dahn
I'm studying to work in...	*J'étudie pour travailler dans...*	zhay-too-dee poor trah-vah-yay dahn
I used to work in...	*Je travaillais dans...*	zhuh trah-vah-yay dahn
I want to work in...	*Je veux travailler dans...*	zhuh vuh trah-vah-yay dahn
...accounting.	*...la comptabilité.*	lah kohmp-tah-bee-lee-tay
...the medical field.	*...le secteur médical.*	luh sehk-tur may-dee-kahl
...social services.	*...le secteur social.*	luh sehk-tur soh-see-ahl
...the legal profession.	*...le secteur légal.*	luh sehk-tur lay-gahl
...banking.	*...le secteur bancaire.*	luh sehk-tur bahn-kair
...business.	*...le commerce.*	luh koh-mehrs
...government.	*...le gouvernement.*	luh goo-vehr-nuh-mahn
...engineering.	*...l'ingéniérie.*	lan-zhay-nee-yay-ree
...public relations.	*...les relations publiques.*	lay reh-lah-see-ohn poob-leek
...science.	*...les sciences.*	lay see-ahns
...teaching.	*...l'enseignement.*	lahn-sehn-yuh-mahn
...the computer field.	*...l'informatique.*	lan-for-mah-teek
...the travel industry.	*...le tourisme.*	luh too-reez-muh
...the arts.	*...les arts.*	layz ar
...journalism.	*...le journalisme.*	luh zhoor-nahl-eez-muh
...a restaurant.	*...un restaurant.*	uhn rehs-toh-rahn
...a store.	*...un magasin.*	uhn mah-gah-zan
...a factory.	*...une usine.*	ewn oo-zeen
I am / We are...	*Je suis / Nous sommes...*	zhuh swee / noo suhm
...unemployed.	*...au chômage.*	oh shoh-mahzh
...retired.	*...à la retraite.*	ah lah ruh-trayt
I'm a professional traveler.	*Je suis voyageur professionnel.*	zhuh swee voy-yah-zhur proh-feh-see-oh-nehl

Do you have a...?	*Vous avez...?*	vooz ah-vay
Here is my / our...	*C'est ma / notre...*	say mah / noh-truh
...business card	*...carte de visite*	kart duh vee-zeet
...e-mail address	*...adresse e-mail*	ah-drehs ee-mayl

Chatting with Children

What's your first name?	*Quel est ton prénom?*	kehl ay toh<u>n</u> pray-noh<u>n</u>
My name is ___.	*Je m'appelle ___.*	zhuh mah-pehl
How old are you?	*Quel âge as-tu?*	kehl ahzh ah-tew
Do you have brothers and sisters?	*Tu as des frères et soeurs?*	tew ahz day frehr ay sur
Do you like school?	*Tu aimes l'école?*	tew ehm lay-kohl
What are you studying?	*Tu étudies quoi?*	tew ay-tew-dee kwah
I'm studying ___.	*J'étudie ___.*	zhay-too-dee
What's your favorite subject?	*Quel est ton sujet préféré?*	kehl ay toh<u>n</u> soo-zhay pray-fuh-ray
Do you have pets?	*As-tu un animal chez toi?*	ah-tew uh<u>n</u> ah-nee-mahl shay twah
I have a...	*J'ai un...*	zhay uh<u>n</u>
We have a...	*Nous avons un...*	nooz ah-voh<u>n</u> ewn
...cat / dog / fish / bird	*...chat / chien / poisson / oiseau*	shah / shee-a<u>n</u> / pwah-soh<u>n</u> / wah-zoh
What is this?	*Qu'est-ce que c'est?*	kes kuh say
Will you teach me...?	*Tu m'apprends...?*	tew mah-prah<u>n</u>
Will you teach us...?	*Tu nous apprend...?*	tew nooz ah-prah<u>n</u>
...some French words	*...quelques mots en français*	kehl-kuh moh ah<u>n</u> frah<u>n</u>-say
...a simple French song	*...une chanson française facile*	ewn shah<u>n</u>-soh<u>n</u> frah<u>n</u>-sehz fah-seel
Guess which country I live in.	*Devine mon pays.*	duh-veen moh<u>n</u> pay-ee
Guess which country we live in.	*Devine notre pays.*	duh-veen noh-truh pay-ee
How old am I?	*J'ai quel âge?*	zhay kehl ahzh

I'm ___ years old.	J'ai ___ ans.	zhay ___ ahn
Want to hear me burp?	Veux-tu m'ententre roter?	vuh-tew mahn-tahn-truh roh-tay
Teach me a fun game.	Apprends-moi un jeu rigolo.	ah-prahn-mwah uhn zhuh ree-goh-loh
Got any candy?	Tu as des bonbons?	tew ah day bohn-bohn
Want to arm wrestle?	Tu veux faire un bras de fer?	tew vuh fair uhn brah duh fehr
Gimme five.	Tape là.	tahp lah

If you want to do a "high five" with a kid, hold up your hand and say, "Tape là" (Hit me here). For a French sing-along, you'll find the words for "Happy Birthday" on page 24 and a couple more songs on page 258.

Travel Talk

I am / Are you...?	Je suis / Vous êtes...?	zhuh sweez / vooz eht
...on vacation	...en vacances	ahn vah-kahns
...on business	...en voyage d'affaires	ahn voy-yahzh dah-fair
How long have you been traveling?	Il y a longtemps que vous voyagez?	eel yah lohn-tahn kuh voo voy-yah-zhay
day / week	jour / semaine	zhoor / suh-mehn
month / year	mois / année	mwah / ah-nay
When are you going home?	Quand allez-vous rentrer?	kahn ah-lay-voo rahn-tray
This is my first time in ___.	C'est ma première fois en ___.	say mah pruhm-yehr fwah ahn
This is our first time in ___.	C'est notre première fois en ___.	say noh-truh pruhm-yehr fwah ahn
It's / It's not a tourist trap.	C'est /Ce n'est pas un piège à touristes.	say / suh nay pah uhn pee-ehzh ah too-reest
This is paradise.	Ceci est le paradis.	say-see ay luh pah-rah-deez
France is wonderful.	La France est magnifique.	lah frahns ay mahn-yee-feek
The French are friendly / boring / rude.	Les Français sont gentils / ennuyeux / impolis.	lay frahn-say sohn zhahn-tee / ahn-noo-yuh / an-poh-lee

So far...	Jusqu'à maintenant...	zhews-kah maη-tuh-nahη
Today...	Aujourd'hui...	oh-zhoor-dwee
...I have / We have seen ___ and ___.	...j'ai / nous avons vu ___ et ___.	zhay / nooz ah-vohη vew ___ ay ___
Next...	Après...	ah-preh
Tomorrow...	Demain...	duh-maη
...I will / We will see ___.	...je vais / nous allons voir ___.	zhuh vay / nooz ahl-lohη vwar
Yesterday...	Hier...	yehr
...I saw / We saw ___.	...j'ai vu / nous avons vu ___.	zhay vew / nooz ah-vohη vew
My / Our vacation is ___ days long, starting in __ and ending in __.	J'ai / Nous avons ___ jours de vacances, qui commencent à __ et qui finissent à __.	zhay / nooz ah-vohη ___ zhoor duh vah-kahηs kee kohη-mahη-sahη ah ___ ay kee fee-nee-sahη ah ___
To travel is to live.	Voyager c'est vivre.	voy-yah-zhay say vee-vruh
Travel is enlightening.	Voyager ouvre l'esprit.	voy-yah-zhay oo-vruh luh-spree
I wish all (American) politicians traveled.	Je souhaite que tous les politiciens (américains) voyagent.	zhuh soo-ayt kuh too lay poh-lee-tee-see-aη (ah-may-ree-kan) voy-yah-zhahη
Have a good trip!	Bon voyage!	bohη voy-yahzh

Map Musings

Use the following maps to delve into family history and explore travel dreams.

I live here.	J'habite ici.	zhah-beet ee-see
We live here.	Nous habitons ici.	nooz ah-bee-tohη ee-see
I was born here.	Je suis né là.	zhuh swee nay lah
My ancestors came from ___.	Mes ancêtres viennent de ___.	mayz ahη-seh-truh vee-ehn duh ___
I've traveled to ___.	J'ai visité à ___.	zhay vee-zee-tay ah ___
We've traveled to ___.	Nous avons visité à ___.	nooz ah-vohη vee-zee-tay ah ___

FRANCE

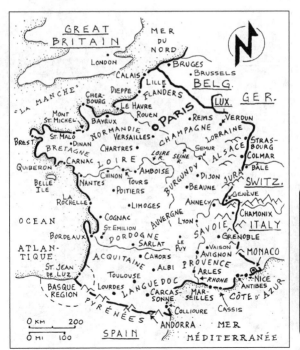

EUROPE

500 KM
300 MI
Trondheim
NORWAY
SOGNE-FJORD
Bergen
Oslo
FINLAND
Helsinki
St. Pete
Turku
Stockholm
Tallinn
ESTONIA
SWEDEN
BALTIC
SEA
LATVIA
Riga
SCOTLAND
NORTH
SEA
Edinburgh
DENMARK
Copenhagen
LITHUANIA
Vilnius
RUSS.
N. IRE.
IRELAND
Dublin
York
ENGLAND
WALES
Lübeck
BELA-RUS
POLAND
DINGLE PENINSULA
London
Amsterdam
Berlin
Warsaw
Bath
NETH.
GERMANY
Bruges
Brussels
BELG.
Mont St. Michel
RHINE
MOSEL
Prague
Krakow
ATLANTIC
NORMANDY
LUX.
ROM. ROAD
CZECH.
UKRAINE
Paris
ALSACE
SLOVAK.
BRITTANY
LOIRE
Colmar
Munich
BAVARIA
Vienna
Budapest
Salzburg
OCEAN
FRANCE
Bern
BERN. OBER.
TIROL
AUST.
HUNG.
ROMANIA
SWITZ.
DOLO-MITES
SLOV.
Chamonix
DORDOGNE
Lyon
Milan
Venice
CRO.
Belgrade
Buch.
CINQUE TERRE
PROVENCE
BOSNIA-HERZ.
Arles
Florence
SERBIA
Sofia
Carc.
MONACO
TUSCANY
SAN MARINO
Dubrov.
SPAIN
ANDORRA
Nice
ADRIATIC SEA
BULG.
CORSICA
MAC.
PORTUGAL
Madrid
Barcelona
Rome
ITALY
ALB.
Lisbon
Toledo
Naples
SARDINIA
CORFU
GREECE
AMALFI COAST
Athens
Sevilla
Gran.
ANDALUSIA
MEDITERRANEAN
PEL. PEN.
ALGARVE
SICILY
DCH
MOROCCO
ALGERIA
TUNISIA
SEA

THE UNITED STATES

THE WORLD

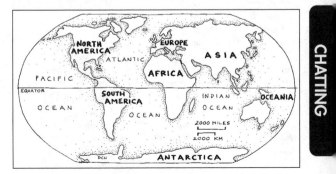

CHATING

Next I'll go to ___.	*Et puis je vais à...*	ay pwee zhuh vay ah
Next we'll go to ___.	*Et puis nous allons à...*	ay pwee nooz ahl-lohn ah
I'd like / We'd like to go to ___.	*Je voudrais / Nous voudrions aller à ___.*	zhuh voo-dray / noo voo-dree-ohn ah-lay ah
Where do you live?	*Où est-ce que vous vivez?*	oo ehs kuh voo vee-vay
Where were you born?	*Où êtes-vous né?*	oo eht-voo nay
Where did your ancestors come from?	*D'où viennent vos ancêtres?*	doo vee-ehn vohz ahn-seh-truh
Where have you traveled?	*Où avez-vous voyagé?*	oo ah-vay-voo voy-yah-zhay
Where are you going?	*Où allez-vous?*	oo ah-lay-voo
Where would you like to go?	*Où voudriez-vous voyager?*	oo voo-dree-yay-voo voy-yah-zhay

Favorite Things

What kind... do you like?	*Quelle sorte... vous aimez?*	kehl sort... vooz eh-may
...of art	*...d'art*	dar
...of books	*...de livres*	duh lee-vruh
...of hobby	*...de hobby, passe temps*	duh oh-bee, pahs tahn
...of ice cream	*...de glace*	duh glahs
...of food	*...de nourriture*	duh noo-ree-tewr
...of movies	*...de films*	duh feelm
...of music	*...de musique*	duh mew-zeek
...of sports	*...de sports*	duh spor
...of vices	*...de vices*	duh vees
Who is your favorite...?	*Qui est votre... préféré?*	kee ay voh-truh... pray-fay-ray

...artist	...artiste	ar-teest
...author	...auteur	ow-tur
...male singer	...chanteur	shahn-tur
...female singer	...chanteuse	shahn-tuhz
...male movie star	...acteur	ahk-tur
...female movie star	...actrice	ahk-trees
Can you recommend a good...?	Vous pouvez me conseiller un bon...?	voo poo-vay muh kohn-seh-yay uhn bohn
...French CD	...français CD	frahn-say say day
...French book	...livre français	lee-vruh frahn-say
translated	traduit	trah-dwee
in English	en anglais	ahn ahn-glay

Thanks a Million

Thank you very much.	Merci beaucoup.	mehr-see boh-koo
You are...	Vous êtes...	vooz eht
...helpful.	...serviable.	sehr-vee-ah-bluh
...wonderful.	...magnifique.	mahn-yee-feek
...generous. (m / f)	...généreux / généreuse.	zhay-nay-ruh / zhay-nay-ruhz
You spoil me / us.	Vous me / nous gâtez.	voo muh / noo gah-tay
You've been a great help!	Vous m'avez beaucoup aider!	voo mah-vay boh-koo ay-day
You are an angel from God.	Vous êtes un ange venu du ciel.	vooz eht uhn ahnzh vuh-new duh see-ehl
I will remember you...	Je me souviendrai de vous...	zhuh muh soov-yan-dreh duh voo
We will remember you...	Nous nous souviendrons de vous...	noo noo soov-yan-dreh duh voo
...always.	...toujours.	too-zhoor
...till Tuesday.	...jusqu'à mardi.	zhews-kah mar-dee

Weather

What's the weather tomorrow?	*Quel temps fera-t-il demain?*	kehl tah<u>n</u> fuh-rah-teel duh-ma<u>n</u>
sunny / cloudy	*ensoleillé / nuageux*	ah<u>n</u>-soh-lay-yay / nwah-zhuh
hot / cold	*chaud / froid*	shoh / frwah
muggy / windy	*humide / venteux*	oo-meed / vah<u>n</u>-tuh
rain / snow	*pluie / neige*	ploo-ee / nehzh
It's raining like cow's piss. (French saying)	*Il pleut comme vâche qui pisse.*	eel pluh kohm vahsh kee pees

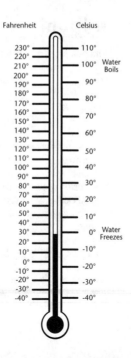

Smoking

Do you smoke?	*Vous fumez?*	voo few-may
Do you smoke pot?	*Vous fumez de l'herbe?*	voo few-may duh lehrb
I (don't) smoke.	*Je (ne) fume (pas).*	zhuh (nuh) fewm (pah)
We (don't) smoke.	*Nous (ne) fumons (pas).*	noo (nuh) few-mohn (pah)
lighter	*briquet*	bree-kay
cigarettes	*cigarette*	see-gah-reht
marijuana	*de l'herbe, marijuana*	duh lehrb, mah-ree-wah-nah
hash	*hachisch*	hah-sheesh
joint	*joint*	"joint"
stoned	*stoned*	"stoned"
Wow!	*Wow!*	"Wow"

Responses for All Occasions

I like that.	*Ça me plaît.*	sah muh play
We like that.	*Ça nous plaît*	sah noo play
I like you.	*Je vous aime bien.*	zhuh vooz ehm bee-an
We like you.	*Nous vous aimons bien.*	noo vooz ehm-ohn bee-an
That's cool.	*C'est chouette.*	say shweht
Great!	*Formidable!*	for-mee-dah-bluh
What a nice place.	*Quell endroit sympa.*	kehl ahn-dwah sahn-pah
Perfect.	*Parfait.*	par-fay
Funny.	*Amusant.*	ah-mew-zahn
Interesting.	*Intéressant.*	an-tay-reh-sahn
Really?	*Vraiment?*	vray-mahn
Wow!	*Wow!*	"Wow"
Congratulations!	*Félicitations!*	fay-lee-see-tah-see-ohn
Well done!	*Bien joué!*	bee-an zhoo-ay
You're welcome.	*Je vous en prie.*	zhuh vooz ahn pree
It's nothing.	*De rien.*	duh ree-an

CHATING

Bless you! (sneeze)	*À vos souhaits!*	ah voh sway
What a pity.	*Quel dommage.*	kehl doh-mahzh
That's life.	*C'est la vie.*	say lah vee
No problem.	*Pas de problème.*	pah duh proh-blehm
O.K.	*D'accord.*	dah-kor
This is the good life!	*Que la vie est belle!*	kuh lah vee ay behl
Have a good day!	*Bonne journée!*	buhn zhoor-nay
Good luck!	*Bonne chance!*	buhn shah<u>n</u>s
Let's go!	*Allons-y!*	ah-loh<u>n</u>-zee

Conversing with Animals

rooster / cock-a-doodle-doo	*coq / cocorico*	kohk / koh-koh-ree-koh
bird / tweet tweet	*oiseau / cui cui*	wah-zoh / kwee kwee
cat / meow	*chat / miaou*	shah / mee-ah-oo
dog / woof woof	*chien / ouah ouah*	shee-a<u>n</u> / wah wah
duck / quack quack	*canard / coin coin*	kah-nar / kwa<u>n</u> kwa<u>n</u>
cow / moo	*vache / meu*	vahsh / muh
pig / oink oink	*cochon / groin groin*	koh-shoh<u>n</u> / grwa<u>n</u> grwa<u>n</u>

Profanity

People make animal noises, too. These words will help you
understand what the more colorful locals are saying...

Damn! (Good God!)	*Bon Dieu!*	boh<u>n</u> dee-uh
bastard	*salaud*	sah-loh
bitch	*salope*	sah-lohp
breasts (colloq.)	*tétons*	tay-toh<u>n</u>
big breasts	*grands tétons*	grah<u>n</u> tay-toh<u>n</u>
penis (colloq.)	*bite*	beet
butthole	*sale con*	sahl koh<u>n</u>
drunk	*bourré*	boo-ray
idiot	*idiot*	ee-dee-oh
imbecile	*imbécile*	a<u>n</u>-bay-seel
jerk	*connard*	kuh-nar

stupid	*stupide*	stew-peed
Did someone fart?	*Est-ce que quelqu'un à péter?*	ehs kuh kehl-ku<u>hn</u> ah pay-tay
I burped.	*J'ai roté.*	zhay roh-tay
This sucks.	*C'est dégueulasse.*	say day-gewl-ahs
Shit.	*Merde.*	mehrd
Bullshit.	*C'est de la merde.*	say duh lah mehrd
You are...	*Vous êtes...*	vooz eht
Don't be...	*Ne soyez pas...*	nuh soh-yay pah
...a son of a bitch.	*...un batard.*	uh<u>n</u> bah-tar
...an asshole.	*...un vieux con.*	uh<u>n</u> vee-uh koh<u>n</u>
...an idiot.	*...un idiot.*	uh<u>n</u> ee-dee-oh
...a creep.	*...un vicieux.*	uh<u>n</u> vee-see-uh
...a cretin.	*...un crétin.*	uh<u>n</u> kray-teen
...a pig.	*...un cochon.*	uh<u>n</u> koh-shoh<u>n</u>

Sweet Curses

My goodness.	*Mon Dieu.*	moh<u>n</u> dee-uh
Goodness gracious.	*Mon bon Dieu.*	moh<u>n</u> boh<u>n</u> dee-uh
Oh, my gosh.	*Oh la la.*	oo lah lah
Shoot.	*Zut.*	zewt
Darn it!	*Mince!*	ma<u>n</u>s

Create Your Own Conversation

The French enjoy good conversations. Join in! You can mix and match these words into a conversation. Make it as deep or silly as you want.

Who

I / you	*je / vous*	zhuh / voo
he / she	*il / elle*	eel / ehl
we / they	*nous / ils*	noo / eel
my / your...	*mes / vos...*	may / voh
...parents / children	*...parents / enfants*	pah-rah<u>n</u> / zah<u>n</u>-fah<u>n</u>
men / women	*hommes / femmes*	ohm / fahm
rich / poor	*riches / pauvres*	reesh / poh-vruh
young /	*jeunes /*	zhuhn /
middle-aged / old	*d'âge mur / vieux*	dahzh mewr / vee-uh
the French	*les Français*	lay frah<u>n</u>-say
the Austrians	*les Autrichiens*	layz oh-treesh-ee-a<u>n</u>
the Belgians	*les Belges*	lay behlzh
the Czechs	*les Tchèques*	lay chehk
the Germans	*les Allemands*	layz ahl-mah<u>n</u>
the Italians	*les Italiens*	layz ee-tah-lee-a<u>n</u>
the Spanish	*les Espagnols*	layz eh-spahn-yohl
the Swiss	*les Suisses*	lay swees
the Europeans	*les Européens*	layz ur-oh-pee-ehn
EU	*UE*	ew uh
(European Union)	*(l'Union Européenne)*	(lewn-yun ur-oh-pee-ehn)
the Americans	*les Américains*	layz ah-may-ree-ka<u>n</u>
liberals	*libéraux*	lee-bay-roh
conservatives	*conservateurs*	koh<u>n</u>-sehr-vah-tur
radicals	*radicaux*	rah-dee-koh
terrorists	*terroristes*	teh-roh-reest
politicians	*politiciens*	poh-lee-tee-see-a<u>n</u>

big business	*grosses affaires*	grohs ah-fair
multinational	*corporations*	kor-por-ah-see-oh<u>n</u>
corporations	*multinationales*	mewl-tee-nah-see-oh-nahl
military	*militaire*	mee-lee-tair
mafia	*mafia*	mah-fee-ah
refugees	*réfugiés*	ray-few-zhee-ay
travelers	*voyageurs*	voy-yah-zhur
God	*Dieu*	dee-uh
Christian	*chrétien*	kray-tee-a<u>n</u>
Catholic	*catholique*	kah-toh-leek
Protestant	*protestant*	proh-tehs-tah<u>n</u>
Jew	*juif*	zhweef
Muslim	*musulmans*	mew-zewl-mah<u>n</u>
everyone	*tout le monde*	too luh moh<u>n</u>d

What

buy / sell	*acheter / vendre*	ah-shuh-tay / vah<u>n</u>-druh
have / lack	*avoir / manquer de*	ahv-wahr / mah<u>n</u>-kay duh
help / abuse	*aider / abuser*	ay-day / ah-boo-zay
learn / fear	*apprendre / craindre*	ah-prah<u>n</u>-druh / cra<u>n</u>-druh
love / hate	*aimer / détester*	eh-may / day-tehs-tay
prosper / suffer	*prospérer / souffrir*	proh-spay-ray / soo-freer
take / give	*prendre / donner*	prah<u>n</u>-druh / duh-nay
want / need	*vouloir / avoir besoin de*	vool-wahr / ahv-wahr buh-swa<u>n</u> duh
work / play	*travailler / jouer*	trah-vah-yay / zhoo-way

Why

(anti-)	*(anti-)*	(ah<u>n</u>-tee-)
globalization	*globalisation*	gloh-bah-lee-zah-see-oh<u>n</u>
class warfare	*lutte sociale*	luht soh-see-ahl
corruption	*corruption*	koh-rewp-see-oh<u>n</u>
democracy	*démocratie*	day-moh-krah-tee
education	*éducation*	ay-dew-kah-see-oh<u>n</u>
family	*famille*	fah-mee-ee
food	*nourriture*	noo-ree-tewr

guns	*armes*	arm
happiness	*bonheur*	boh<u>n</u>-ur
health	*santé*	sah<u>n</u>-tay
hope	*espoir*	ehs-pwahr
imperialism	*impérialisme*	a<u>n</u>-pay-ree-ahl-eez-muh
lies	*mensonges*	mah<u>n</u>-soh<u>n</u>zh
love / sex	*amour / sexe*	ah-moor / "sex"
marijuana	*marijuana*	mah-ree-wah-nah
money / power	*argent / pouvoir*	ar-zhah<u>n</u> / poov-wahr
pollution	*pollution*	poh-lew-see-oh<u>n</u>
racism	*racisme*	rah-seez-muh
regime change	*changement de régime*	shah<u>n</u>-zhuh-mah<u>n</u> duh ray-zheem
relaxation	*relaxation*	ruh-lahk-sah-see-oh<u>n</u>
religion	*religion*	ruh-lee-zhee-oh<u>n</u>
respect	*respect*	ruh-speh
taxes	*taxes*	tahks
television	*télévision*	tay-lay-vee-zee-oh<u>n</u>
violence	*violence*	vee-oh-lah<u>n</u>s
war / peace	*guerre / paix*	gehr / peh
work	*travail*	trah-vah-ee
global perspective	*perspective globale*	pehr-spehk-teev gloh-bahl

You Be the Judge

(no) problem	*(pas de) problème*	(pah duh) proh-blehm
(not) good	*(pas) bon*	(pah) boh<u>n</u>
(not) dangerous	*(pas) dangereux*	(pah) dah<u>n</u>-zhay-ruh
(not) fair	*(pas) juste*	(pah) zhewst
(not) guilty	*(pas) coupable*	(pah) koo-pah-bluh
(not) powerful	*(pas) puissant*	(pah) pwee-sah<u>n</u>
(not) stupid	*(pas) stupide*	(pah) stew-peed
(not) happy	*(pas) content*	(pah) koh<u>n</u>-tah<u>n</u>
because / for	*parce que / pour*	pars kuh / poor
and / or / from	*et / ou / de*	ay / oo / duh

too much	*trop*	troh
(never) enough	*(jamais) assez*	(zhah-may) ah-say
same	*même*	mehm
better / worse	*mieux / pire*	mee-uh / peer
here / everywhere	*ici / partout*	ee-see / par-too

Beginnings and Endings

I like...	*J'aime...*	zhehm
We like...	*Nous aimons...*	nooz eh-mohn
I don't like...	*Je n'aime pas...*	zhuh nehm pah
We don't like...	*Nous n'aimons pas...*	noo neh-mohn pah
Do you like...?	*Vous aimez...?*	vooz eh-may
In the past...	*Dans le passé...*	dahn luh pah-say
When I was younger,	*Quand j'étais jeune,*	kahn zhay-tay zhuhn
I thought...	*je pensais...*	zhuh pahn-say
Now, I think...	*Maintenant,*	man-tuh-nahn
	je pense...	zhuh pahns
I am / Are you...?	*Je suis / Vous êtes...?*	zhuh swee / vooz eht
...optimistic /	*...optimiste /*	ohp-tee-meest /
pessimistic	*pessimiste*	peh-see-meest
I believe...	*Je crois...*	zhuh krwah
I don't believe...	*Je ne crois pas...*	zhuh nuh krwah pah
Do you believe...?	*Croyez-vous...?*	krwah-yay-voo
...in God	*...en Dieu*	ahn dee-uh
...in life after death	*...en la vie après*	ahn lah vee ah-preh
	la mort	lah mor
...in extraterrestrial	*...dans la vie*	dahn lah vee
life	*extraterrestre*	ehk-strah-tuh-rehs-truh
...in Santa Claus	*...au Père Noël*	oh pehr noh-ehl
Yes. / No.	*Oui. / Non.*	wee / nohn
Maybe. /	*Peut-être. /*	puh-teh-truh /
I don't know.	*Je ne sais pas.*	zhuh nuh say pah
What's most	*Quel est le plus*	kehl ay luh plewz
important in life?	*important dans*	an-por-tahn dahn
	la vie?	lah vee

CHATING

The problem is...	*Le problème, c'est que...*	luh proh-blehm say kuh
The answer is...	*La solution, c'est...*	luh soh-lew-see-ohn say
We have solved the world's problems.	*Nous avons résolu les problèmes du monde.*	nooz ah-vohn ray-zoh-lew lay proh-blehm dew mohnd

The French Political Scene

These are the top six political parties in France, listed the same way you read, from left to right.

Parti Communiste: Beloved by labor unions, the communist party has become almost irrelevant.

Parti Écologiste: Also known as **Les Vert** (the greens), this is France's environmental party.

Parti Socialiste: The socialist party is France's mainstream left-leaning party.

Républicains pour la Rassemblement (RPR): Founded by Charles de Gaulle and led by Jacques Chirac, this traditionally conservative party vies with the Parti Socialiste for control.

Front Nationale: Headed by Jean-Marie le Pen, this racist extreme right party advocates deportation of North African residents. Drawing about 10 to 15 percent of the vote, this party is fueled mainly by France's southern regions.

A French Romance

Words of Love

I / me / you / we	*je / moi / tu / nous*	zhuh / mwah / tew / noo
flirt	*flirter*	fleer-tay
kiss	*baiser*	bay-zay
hug	*se serrer dans les bras*	suh suh-ray dah<u>n</u> lay brah
love	*amour*	ah-moor
make love	*faire l'amour*	fair lah-moor
condom	*préservatif*	pray-zehr-vah-teef
contraceptive	*contraceptif*	koh<u>n</u>-trah-sehp-teef
safe sex	*safe sex*	"safe sex"
sexy	*sexy*	"sexy"
cozy	*douillet*	doo-yay
romantic	*romantique*	roh-mah<u>n</u>-teek
my angel	*mon ange*	moh<u>n</u> ah<u>n</u>zh
my doe	*ma biche*	mah beesh
my love	*mon amour*	moh<u>n</u> ah-moor
my little cabbage	*mon petit chou*	moh<u>n</u> puh-tee shoo
my flea (endearing)	*ma puce*	mah poos
my treasure	*mon trésor*	moh<u>n</u> tray-sor

Ah, l'Amour

What's the matter?	*Qu'est-ce qu'il y a?*	kehs keel yah
Nothing.	*Rien.*	ree-a<u>n</u>
I am / Are you...?	*Je suis / Vous êtes...?*	zhuh swee / vooz eht
...gay	*...homosexual, gay*	oh-moh-sehk-soo-ehl, "gay"
...straight	*...hétéro*	ay-tay-roh
...bisexual	*...bisexuel*	bee-sehk-swehl

...undecided	...indécis	an-day-see
...prudish (m / f)	...pudibond / pudibonde	pew-dee-bohn / pew-dee-bohnd
...horny	...excité	ehk-see-tay
We are on our honeymoon.	C'est notre lune de miel.	say noh-truh lewn duh mee-ehl
I have a boyfriend.	J'ai un petit ami.	zhay uhn puh-teet ah-mee
I have a girlfriend.	J'ai une petite amie.	zhay ewn puh-teet ah-mee
I'm married.	Je suis marié.	zhuh swee mah-ree-ay
I'm married (but...).	Je suis marié (mais...).	zhuh swee mah-ree-ay (may)
I'm not married.	Je ne suis pas marié.	zhuh nuh swee pah mah-ree-ay
Do you have a boyfriend / a girlfriend?	Vous avez un petit ami / une petite amie?	vooz ah-vay uhn puh-teet ah-mee / ewn puh-teet ah-mee
I am adventurous.	Je suis aventureux(se).	zhuh swee ah-vahn-too-ruh(z)
I'm lonely (tonight).	Je me sens seul (ce soir).	zhuh muh sahn suhl (suh swar)
I am rich and single.	Je suis riche et célibataire.	zhuh swee reesh ay say-lee-bah-tair
Do you mind if I sit here?	Ça vous embête si je m'assieds ici?	sah vooz ahn-beht see zhuh mah-seed ee-see
Would you like a drink?	Vous voulez un verre?	voo voo-lay uhn vehr
Will you go out with me?	Vous voulez sortir avec moi?	voo voo-lay sor-teer ah-vehk mwah
Would you like to go out tonight for...?	Vous voulez m'accompagner ce soir pour...?	voo voo-lay mah-kohn-pahn-yay suh swar poor
...a walk	...une promenade	ewn proh-muh-nahd
...dinner	...dîner	dee-nay
...a drink	...boire un pot	bwar uhn poh

Where's the best place to dance nearby?	*Où est le meilleur endroit pour danser?*	oo ay luh meh-yur ahn-dwah poor dahn-say
Do you want to dance?	*Vous voulez danser?*	voo voo-lay dahn-say
Again?	*De nouveau?*	duh noo-voh
Let's celebrate!	*Faisons la fête!*	fay-zohn lah feht
Let's have fun like idiots!	*Amusons-nous comme des fous!*	ah-mew-zohn-noo kohm day foo
Let's have a wild and crazy night!	*On va s'éclater ce soir!*	ohn vah say-klah-tay suh swar
I have no diseases.	*Je n'ai pas de maladies.*	zhuh nay pah duh mah-lah-dee
I have many diseases.	*J'ai plusieurs maladies.*	zhay plewz-yur mah-lah-dee
I have only safe sex.	*Je pratique que le safe sex.*	zhuh prah-teek kuh luh "safe sex"
Can I take you home?	*Tu veux venir chez moi?*	tew vuh vuh-neer shay mwah
Why not?	*Pourquoi pas?*	poor-kwah pah
How can I change your mind?	*Qu'est-ce que je peux faire pour te faire changer d'avis?*	kehs kuh zhuh puh fair poor tuh fair shan-zhay dah-vee
Kiss me.	*Embrasse-moi.*	ahn-brah-say-mwah
May I kiss you?	*Je peux t'embrasser?*	zhuh puh tahn-brah-say
Can I see you again?	*On peut se revoir?*	ohn puh suh ruh-vwahr
Your place or mine?	*Chez toi ou chez moi?*	shay twah oo shay mwah
How does this feel?	*Comment tu te sens?*	koh-mahn tew tuh sahn
Is this an aphrodisiac?	*C'est un aphrodisiaque?*	sayt uhn ah-froh-dee-zee-yahk

This is my first time.	C'est la première fois.	seht lah pruhm-yehr fwah
This is not my first time.	Ce n'est pas la première fois.	seh nay pah lah pruhm-yehr fwah
You are my most beautiful souvenir.	Tu es mon plus beau souvenir.	tew ay mohn plew boh soo-vuh-neer
Do you do this often?	Tu fais ça souvent?	tew fay sah soo-vahn
How's my breath?	Comment tu trouves mon haleine?	koh-mahn tew troo-vay mohn ah-lehn
Let's just be friends.	Soyons amis.	swah-yohnz ah-mee
I'll pay for my share.	Je paie mon partage.	zhuh pay mohn par-tahzh
Would you like a massage...?	Tu veux un massage...?	tew vuh uhn mah-sahzh
...for your back	...pour le dos	poor luh doh
...for your feet	...des pieds	day pee-yay
Why not?	Pourquoi pas?	poor-kwah pah
Try it.	Essaies.	eh-say
That tickles.	Ça chatouille.	sah shah-too-ee
Oh my God.	Mon Dieu.	mohn dee-uh
I love you.	Je t'aime.	zhuh tehm
Darling, will you marry me?	Chéri, tu veux m'épouser?	shay-ree tew vuh may-poo-zay

DICTIONARY

French/English

A

French	English
à	to; at
à la retraite	retired
à l'heure	on time
à remplir de nouveau	refill (v)
à travers	through
abstrait	abstract
abuser	abuse (v)
accès internet	Internet access
accessible à un fauteuil roulant	wheelchair-accessible
accident	accident
acheter	buy
adaptateur électrique	electrical adapter
addition	bill (payment)
adolescent	teenager
adresse	address
adresse e-mail	e-mail address
adulte	adult
aéroport	airport
affaires	business
affiche	poster
Afrique	Africa
âge	age
agence de voyage	travel agency
âgés, gens	seniors
aggressif	aggressive
agneau	lamb
agnostique	agnostic
agraffeuse	stapler
aider	help (v)
aigre	sour
aiguille	needle
aile	wing
aimable	kind
aimer	love (v)
aimer bien	like (v)

air, l'	air	**après-**	conditioner (hair)
alcool	alcohol	**shampoing**	
Allemagne	Germany	**araignée**	spider
aller	go	**arbre**	tree
aller simple	one way (ticket)	**arc-en-ciel**	rainbow
allergies	allergies	**argent**	money; silver
allergique	allergic	**arobase, signe**	"at" sign (@)
aller-retour	round trip	**arrêt**	stop (n)
allumettes	matches	**arrêt de bus**	bus stop
amant	lover	**arrêt de Métro**	subway stop
ambassade	embassy	**arrêter**	stop (v)
ami	friend	**arrivées**	arrivals
amitié	friendship	**arriver**	arrive
amour	love (n)	**art, l'**	art
ampoule	bulb, light bulb	**arthrite**	arthritis
ampoules	blisters	**artiste**	artist
amusement	fun	**arts**	crafts
ancêtre	ancestor	**ascenseur**	elevator
ancien	ancient	**aspirine**	aspirin
âne	donkey	**assez**	enough
anglais	English	**assiette**	plate
année	year	**assurance**	insurance
anniversaire	birthday	**assurance**	health insurance
annuler	cancel; delete	**maladie**	
anti-acide	antacid	**assuré**	insured
antibiotique	antibiotic	**asthme**	asthma
antiquités	antiques	**athée**	atheist
août	August	**attendre**	wait
appareil-photo	camera	**attirant**	attractive
appartement	apartment	**attraper**	catch (v)
apprécier	enjoy	**au chômage**	unemployed
apprendre	learn	**au dessus**	above
après	after, afterwards	**au lieu de**	instead
après	day after tomorrow	**au revoir**	goodbye
demain		**aube**	sunrise
après rasage	aftershave	**auberge de**	youth hostel
après-midi	afternoon	**jeunesse**	

aujourd'hui	today	bas, en	down
autel	altar	basket	basketball
authentique	genuine	baskettes	tennis shoes
automne	autumn	bateau	boat
autostop, faire de l'	hitchhike	bâtiment	building
autre	other	batterie	battery
Autriche	Austria	bavoir	bib
aux urgences	emergency room	beau	handsome
avaler	swallow (v)	beaucoup	much; many
avant	before	beaume pour les lèvres	lip salve
avec	with		
avenir	future	beau-père	father-in-law
avion	plane	bébé	baby
avion, par	air mail	Belgique	Belgium
avocat	lawyer	belle	beautiful
avoir	have	belle-mère	mother-in-law
avoir besoin de	need (v)	besoin de, avoir	need (v)
avoir sommeil	sleepy	bibliothèque	library
avortement	abortion	bien	good
avril	April	bientôt	soon
		bienvenue	welcome
B		bière	beer
bac	ferry	bijouterie	jewelry shop
bagage	baggage	bijoux	jewelry
bagage en cabine	carry-on luggage	billet	ticket
		bizarre	strange
bague	ring (n)	blague	joke (n)
baignoire	bathtub	blanc	white
bain	bath	blessé	injured
baiser	kiss (n, v)	bleu	blue
balcon	balcony	blonde	blond
balle	ball	blush	blush (makeup)
banane	banana	boeuf	beef
bandage adhésif	Band-Aid	boire	drink (v)
banque	bank	bois	wood
barbe	beard	boisson	drink (n)
bas	low	boîte	box

boîte de conserve	can (n)
bol	bowl
bombe	bomb
bombe contre les insectes	insect repellant
bon	fine (good); valid
bon marché	cheap
bonbon	candy
bonheur	happiness
bonjour	hello, good day
bonne santé	healthy
bottes	boots
bouche	mouth
bouchon	cork
bouchon pour le lavabo	sink stopper
boucle d'oreille	earrings
bougies	sparkplugs
bouilli	boiled
bouilloire	kettle
boulangerie	bakery
boules quiès	earplugs
boulot	job
bouteille	bottle
boutique	clothing boutique
boutique de souvenirs	souvenir shop
bouton	button
boutons	rash
bracelet	bracelet
bras	arm
briquet	lighter (n)
broche	brooch
bronzage	suntan (n)
brosse	hairbrush
brosse à dents	toothbrush
brouillard	fog
bruillant	noisy
brûlure	burn (n)
brun	brown
bruyant	loud
bureau	office
bus	city bus

C

cabine téléphonique	phone booth
cachot	dungeon
cadeau	gift
cafards	cockroach
café	coffee; coffee shop
caisse	cashier
calendrier	calendar
calepin	notebook
calmant	pain killer
camp, lit de	cot
camping-car	R.V.
canoë	canoe
canot	rowboat
capitaine	captain
car	long-distance bus
carafe	carafe
caroussel des bagages	baggage claim
carrefour	intersection
carte	card; menu; map
carte de crédit	credit card
carte de visite	business card
carte postale	postcard
carte téléphonique	telephone card
cascade	waterfall
casquette	cap

cassette	tape (cassette)	chaud	hot
cathédrale	cathedral	chauffage	heat (n)
catholique	Catholic (adj)	chauffer	heat (v)
caution	deposit	chauffeur	driver
cave	cellar	chaussettes	socks
ce soir	tonight	chaussons	slippers
ceinture	belt	chaussures	shoes
célibataire	single	chaussures	tennis shoes
cendrier	ashtray	de tennis	
centre	center	chef	boss
centre	shopping mall	chemin de fer	railway
commercial		chemise	shirt
centre-ville	downtown	chemise de nuit	nightgown
céramique	ceramic	chèque	check
chaire	pulpit	chèque	travelers check
chaise	chair	de voyage	
chaise haute	high chair	cher	expensive
chambre	room	cheval	horse
chambre libre	vacancy (hotel)	chevaliers	knights
champ	field	cheveux	hair
championnat	championship	cheveux, coupe de	haircut
chance	luck	cheville	ankle
chandelle	candle	chien	dog
change	change (n);	chinois	Chinese (adj)
	exchange (n)	chocolat	chocolate
changer	change (v)	choeur	choir
chanson	song	chômage, au	unemployed
chanter	sing	chose	thing
chanteur	singer	chose, quelque	something
chapeau	hat	chrétien	Christian (adj)
chapelle	chapel	ciel	sky
chaque	each, every	cigarette	cigarette
charcuterie-	delicatessen	cinéma	cinema
traiteur		cintre	coat hanger
charmant	charming	circulation	traffic
chat	cat	ciseaux	scissors
château	castle	clair	clear

classe	class	**compteur**	taxi meter
classe, deuxième	second class	**concert**	concert
classe, première	first class	**conducteur**	conductor
classique	classical	**conduire**	drive (v)
clef	key	**confirmer**	confirm
clignotant	turn signal	**confiserie**	sweets shop
climatisé	air-conditioned	**confortable**	comfortable, cozy
clinique médicale	medical	**congestion**	congestion (sinus)
	clinic	**conserve, boîte de**	can (n)
cloches	bells	**consigne**	lockers
cloître	cloister	**constipation**	constipation
cochon	pig	**contagieux**	contagious
code	PIN code	**contraceptif**	contraceptive
code postal	Zip code	**coquille**	shell
coeur	heart	**corde**	rope
coiffeur	barber, barber shop	**corde à linge**	clothesline
coiffeur pour	beauty	**corps**	body
dames	salon	**correspondance**	connection
coin	corner		transfer (n) (train)
coincé	stuck	**correspondance,**	transfer (v)
colis	package	**prendre une**	
collants	nylons (pantyhose)	**corruption**	corruption
collier	necklace	**costume de bain**	swimsuit
colline	hill	**côte**	coast
combattre	fight (v)	**coton**	cotton
combien	how many,	**cou**	neck
	how much	**couche**	diaper
commencer	begin	**coucher de soleil**	sunset
comment	how	**couchette**	berth (train)
compagne	company	**coude**	elbow
compartiment	sleeper (train)	**couleurs**	colors
privé		**couloir**	aisle
complet	no vacancy	**coup de soleil**	sunburn
compliqué	complicated	**coupable**	guilty
composter	validate	**coupe de cheveux**	haircut
comprendre	understand	**courir**	run (v)
comptable	accountant	**courrier**	mail (n)

courroie du ventilateur	fan belt
court	short
couteau	knife
coûter	cost (v)
couverture	blanket
craindre	fear (v)
crampes	cramps
crampes de menstruation	menstrual cramps
crayon	pencil
crayon pour les yeux	eyeliner
crème	cream
crème à raser	shaving cream
crème antiseptique	first-aid cream
crème chantilly	whipped cream
crème hydratante	moisturizer
crème pour les mains	hand lotion
croix	cross
cru	raw
crypte	crypt
cuillère	spoon
cuir	leather
cuisine	kitchen
cuisinier	cook (v)
cuisse	thigh
cuivre	copper
cuivre jaune	brass
cure-dent	toothpick

D

d'accord	agree; O.K.
dames	women
dangereux	dangerous
dans	in
danser	dance (v)
de	of; from
de l'herbe	marijuana
décembre	December
déclarer	declare (customs)
décongestant	decongestant
dedans	inside
déjà	already
délicieux	delicious
demain	tomorrow
demain, après	day after tomorrow
demander	ask
démangeaison	itch (n)
démocratie	democracy
dent	tooth
dentelle	lace
dentifrice	toothpaste
dentiste	dentist
dents	teeth
dents, mal aux	toothache
dépanneur	tow truck
départs	departures
dépêcher (se)	hurry (v)
dépenser	spend
déranger	disturb
dernier	last (adj.)
derrière	behind
désinfectant	disinfectant
désodorisant	deodorant
désolé	sorry
dessus, au	above
détester	hate (v)
deuxième	second
deuxième classe	second class

déviation	detour (n)
diabète	diabetes
diabétique	diabetic
diamant	diamond
diaphragme	diaphragm (birth control)
diapositive	slide (photo)
diarrhée	diarrhea
dictionnaire	dictionary
Dieu	God
difficile	difficult
dimanche	Sunday
dîner	dinner; dine
direct	direct
directeur	manager
disque compact	compact disc
dissolvant	nail polish remover
distributeur automatique	cash machine
divorcé	divorced
docteur	doctor
doigt	finger
dôme	dome
dommage, quel	it's a pity
donner	give
dormir	sleep (v)
dortoire	dormitory
dos	back
douane	customs
douche	shower
douleur	pain
doux	sweet; mild
douzaine	dozen
drap	sheet
drapeau	flag
draps	bedsheet

droit	straight
droite	right (direction)
drôle	funny
du scotch	scotch tape
dur	hard; tough

E

eau	water
eau du robinet	tap water
eau minérale	mineral water
eau potable	drinkable water
échelle	ladder
école	school
écouter	listen
écrire	write
éducation	education
église	church
elle	she; her
e-mail, adresse	e-mail address
emballer	wrap (v)
emplacement	campsite
emploi	occupation
empoisonement alimentaire	food poisoning
emporter	take out (food)
emprunter	borrow
en	in, by (via)
en bas	down
en haut	up; upstairs
en panne	broken
en plein air	outdoors
en sécurité	safe
enceinte	pregnant
encore	again; more
enfants	children
enflure	swelling (n)
ensemble	together

ensoleillé	sunny
entendre	hear
enterrement	funeral
entrée	entrance
entrée du Metro	subway entrance
enveloppe	envelope
envoyer	send
épais	thick
épaule	shoulder
épicerie	grocery store
épilepsie	epilepsy
épingle	pin (n)
épingle à nourrice	safety pin
épuisé	exhausted
équipe	team
équitation	horse riding
erreur	mistake (n)
érythème fessier	diaper rash
escalier	stairs
Espagne	Spain
espoir	hope
essence	fuel
essuie-glace	windshield wiper
est	is; east
estomac	stomach
estomac, mal à l'	stomachache
et	and
étage	story (floor)
état	state (n)
États-Unis	United States
été	summer
éternuer	sneeze (v)
étoile	star (in sky)
étranger	foreign
étroit	narrow
étudiant	student

exactement	exactly
excuse	apology
exemple	example
expliquer	explain

F

fâché	angry
facile	easy
faim	hungry
faire	make (v)
faire bronzer (se)	sunbathe
faire du ski	ski (v)
fait à la maison	homemade
falaise	cliff
fameux	famous
famille	family
fantastique	fantastic
fatigué	tired
fausse couche	miscarriage
fauteuil roulant, accessible à un	wheelchair-accessible
faux	false
félicitations	congratulations
femelle	female
femme	woman, wife
femme de sciences	female scientist
fenêtre	window
ferme	farm (n)
fermé	closed
fermer à clef	lock (v)
fermeture éclair	zipper
fermier	farmer
fesses	buttocks
feu	fire; stoplight
feux arrières	tail lights

feux d'artifices	fireworks
février	February
ficelle	string (n)
fièvre	fever
fil	thread (n)
fil dentaire	dental floss
fille	girl; daughter
film	movie
fils	son
fini	over (finished)
finir	finish (v)
flash	flash (camera)
fleur	flower
fois, une	once
fond	bottom
fond de teint	foundation (makeup)
fond de teint compact	face powder
fontaine	fountain
football	soccer
football américain	American football
fort	strong
fossé	moat
foule	crowd (n)
four	oven
fourchette	fork
fraîche	fresh
frais	cool
français	French
freins	brakes
frère	brother
frissons	chills
froid	cold (adj)
fromage	cheese
fromagerie	cheese shop

frontière	border (n)
fruit	fruit
fruits de mer	seafood
fumée	smoke (n)
fumeur	smoking
fumeur, non	non-smoking
fusibles	fuses
fusil	gun

G

gallerie	gallery
gallerie d'art	art gallery
gants	gloves
garçon	boy; waiter
garder	keep
gare routière	bus station
garer	park (v)
gauche	left
gaze	gauze
gênant	embarrassing
généreux	generous
genou	knee
gens	people
gens âgés	seniors
gilet	vest
glace	ice cream
glaçons	ice
glissant	slippery
gomme	eraser
gorge	throat
gorge, mal à la	sore throat
gothique	Gothic
goût	taste (n)
goûter	taste (v)
grain de beauté	moleskin
graisseux	greasy
grammaire	grammar

grand	big; tall
grand magasin	department store
grande route	highway
Grande-Bretagne	Great Britain
grand-mère	grandmother
grand-père	grandfather
grasse, matière	fat (n)
gratuit	free (no cost); toll-free
Grèce	Greece
grippe	flu
gris	gray
gros	fat (adj)
grossesse	pregnancy
grotte	cave
guarantie	guarantee (n)
guerre	war
guide	guide; guidebook
guide audio	audioguide
guitare	guitar
gymnastique	gymnastics
gynécologue	gynecologist

H

hachisch	hash
haleine	breath
handicapé	handicapped
haut	high
haut, en	up; upstairs
hémorroïdes	hemorrhoids
herbe, de l'	marijuana
heure	hour
heure, à l'	on time
heures d'ouverture	opening hours
heureux	happy
hier	yesterday

histoire	history
hiver	winter
homme	man
homme de sciences	male scientist
hommes	men
homosexuel	gay
honnête	honest
hôpital	hospital
horaire	timetable
horloge	clock
horrible	horrible
hors taxe	duty free
hors d'oeuvre	appetizer
hôtel	hotel
huile	oil
huile solaire	sunscreen
humide	muggy
hydroptère	hydrofoil
hypertension	high blood pressure

I

ici	here
il	he
île	island
immédiatement	immediately
imperméable	raincoat
importé	imported
impressionniste	Impressionist
imprimer	print
inclus	included
inconscient	unconscious
incroyable	incredible
indépendant	independent
indiquer	point (v)
industrie	industry

infection	urinary infection
urinarire	
infirmière	nurse
inflation	inflammation
ingénieur	engineer
insecte	insect
insolation	sunstroke
inspection des bagages	baggage check
interdit	prohibited
intéressant	interesting
intestins	intestines
invité	guest
Irlande	Ireland
Italie	Italy
ivre	drunk

J

jamais	never
jambe	leg
janvier	January
jardin	garden
jardinage	gardening
jaune	yellow
je	I
jeter	throw (v)
jeton	token
jeu	game
jeu de cartes	cards (deck)
jeudi	Thursday
jeune	young
jeunes	youths
jeunesse, auberge de	youth hostel
jeux, parc avec des	playground
joint	joint (marijuana)

jolie	pretty
jouer	play (v); athlete
jouet	toy
jour	day
jour férié	holiday
journal	newspaper
juif	Jewish
juillet	July
juin	June
jumeaux	twins
jupe	skirt
jupon	slip (n)
jus	juice
juste	fair (just)

L

l'herbe, de	marijuana
la pilule	birth control pill
lac	lake
lacets	shoelaces
laid	ugly
laine	wool
lait nettoyant	face cleanser
lait pour bébé	baby formula
laiton	pewter
lampe de poche	flashlight
langue	language
lapin	rabbit
lavabo	sink
laver	wash (v)
laverie	launderette
laxatif	laxative
le meilleur	best
le pire	worst
lent	slow
lentilles de contact	contact lenses

lessive	laundry detergent
lettre	letter
lèvre	lip
l'heure, à	on time
librairie	book shop
libre	vacant
libre service	self-service
lieu de, au	instead
ligne aérienne	airline
lin	linen
liquide	cash
liquide de transmission	transmission fluid
liste	list
lit	bed
lit de camp	cot
litre	liter
lits superposés	bunk beds
livre	book (n)
loin	far
lotion solaire	suntan lotion
louer	rent (v)
lourd	heavy
lumière	light (n)
lundi	Monday
lune	moon
lune de miel	honeymoon
lunettes	glasses (eye)
lunettes de soleil	sunglasses
lutte	fight (n)

M

ma	my
machine à laver	washer
machine à sécher	dryer
machoire	jaw
Madame	Mrs.
Mademoiselle	Miss
magasin	shop (n), store
magasin d'antiquités	antiques shop
magasin de jouets	toy store
magasin de photo	camera shop
magasin de photocopie	photocopy shop
magasin de portables	cell phone shop
magasin de vêtements	clothing boutique
magnétoscope	video recorder
mai	May
maigre	skinny
maillot de bain	swim trunks
main	hand
maintenant	now
mais	but
maison	house
maison de la presse	newsstand
maison, fait à la	homemade
mal à la gorge	sore throat
mal à l'estomac	stomachache
mal aux dents	toothache
mal aux oreilles	earache
mal de tête	headache
malade	sick
maladie	disease
maladie vénérienne	venereal disease
mâle	male
malentendu	misunderstanding
malheureusement	unfortunately

manches	sleeves	mesdames	ladies
manger	eat	messe	church service
maquillage	makeup	métal	metal
marbre	marble (material)	météo	weather forecast
marchand de vin	wine shop	Métro	subway
marché	market	meubles	furniture
marché aux fleurs	flower market	midi	noon
		migraine	migraine
marché aux puces	flea market	militaire	military
marché en plein air	open-air market	mince	thin
		minuit	midnight
marché, bon	cheap	miroir	mirror
marcher	walk (v)	mode	fashion, style
mardi	Tuesday	moderne	modern
mari	husband	mois	month
mariage	wedding	mon	my
marié	married	monastère	monastery
mars	March	monde	world
matière grasse	fat (n)	monsieur	gentleman; sir
matin	morning	Monsieur	Mr.
mauvais	bad	montagne	mountain
maux de poitrine	chest pains	montre	watch (n)
maximum	maximum	montrer	show (v)
mécanicien	mechanic	moquette	carpet
médicament pour la diarrhée	diarrhea medicine	morceau	piece
		mort	dead
médicaments	medicine	mosquée	mosque
médiéval	medieval	mot	word
meilleur	better	motocyclette	motorcycle
meilleur, le	best	mouchoirs en papier	facial tissue
mélange	mix (n)		
même	same	mouillé	wet
mensonges	lies	mourir	die
mer	sea	moustache	moustache
merci	thanks	moustique	mosquito
mercredi	Wednesday	moyen	medium
mère	mother	mûr	ripe

musée	museum
musique	music
musulman	Muslim (n, adj)
mycose	athlete's foot

N

nager	swim
nationalité	nationality
nature	nature
naturel	natural
nausée	nausea
navire	ship (n)
nécessaire	necessary
néoclassique	neoclassical
nerveux	nervous
neveu	nephew
nez	nose
nièce	niece
Noël	Christmas
noir	black
nom	name
non	no
non fumeur	non-smoking
nord	north
normale	normal
nostalgique	homesick
nourriture	food
nourriture pour bébé	baby food
nous	we; us
nouveau	new
novembre	November
nu	naked
nuageux	cloudy
nuit	night
nylon	nylon (material)

O

occupé	occupied
océan	ocean
octobre	October
odeur	smell (n)
oeil	eye
oiseau	bird
Olympiques	Olympics
ombre à paupières	eye shadow
oncle	uncle
ongle	fingernail
opéra	opera
opticien	optician
or	gold
ordinateur	computer
ordonnance	prescription
oreille	ear
oreiller	pillow
oreilles, mal aux	earache
orgue	organ
orteil	toe
ou	or
où	where
oublier	forget
ouest	west
oui	yes
ouvert	open (adj)
ouvre-boîte	can opener
ouvrir	open (v)

P

pain	bread
paix	peace
palais	palace
panne, en	broken

panneau	sign
pannier	basket
pansement élastique	support bandage
pantalon	pants
papa	dad
papeterie	office supplies store
papier	paper
papier hygiénique	toilet paper
Pâques	Easter
par avion	air mail
paradis	heaven
parapluie	umbrella
parc	park (garden); playpen
parc avec des jeux	playground
parce que	because
pardon	excuse me
paresseux	lazy
parfait	perfect
parfum	flavor (n); perfume
parking	parking lot
parler	talk
partir	leave
pas	not
passager	passenger
passé	past
passeport	passport
passer	go through
pastille	cough drop
paté de maisons	block (street)
patinage	skating
patins à roulettes	roller skates
patisserie	pastry shop
pauvre	poor
payer	pay
pays	country

Pays-Bas	Netherlands
péage	toll
peau	skin
pêcher	fish (v)
pédalo	paddleboat
peigne	comb (n)
peignoir de bain	bathrobe
pénis	penis
penser	think
perdu	lost
père	father
Père Noël	Santa Claus
période	period (time)
personne	person
pétillant	fizzy
petit	small
petit déjeuner	breakfast
petite-fille	granddaughter
petit-fils	grandson
peu	few
peur	afraid
peut-être	maybe
phares	headlights
pharmacie	pharmacy
photocopie	photocopy (n)
pièces	coins
pied	foot
piéton	pedestrian
pilule	pill
pilule, la	birth control pill
pince à épiler	tweezers
pince à linge	clothes pins
pince à ongles	nail clipper
pinces	pliers
piquant	spicy
pique-nique	picnic (n)
piquets de tente	tent pegs

pire	worse	**porter**	carry
pire, le	worst	**posséder**	own (v)
piscine	swimming pool	**potable, eau**	drinkable water
place	square (town); seat	**poul**	pulse
plage	beach	**poulet**	chicken
plaindre (se)	complain	**poumons**	lungs
plaisant	nice	**poupée**	doll
plaît, s'il vous	please	**pour**	for
plan du Métro	subway map	**pourcentage**	percent
planche à voile	windsurfing	**pourquoi**	why
planche de surf	surfboard	**pourri**	rotten
plante	plant	**poussée**	teething (baby)
plastique	plastic	**des dents**	
plein air, en	outdoors	**pousser**	push
pleurer	cry (v)	**poussette**	stroller
pluie	rain (n)	**pouvoir**	can (v); power
plus tard	later	**pratique**	practical
pneu	tire	**premier**	first
pneumonie	pneumonia	**première classe**	first class
poche	pocket	**premiers secours**	first aid
poids	weight	**prendre**	take
poignée	handle (n)	**prendre une**	transfer (v)
poignet	wrist	**correspondance**	(train)
point	dot (computer)	**Préparation H**	Preparation H
poisson	fish (n)	**près**	near
poitrine	chest	**préservatif**	condom
poitrine, maux de	chest pains	**presque**	approximately
politiciens	politicians	**prêt**	ready
pomme	apple	**prêter**	lend
pompe	pump (n)	**prêtre**	priest
pont	bridge	**principal**	main
porc	pork	**printemps**	spring
porcelaine	porcelain	**privé**	private
port	harbor	**prix**	price
portable	cell phone	**problème**	problem
porte	door	**problème**	heart condition
portefeuille	wallet	**cardiaque**	

problèmes de sinus	sinus problems	réceptioniste	receptionist
prochain	next	recette	recipe
produits artisanaux	handicrafts	recevoir	receive
professeur	teacher	reçu	receipt
propre	clean (adj)	réduction	discount (n)
propriétaire	owner	réfugiés	refugees
prospérer	prosper	regarder	look, watch (v)
prudent	careful	régional	local
publique	public	règles	period (woman's)
puce	flea	réhausseur	booster seat
puissant	powerful	reine	queen
pullover	sweater	relaxation	relaxation
pyjama	pajamas	relique	relic
		remboursement	refund (n)
		remède contre le rhume	cold medicine

Q

quai	platform (train)	remparts	foritfed wall
qualité	quality	remplir	refill (v)
quand	when	renaissance	Renaissance
quart	quarter (1/4)	rendez-vous	appointment
que	what	réparer	repair (v)
quel dommage	it's a pity	répéter	repeat (v)
quelque chose	something	réponse	answer (n)
quelques	some	reposer (se)	relax (v)
queue	tail	reproduction	copy (n)
qui	who	Republique Tchéque	Czech Republic
quiès, boules	earplugs	réservation	reservation
quincaillerie	hardware store	reserver	reserve
		retardement	delay (n)

R

		retraite, à la	retired
racisme	racism	rêve	dream (n)
radeau	raft	réveille-matin	alarm clock
radiateur	radiator	réveiller (se)	wake up
radio	radio; X-ray	rêver	dream (v)
rasage, après	aftershave	revoir, au	goodbye
rasoir	razor	rhume	cold (n)

French	English
rhume des foins	hay fever
riche	rich
rien	nothing
rire	laugh (v)
rivière	river
robe	dress (n)
robinet	faucet
robinet, eau du	tap water
robuste	sturdy
rocade	ring road
rocher	rock (n)
roi	king
romanesque	Romanesque
romantique	romantic; Romantic
rondpoint	roundabout
ronfler	snore (v)
rose	pink
roue	wheel
rouge	red
rouge à joues	blush (makeup)
rouge à lèvres	lipstick
routière, gare	bus station
rue	street
ruines	ruins
ruisseau	stream (n)
Russie	Russia

S

French	English
sac	bag, purse
sac à dos	backpack
sac de couchage	sleeping bag
sac en plastique	plastic bag
sac en plastique à fermeture	Ziplock bag
saignement	bleeding
sale	dirty

French	English
salle	hall (big room)
salle d'attente	waiting room
salle de bains	bathroom
salut	hi
samedi	Saturday
sandales	sandals
sang	blood
sans	without
santé	health
Santé!	Cheers!
santé, bonne	healthy
sauf	except
sauter	jump (v)
sauvage	wild
sauver	save (computer)
savoir	know
savon	soap
scandaleux	scandalous
Scandinavie	Scandinavia
scotch	tape (adhesive)
scotch, du	scotch tape
sculpteur	sculptor
sculpture	sculpture
se dépêcher	hurry (v)
se faire bronzer	sunbathe
se plaindre	complain
se reposer	relax (v)
se réveiller	wake up
se souvenir	remember
seau	bucket
sec	dry (adj)
sécher	dry (v)
secours	help (n)
sécurité, en	safe
seins	breast
semaine	week
semblable	similar

French	English
sens unique	one way (street)
séparé	separate (adj)
septembre	September
sérieux	serious
serré	tight
serrure	lock (n)
serveuse	waitress
serviable	helpful
service de babysitting	babysitting service
serviette	napkin
serviette de bain	towel
serviettes hygiéniques	sanitary napkins
seule	alone
seulement	only
sexe	sex
sexy	sexy
shampooing	shampoo
short	shorts
si	if
SIDA	AIDS
siècle	century
siège voiture	car seat (baby)
signe arobase	"at" sign (@)
s'il vous plaît	please
simple, aller	one way (ticket)
site web	Web site
ski	skiing
ski nautique	waterskiing
slip	underpants; panties; briefs
sobriquet	nickname
soeur	sister
soie	silk
soif	thirsty
soir	evening
soir, ce	tonight
soirée	party (n)
solaire, huile	sunscreen
solaire, lotion	suntan lotion
solde	sale
soleil	sun; sunshine
soleil, coucher de	sunset
soleil, coup de	sunburn
soleil, lunettes de	sunglasses
sombre	dark
sommeil, avoir	sleepy
sortie	exit (n)
sortie de secours	emergency exit
soudain	suddenly
souffrir	suffer
souhaiter	wish (v)
souligne	underscore (_)
sourire	smile (v)
sous	under; below
sous vêtements	underwear
sous-sol	basement
soutien-gorge	bra
souvenir (se)	remember
spécialement	especially
spécialité	specialty
spectacle	show (n)
standardiste	operator
station de Métro	subway station
station de service	gas station
stoned	stoned
stupide	stupid
stylo	pen
sud	south
suggérer	recommend

Suisse	Switzerland	**théâtre**	theater; play (n)
super	great	**thermomètre**	thermometer
supermarché	supermarket	**tiède**	lukewarm
supplément	supplement	**timbre**	stamp
sur	on	**timide**	shy
surfeur	surfer	**tire-bouchon**	corkscrew
synthétique	synthetic	**tirer**	pull
		tiret	hyphen (-)
T		**tissu**	cloth
tableau	painting	**toilette**	toilet
taille	size; waist	**toit**	roof
talc	talcum powder	**tomber**	fall (v)
tante	aunt	**tongues**	flip-flops
tapis	rug	**tôt**	early
tard	late	**total**	total
tard, plus	later	**toucher**	touch (v)
tasse	cup	**toujours**	always
taxe	tax	**tour**	tour; tower
taxe, hors	duty free	**touriste**	tourist
teinture d'iode	iodine	**tournevis**	screwdriver
télécharge	download (n)	**tousser**	cough (v)
téléphone	telephone	**tout**	everything
télévision	television	**toux**	cough (n)
température	temperature	**traditionnel**	traditional
tempête	storm	**traduire**	translate
temps	weather	**train**	train
tendre	tender (adj.)	**tranche**	slice (n)
tennis	tennis	**transpirer**	sweat (v)
tente	tent	**travail**	work (n)
terre	earth	**travailler**	work (v)
terroristes	terrorists	**travaux**	construction (sign)
test de grossesse	pregnancy test	**travers, à**	through
		trépied	tripod
testicules	testicles	**très**	very
tête	head	**trésorerie**	treasury
tête, mal de	headache	**triste**	sad
tétine	pacifier	**trombone**	paper clip

trop	too (much)	vertige	dizziness
trou	hole	vessie	bladder
tu	you (informal)	veste	jacket
tuba	snorkel	vêtements	clothes
tuer	kill (v)	veuf	widower
Turquie	Turkey	veuve	widow
		viande	meat
U		vide	empty
une fois	once	vidéo	video
univerisité	university	vie	life
urèthre	urethra	vieux	old
urgence	emergency	vignoble	vineyard
urgences, aux	emergency room	village	town
		ville	city
urgent	urgent	vin	wine
usine	factory	viol	rape (n)
utérus	uterus	violet	purple
utiliser	use (v)	visage	face
		visite	visit (n)
V		visite guidée	guided tour
vacances	vacation	visiter	visit (v)
vache	cow	vitamines	vitamins
vagin	vagina	vitesse	speed
valise	suitcase	voie	track (train)
vallée	valley	voile	sailing
végétarien	vegetarian (n)	voilier	sailboat
vélo	bicycle	voir	see
vélomoteur	motor scooter	voiture	car; train car
velours	velvet	voiture restaurant	dining car (train)
vendre	sell		
vendredi	Friday	voix	voice
venir	come	vol	flight
vent	wind (n)	volé	robbed
venteux	windy	voler	fly (v)
vernis à ongles	nail polish	voleur	thief
verre	glass	vomir	vomit (v)
vert	green	vouloir	want (v)

vous	you (formal)
voyage	trip
voyage, agence de	travel agency
voyage, chèque de	travelers check
voyager	travel
voyageurs	travelers
vue	view (n)

W

wagon-lit	sleeper car (train)

Z

zéro	zero
zoo	zoo

5

English/French

A

abortion	avortement	**alone**	seule
above	au dessus	**already**	déjà
abstract	abstrait	**altar**	autel
abuse (v)	abuser	**always**	toujours
accident	accident	**ambulance**	ambulance
accountant	comptable	**ancestor**	ancêtre
adapter, electrical	adaptateur électrique	**ancient**	ancien
address	adresse	**and**	et
address, e-mail	adresse e-mail	**angry**	fâché
adult	adulte	**animal**	animal
afraid	peur	**ankle**	cheville
Africa	Afrique	**another**	encore
after	après	**answer**	réponse
afternoon	après-midi	**antacid**	anti-acide
aftershave	après rasage	**antibiotic**	antibiotique
afterwards	après	**antiques**	antiquités
again	encore	**antiques shop**	magasin d'antiquités
age	âge	**apartment**	appartement
aggressive	aggressif	**apology**	excuses
agnostic	agnostique	**appetizer**	hors d'oeuvre
agree	d'accord	**apple**	pomme
AIDS	SIDA	**appointment**	rendez-vous
air	l'air	**approximately**	presque
air mail	par avion	**April**	avril
air-conditioned	climatisé	**arm**	bras
airline	ligne aérienne	**arrivals**	arrivées
airport	aéroport	**arrive**	arriver
aisle	couloir	**art**	l'art
alarm clock	réveille-matin	**art gallery**	gallerie d'art
alcohol	alcool	**Art Nouveau**	art nouveau
allergic	allergique	**arthritis**	arthrite
allergies	allergies	**artificial**	artificial

artist	artiste
ashtray	cendrier
ask	demander
aspirin	aspirine
asthma	asthme
at	à
"at" sign (@)	signe arobase
atheist	athée
athlete	jouer
athlete's foot	mycose
attractive	attirant
audioguide	guide audio
August	août
aunt	tante
Austria	Autriche
autumn	automne

B

baby	bébé
baby booster seat	réhausseur
baby car seat	siège voiture
baby food	nourriture pour bébé
baby formula	lait pour bébé
babysitter	babysitter
babysitting service	service de babysitting
back	dos
backpack	sac à dos
bad	mauvais
bag	sac
bag, plastic	sac en plastique
bag, Ziplock	sac en plastique à fermeture
baggage	bagages
baggage check	inspection des bagages
baggage claim	caroussel des bagages

bakery	boulangerie
balcony	balcon
ball	balle
banana	banane
bandage	bandage
bandage, support	pansement élastique
Band-Aid	bandage adhésif
bank	banque
barber	coiffeur
barber shop	coiffeur
baseball	baseball
basement	sous-sol
basket	pannier
basketball	basket
bath	bain
bathrobe	peignoir de bain
bathroom	salle de bain
bathtub	baignoire
battery	batterie
beach	plage
beard	barbe
beautiful	belle
beauty salon	coiffeur pour dames
because	parce que
bed	lit
bedbugs	insectes
bedroom	chambre
bedsheet	draps
beef	boeuf
beer	bière
before	avant
begin	commencer
behind	derrière
Belgium	Belgique
bells	cloches
below	sous

belt	ceinture	boutique, clothing	boutique; magasin de vêtements
berth (train)	couchette	bowl	bol
best	le meilleur	box	boîte
better	meilleur	boy	garçon
bib	bavoir	bra	soutien-gorge
bicycle	vélo	bracelet	bracelet
big	grand	brakes	freins
bill (payment)	addition	brass	cuivre jaune
bird	oiseau	bread	pain
birth control pill	la pilule	breakfast	petit déjeuner
birthday	anniversaire	breast	seins
black	noir	breath	haleine
bladder	vessie	bridge	pont
blanket	couverture	briefs	slip
bleeding	saignement	broken	en panne
blisters	ampoules	bronze	bronze
block (street)	paté de maisons	brooch	broche
blond	blonde	brother	frère
blood	sang	brown	brun
blood pressure, high	hypertension	bucket	seau
blue	bleu	building	bâtiment
blush (makeup)	blush; rouge à joues	bulb	ampoule
boat	bateau	bulb, light	ampoule
body	corps	bunk beds	lits superposés
boiled	bouilli	burn (n)	brûlure
bomb	bombe	bus	bus
book (n)	livre	bus station	gare routière
book shop	librairie	bus stop	arrêt de bus
booster seat	réhausseur	bus, city	bus
boots	bottes	bus, long-distance	car
border	frontière	business	affaires
borrow	emprunter	business card	carte de visite
boss	chef	but	mais
bottle	bouteille	buttocks	fesses
bottom	fond	button	bouton
		buy	acheter
		by (via)	en

C

calendar	calendrier
calorie	calorie
camera	appareil-photo
camera shop	magasin de photo
camping	camping
campsite	emplacement
can (n)	boîte de conserve
can (v)	pouvoir
can opener	ouvre-boîte
Canada	Canada
canal	canal
cancel	annuler
candle	chandelle
candy	bonbon
canoe	canoë
cap	casquette
captain	capitaine
car	voiture
car (train)	voiture
car, dining (train)	voiture restaurant
car seat (baby)	siège voiture
car, sleeper (train)	wagon-lit
carafe	carafe
card	carte
card, telephone	carte téléphonique
cards (deck)	jeu de cartes
careful	prudent
carpet	moquette
carry	porter
carry-on luggage	bagage en cabine
cash	liquide
cash machine	distributeur automatique

cashier	caisse
cassette	cassette
castle	château
cat	chat
catch (v)	attraper
cathedral	cathédrale
Catholic (adj)	catholique
cave	grotte
cell phone	portable
cell phone shop	magasin de portables
cellar	cave
center	centre
century	siècle
ceramic	céramique
chair	chaise
championship	championnat
change (n)	change
change (v)	changer
chapel	chapelle
charming	charmant
cheap	bon marché
check	chèque
Cheers!	Santé!
cheese	fromage
cheese shop	fromagerie
chest	poitrine
chest pains	maux de poitrine
chicken	poulet
children	enfants
chills	frissons
Chinese (adj)	chinois
chocolate	chocolat
choir	choeur
Christian (adj)	chrétien
Christmas	Noël
church	église
church service	messe

cigarette	cigarette	computer	ordinateur
cinema	cinéma	concert	concert
city	ville	conditioner (hair)	après-shampoing
class	classe		
classical	classique	condom	préservatif
clean (adj)	propre	conductor	conducteur
clear	clair	confirm	confirmer
cliff	falaise	congestion (sinus)	congestion
clinic, medical	clinique médicale	congratulations	félicitations
		connection (train)	correspondance
clock	horloge		
clock, alarm	réveille-matin	constipation	constipation
cloister	cloître	construction (sign)	travaux
closed	fermé	contact lenses	lentilles de contact
cloth	tissu		
clothes	vêtements	contagious	contagieux
clothes pins	pince à linge	contraceptive	contraceptif
clothesline	corde à linge	cook (v)	cuisinier
clothing boutique	boutique, magasin de vêtements	cool	frais
		copper	cuivre
cloudy	nuageux	copy (n)	reproduction
coast	côte	copy shop	magasin de photocopie
coat hanger	cintre		
cockroach	cafards	cork	bouchon
coffee	café	corkscrew	tire-bouchon
coffee shop	café	corner	coin
coins	pièces	corridor	couloir
cold (adj)	froid	corruption	corruption
cold (n)	rhume	cost (v)	coûter
cold medicine	remède contre le rhume	cot	lit de camp
		cotton	coton
colors	couleurs	cough (n)	toux
comb (n)	peigne	cough (v)	tousser
come	venir	cough drop	pastille
comfortable	confortable	country	pays
compact disc	disque compact	countryside	compagne
complain	se plaindre	cousin	cousin
complicated	compliqué	cow	vache

cozy	confortable	democracy	démocratie
crafts	arts	dental floss	fil dentaire
cramps	crampes	dentist	dentiste
cramps, menstrual	crampes de menstruation	deodorant	désodorisant
cream	crème	depart	partir
cream, first-aid	crème antiseptique	department store	grand magasin
credit card	carte de crédit	departures	départs
cross	croix	deposit	caution
crowd (n)	foule	dessert	dessert
cry (v)	pleurer	detergent	lessive
crypt	crypte	detour (n)	déviation
cup	tasse	diabetes	diabète
customs	douane	diabetic	diabétique
Czech Republic	République Tchéque	diamond	diamant
		diaper	couche
		diaper rash	érythème fessier

D

		diaphragm (birth control)	diaphragme
dad	papa	diarrhea	diarrhée
dance (v)	danser	diarrhea medicine	médicament pour la diarrhée
danger	danger	dictionary	dictionnaire
dangerous	dangereux	die	mourir
dark	sombre	difficult	difficile
dash (-)	tiret	dine (v)	dîner
daughter	fille	dining car (train)	voiture restaurant
day	jour	dinner (n)	dîner
day after tomorrow	après demain	direct (adj)	direct
dead	mort	direction	direction
December	décembre	dirty	sale
declare (customs)	déclarer	discount (n)	réduction
decongestant	décongestant	disease	maladie
delay (n)	retardement	disease, venereal	maladie vénérienne
delete	annuler	disinfectant	désinfectant
delicatessen	charcuterie-traiteur	disturb	déranger
delicious	délicieux		

divorced	divorcé	**Easter**	Pâques
dizziness	vertige	**easy**	facile
doctor	docteur	**eat**	manger
dog	chien	**education**	éducation
doll	poupée	**elbow**	coude
dome	dôme	**electrical adapter**	adaptateur électrique
donkey	âne		
door	porte	**elevator**	ascenseur
dormitory	dortoire	**e-mail**	e-mail
dot (computer)	point	**e-mail address**	adresse d'e-mail
double	double	**embarrassing**	gênant
down	en bas	**embassy**	ambassade
download (n)	télécharge	**emergency**	urgence
downtown	centre-ville	**emergency exit**	sortie de secours
dozen	douzaine		
dream (n)	rêve	**emergency room**	aux urgences
dream (v)	rêver		
dress (n)	robe	**empty**	vide
drink (n)	boisson	**engineer**	ingénieur
drink (v)	boire	**English**	anglais
drive (v)	conduire	**enjoy**	apprécier
driver	chauffeur	**enough**	assez
drunk	ivre	**entrance**	entrée
dry (adj)	sec	**entry**	entrée
dry (v)	sécher	**envelope**	enveloppe
dryer	machine à sécher	**epilepsy**	épilepsie
dungeon	cachot	**eraser**	gomme
duty free	hors taxe	**especially**	spécialement
		Europe	Europe
E		**evening**	soir
		every	chaque
each	chaque	**everything**	tout
ear	oreille	**exactly**	exactement
earache	mal aux oreilles	**example**	exemple
early	tôt	**excellent**	excellent
earplugs	boules quiès	**except**	sauf
earrings	boucle d'oreille	**exchange (n)**	change
earth	terre	**excuse me**	pardon
east	est		

exhausted	épuisé	female	femelle
exit (n)	sortie	ferry	bac
exit, emergency	sortie de secours	fever	fièvre
expensive	cher	few	peu
explain	expliquer	field	champ
eye	oeil	fight (n)	lutte
eye shadow	ombre à paupières	fight (v)	combattre
eyeliner	eyeliner; crayon pour les yeux	fine (good)	bon
		finger	doigt
		fingernail	ongle
		finish (v)	finir

F

		fire	feu
face	visage	fireworks	feux d'artifices
face cleanser	lait nettoyant	first	premier
face powder	fond de teint compact	first aid	premiers secours
		first class	première classe
facial tissue	kleenex; mouchoirs en papier	first-aid cream	crème antiseptique
factory	usine	fish (n)	poisson
fair (just)	juste	fish (v)	pêcher
fall (v)	tomber	fix (v)	réparer
false	faux	fizzy	pétillant
family	famille	flag	drapeau
famous	fameux	flash (camera)	flash
fan belt	courroie du ventilateur	flashlight	lampe de poche
fantastic	fantastique	flavor (n)	parfum
far	loin	flea	puce
farm (n)	ferme	flea market	marché aux puces
farmer	fermier	flight	vol
fashion	mode	flip-flops	tongues
fat (adj)	gros	floss, dental	fil dentaire
fat (n)	matière grasse	flower	fleur
father	père	flower market	marché aux fleurs
father-in-law	beau-père		
faucet	robinet	flu	grippe
fax (n)	fax	fly (v)	voler
fear (v)	craindre	fog	brouillard
February	février	food	nourriture

food poisoning	empoisonement alimentaire	**gardening**	jardinage
foot	pied	**gas station**	station de service
football, American	football américain	**gauze**	gaze
for	pour	**gay**	homosexuel
forbidden	interdit	**generous**	généreux
foreign	étranger	**gentleman**	monsieur
forget	oublier	**genuine**	authentique
fork	fourchette	**Germany**	Allemagne
formula (for baby)	lait pour bébé	**gift**	cadeau
foundation (makeup)	fond de teint	**girl**	fille
		give	donner
		glass (drinking)	verre
fountain	fontaine	**glasses (eye)**	lunettes
fragile	fragile	**gloves**	gants
free (no cost)	gratuit	**go**	aller
French	français	**go through**	passer
fresh	fraîche	**God**	Dieu
Friday	vendredi	**gold**	or
friend	ami	**golf**	golf
friendship	amitié	**good**	bien
Frisbee	frisbee	**good day**	bonjour
from	de	**goodbye**	au revoir
fruit	fruit	**Gothic**	gothique
fuel	essence	**grammar**	grammaire
fun	amusement	**granddaughter**	petite-fille
funeral	enterrement	**grandfather**	grand-père
funny	drôle	**grandmother**	grand-mère
furniture	meubles	**grandson**	petit-fils
fuses	fusibles	**gray**	gris
future	avenir	**greasy**	graisseux
		great	super
		Great Britain	Grande-Bretagne
		Greece	Grèce
		green	vert
gallery	gallerie	**grocery store (n)**	épicerie
game	jeu	**guarantee**	guarantie
garage	garage	**guest**	invité
garden	jardin	**guide (n)**	guide

G

guidebook	guide	healthy	bonne santé
guided tour	visite guidée	hear	entendre
guilty	coupable	heart	coeur
guitar	guitare	heart condition	problème cardiaque
gum	chewing-gum	heat (n)	chauffage
gun	fusil	heat (v)	chauffer
gymnastics	gymnastique	heaven	paradis
gynecologist	gynécologue	heavy	lourd
		hello	bonjour
H		help (n)	secours
hair	cheveux	help (v)	aider
hairbrush	brosse	helpful	serviable
haircut	coupe de cheveux	hemorrhoids	hémorroïdes
hall (big room)	salle	her	elle
hand	main	here	ici
hand lotion	crème pour les mains	hi	salut
handicapped	handicapé	high	haut
handicrafts	produits artisanaux	high blood pressure	hypertension
handle (n)	poignée	high chair	chaise haute
handsome	beau	highway	grande route
happiness	bonheur	hill	colline
happy	heureux	history	histoire
harbor	port	hitchhike	autostop
hard	dur	hobby	hobby
hardware store	quincaillerie	hockey	hockey
hash	hachisch	hole	trou
hat	chapeau	holiday	jour férié
hate (v)	détester	homemade	fait à la maison
have	avoir	homesick	nostalgique
hay fever	rhume des foins	honest	honnête
he	il	honeymoon	lune de miel
head	tête	hope (n)	espoir
headache	mal de tête	horrible	horrible
headlights	phares	horse	cheval
health	santé	horse riding	équitation
health insurance	assurance maladie	hospital	hôpital

hot	chaud	**insect**	bombe contre les
hotel	hôtel	**repellant**	insectes
hour	heure	**inside**	dedans
house	maison	**instant**	instant
how	comment	**instead**	au lieu de
how many	combien	**insurance**	assurance
how much ($)	combien	**insurance,**	assurance maladie
hungry	faim	**health**	
hurry (v)	se dépêcher	**insured**	assuré
husband	mari	**intelligent**	intelligent
hydrofoil	hydroptère	**interesting**	intéressant
hyphen (-)	tiret	**Internet**	internet
		Internet access	accès internet
I		**Internet café**	café internet
I	je	**intersection**	carrefour
ice	glaçons	**intestines**	intestins
ice cream	glace	**invitation**	invitation
if	si	**iodine**	teinture d'iode
ill	malade	**Ireland**	Irlande
immediately	immédiatement	**is**	est
important	important	**island**	île
imported	importé	**Italy**	Italie
impossible	impossible	**itch (n)**	démangeaison
Impressionist	impressionniste	**it's a pity**	quel dommage
in	en; dans		
included	inclus	**J**	
incredible	incroyable	**jacket**	veste
independent	indépendant	**January**	janvier
indigestion	indigestion	**jaw**	machoire
industry	industrie	**jeans**	jeans
infection	infection	**jewelry**	bijoux
infection,	infection urinarire	**jewelry shop**	bijouterie
urinary		**Jewish**	juif
inflammation	inflation	**job**	boulot
information	information	**jogging**	jogging
injured	blessé	**joint (marijuana)**	joint
innocent	innocent	**joke (n)**	blague
insect	insecte	**journey**	voyage

juice	jus	leather	cuir
July	juillet	leave	partir
jump (v)	sauter	left	gauche
June	juin	leg	jambe
		lend	prêter
K		lenses, contact	lentilles de contact
keep	garder		
kettle	bouilloire	letter	lettre
key	clef	library	bibliothèque
kill (v)	tuer	lies	mensonges
kind	aimable	life	vie
king	roi	light (n)	lumière
kiss (n, v)	baiser	light bulb	ampoule
kitchen	cuisine	lighter (n)	briquet
kitchenette	kitchenette	like	aimer bien
knee	genou	linen	lin
knife	couteau	lip	lèvre
knights	chevaliers	lip salve	beaume pour les lèvres
know	savoir		
		lipstick	rouge à lèvres
L		list (n)	liste
lace	dentelle	listen	écouter
ladder	échelle	liter	litre
ladies	mesdames	little (adj)	petit
lake	lac	local	régional
lamb	agneau	lock (n)	serrure
language	langue	lock (v)	fermer à clef
large	grand	locker	consigne
last	dernier	look (v)	regarder
late	tard	lost	perdu
later	plus tard	lotion, hand	crème pour les mains
laugh (v)	rire		
launderette	laverie	loud	bruyant
laundry soap	lessive	love (n)	amour
lawyer	avocat	love (v)	aimer
laxative	laxatif	lover	amant
lazy	paresseux	low	bas
learn	apprendre	lozenges	pastilles

luck	chance	meat	viande
luggage	bagage	mechanic	mécanicien
luggage, carry-on	baggage en cabine	medicine	médicaments
lukewarm	tiède	medicine for a cold	remède contre le rhume
lungs	poumons	medicine, non-aspirin substitute	Tylenol

M

macho	macho	medieval	médiéval
mad	fâché	medium	moyen
magazine	magazine	men	hommes
mail (n)	courrier	menstrual cramps	crampes de menstruation
main	principal	menstruation	menstruation
make (v)	faire	menu	carte
makeup	maquillage	message	message
male	mâle	metal	métal
mall (shopping)	centre commercial	meter, taxi	compteur
man	homme	midnight	minuit
manager	directeur	migraine	migraine
many	beaucoup	mild	doux
map	carte	military	militaire
marble (material)	marbre	mineral water	eau minérale
March	mars	minimum	minimum
marijuana	de l'herbe; marijuana	minutes	minutes
market (n)	marché	mirror	miroir
market, flea	marché aux puces	miscarriage	fausse couche
market, flower	marché aux fleurs	Miss	Mademoiselle
market, open-air	marché en plein air	mistake	erreur
		misunderstanding	malentendu
married	marié	mix (n)	mélange
mascara	mascara	moat	fossé
matches	allumettes	modem	modem
maximum	maximum	modern	moderne
May	mai	moisturizer	crème hydratante
maybe	peut-être	moleskin	grain de beauté
		moment	moment
		monastery	monastère
		Monday	lundi

money	argent	nature	nature
month	mois	nausea	nausée
monument	monument	near	près
moon	lune	necessary	nécessaire
more	encore	neck	cou
morning	matin	necklace	collier
mosque	mosquée	need (v)	avoir besoin de
mosquito	moustique	needle	aiguille
mother	mère	neoclassical	néoclassique
mother-in-law	belle-mère	nephew	neveu
motor scooter	vélomoteur	nervous	nerveux
motorcycle	motocyclette	Netherlands	Pays-Bas
mountain	montagne	never	jamais
moustache	moustache	new	nouveau
mouth	bouche	newspaper	journal
movie	film	newsstand	maison de
Mr.	Monsieur		la presse
Mrs.	Madame	next	prochain
much	beaucoup	nice	plaisant
muggy	humide	nickname	sobriquet
muscle	muscle	niece	nièce
museum	musée	night	nuit
music	musique	nightgown	chemise de nuit
Muslim (n, adj)	musulman	no	non
my	mon; ma	no vacancy	complet
		noisy	bruillant
		non-aspirin	Tylenol

N

nail (finger)	ongle	substitute	
nail clipper	pince à ongles	non-smoking	non fumeur
nail polish	vernis à ongles	noon	midi
nail polish	dissolvant	normal	normale
remover		north	nord
naked	nu	nose	nez
name	nom	not	pas
napkin	serviette	notebook	calepin
narrow	étroit	nothing	rien
nationality	nationalité	November	novembre
natural	naturel		

now	maintenant
nurse	infirmière
nylon (material)	nylon
nylons (pantyhose)	collants

O

occupation	emploi
occupied	occupé
ocean	océan
October	octobre
of	de
office	bureau
office supplies store	papeterie
oil	huile
O.K.	d'accord
old	vieux
Olympics	Olympiques
on	sur
on time	à l'heure
once	une fois
one way (street)	sens unique
one way (ticket)	aller simple
only	seulement
open (adj)	ouvert
open (v)	ouvrir
open-air market	marché en plein air
opening hours	heures d'ouverture
opera	opéra
operator	standardiste
optician	opticien
or	ou
orange	orange
organ	orgue
original	original
other	autre
outdoors	en plein air

oven	four
over (finished)	fini
own (v)	posséder
owner	propriétaire

P

pacifier	tétine
package	colis
paddleboat	pédalo
page	page
pail	seau
pain	douleur
pain killer	calmant
pains, chest	maux de poitrine
painting	tableau
pajamas	pyjama
palace	palais
panties	slip
pants	pantalon
paper	papier
paper clip	trombone
parents	parents
park (garden)	parc
park (v)	garer
parking lot	parking
party	soirée
passenger	passager
passport	passeport
past	passé
pastry shop	patisserie
pay	payer
peace	paix
pedestrian	piéton
pen	stylo
pencil	crayon
penis	pénis
people	gens
percent	pourcentage

perfect	parfait	**pliers**	pinces
perfume	parfum	**pneumonia**	pneumonie
period (time)	période	**pocket**	poche
period (woman's)	règles	**point (v)**	indiquer
person	personne	**police**	police
pewter	laiton	**politicians**	politiciens
pharmacy	pharmacie	**pollution**	pollution
phone	cabine téléphonique	**polyester**	polyester
booth		**poor**	pauvre
phone, cellular	portable	**porcelain**	porcelaine
photo	photo	**pork**	porc
photocopy (n)	photocopie	**Portugal**	Portugal
photocopy	magasin de	**possible**	possible
shop	photocopie	**postcard**	carte postale
pickpocket	pickpocket	**poster**	affiche
picnic	pique-nique	**power**	pouvoir
piece	morceau	**powerful**	puissant
pig	cochon	**practical**	pratique
pill (n)	pilule	**pregnancy**	grossesse
pill, birth control	la pilule	**pregnancy**	test de grossesse
pillow	oreiller	**test**	
pin	épingle	**pregnant**	enceinte
PIN code	code	**Preparation H**	Préparation H
pink	rose	**prescription**	ordonnance
pity, it's a	quel dommage	**present (gift)**	cadeau
pizza	pizza	**pretty**	jolie
plain	simple	**price**	prix
plane	avion	**priest**	prêtre
plant (n)	plante	**print (v)**	imprimer
plastic	plastique	**private**	privé
plastic bag	sac en plastique	**problem**	problème
plate	assiette	**profession**	profession
platform (train)	quai	**prohibited**	interdit
play (n)	théâtre	**pronunciation**	prononciation
play (v)	jouer	**prosper**	prospérer
playground	parc avec des jeux	**Protestant (adj)**	protestant
playpen	parc	**public**	publique
please	s'il vous plaît	**pull**	tirer

pulpit	chaire	red	rouge
pulse	poul	refill (V)	à remplir de nouveau
pump (n)	pompe	refugees	réfugiés
punctual	à l'heure	refund (n)	remboursement
purple	violet	relax (v)	se reposer
purse	sac	relaxation	relaxation
push	pousser	relic	relique
		religion	religion
Q		remember	se souvenir
quality	qualité	Renaissance	renaissance
quarter (1/4)	quart	rent (v)	louer
queen	reine	repair (v)	réparer
question (n)	question	repeat (v)	répéter
quiet	silence	reservation	réservation
		reserve	reserver
		respect	respect
R		retired	à la retraite
R.V.	camping-car	rich	riche
rabbit	lapin	right (direction)	droite
racism	racisme	ring (n)	bague
radiator	radiateur	ring road	rocade
radio	radio	ripe	mûr
raft	radeau	river	rivière
railway	chemin de fer	robbed	volé
rain (n)	pluie	rock (n)	rocher
rainbow	arc-en-ciel	roller skates	patins à
raincoat	imperméable		roulettes
rape (n)	viol	Romanesque	romanesque
rash	boutons	Romantic	romantique
rash, diaper	érythème fessier	romantic	romantique
raw	cru	roof	toit
razor	rasoir	room	chambre
ready	prêt	rope	corde
receipt	reçu	rotten	pourri
receive	recevoir	round trip	aller-retour
receptionist	réceptioniste	roundabout	rondpoint
recipe	recette	rowboat	canot
recommend	suggérer	rucksack	sac à dos
rectum	rectum		

rug	tapis	secret	secret
ruins	ruines	see	voir
run (v)	courir	self-service	libre service
Russia	Russie	sell	vendre
		send	envoyer
S		seniors	gens âgés
sad	triste	separate (adj)	séparé
safe	en sécurité	September	septembre
safety pin	épingle à	serious	sérieux
	nourrice	service	service
sailboat	voilier	service, church	messe
sailing	voile	sex	sexe
saint	saint	sexy	sexy
sale	solde	shampoo	shampooing
same	même	shaving cream	crème à raser
sandals	sandales	she	elle
sandwich	sandwich	sheet	drap
sanitary napkins	serviettes hygiéniques	shell	coquille
Santa Claus	Père Noël	ship (n)	navire
Saturday	samedi	shirt	chemise
save (computer)	sauver	shoelaces	lacets
scandalous	scandaleux	shoes	chaussures
Scandinavia	Scandinavie	shoes, tennis	baskettes, chaussures de tennis
school	école	shop (n)	magasin
science	science	shop, antique	magasin d'antiquités
scientist (m/f)	homme/femme de sciences	shop, barber	coiffeur
scissors	ciseaux	shop, camera	magasin de photo
scotch tape	du scotch	shop, cell phone	magasin de portables
screwdriver	tournevis	shop, cheese	fromagerie
sculptor	sculpteur	shop, coffee	café
sculpture	sculpture	shop, jewelry	bijouterie
sea	mer	shop, pastry	patisserie
seafood	fruits de mer	shop, photocopy	magasin de photocopie
seat	place		
second	deuxième		
second class	deuxième classe		

shop, souvenir	boutique de souvenirs	**skirt**	jupe
		sky	ciel
shop, sweets	confiserie	**sleep (v)**	dormir
shop, wine	marchand de vin	**sleeper (train)**	compartiment privé
shopping	shopping		
shopping mall	centre commercial	**sleeper car (train)**	wagon-lit
		sleeping bag	sac de couchage
short	court		
shorts	short	**sleepy**	avoir sommeil
shoulder	épaule	**sleeves**	manches
show (n)	spectacle	**slice (n)**	tranche
show (v)	montrer	**slide (photo)**	diapositive
shower	douche	**slip (n)**	jupon
shy	timide	**slippers**	chaussons
sick	malade	**slippery**	glissant
sign	panneau	**slow**	lent
signature	signature	**small**	petit
silence	silence	**smell (n)**	odeur
silk	soie	**smile (v)**	sourire
silver	argent	**smoke (n)**	fumée
similar	semblable	**smoking**	fumeur
simple	simple	**snack**	snack
sing	chanter	**sneeze (v)**	éternuer
singer (male)	chanteur	**snore**	ronfler
single	célibataire	**snorkel**	tuba
sink	lavabo	**soap**	savon
sink stopper	bouchon pour le lavabo	**soap, laundry**	lessive
		soccer	football
sinus problems	problèmes de sinus	**socks**	chaussettes
		some	quelques
sir	monsieur	**something**	quelque chose
sister	soeur	**son**	fils
size	taille	**song**	chanson
skating	patinage	**soon**	bientôt
ski (v)	faire du ski	**sore throat**	mal à la gorge
skiing	ski	**sorry**	désolé
skin	peau	**sour**	aigre
skinny	maigre	**south**	sud

souvenir shop	boutique de souvenirs	strange	bizarre
Spain	Espagne	stream (n)	ruisseau
sparkplug	bougies	street	rue
speak	parler	string	ficelle
specialty	spécialité	stroller	poussette
speed (n)	vitesse	strong	fort
spend	dépenser	stuck	coincé
spicy	piquant	student	étudiant
spider	araignée	stupid	stupide
spoon	cuillère	sturdy	robuste
sport	sport	style	mode
spring	printemps	subway	Métro
square (town)	place	subway entrance	l'entrée du Métro
stairs	escalier	subway exit	sortie
stamp	timbre	subway map	plan du Métro
stapler	agraffeuse	subway station	station de Métro
star (in sky)	étoile		
state (n)	état	subway stop	arrêt de Métro
station	station	suddenly	soudain
stomach	estomac	suffer	souffrir
stomachache	mal à l'estomac	suitcase	valise
stoned	stoned	summer	été
stop (n)	stop; arrêt	sun	soleil
stop (v)	arrêter	sunbathe	se faire bronzer
stoplight	feu	sunburn	coup de soleil
stopper, sink	bouchon pour le lavabo	Sunday	dimanche
		sunglasses	lunettes de soleil
store (n)	magasin	sunny	ensoleillé
store, department	grand magasin	sunrise	aube
		sunscreen	huile solaire
store, hardware	quincaillerie	sunset	coucher de soleil
store, office supplies	papeterie	sunshine	soleil
		sunstroke	insolation
store, toy	magasin de jouets	suntan (n)	bronzage
storm	tempête	suntan lotion	lotion solaire
story (floor)	étage	supermarket	supermarché
straight	droit	supplement (n)	supplément

surfboard	planche de surf
surfer	surfeur
surprise (n)	surprise
swallow (v)	avaler
sweat (v)	transpirer
sweater	pullover
sweet	doux
sweets shop	confiserie
swelling (n)	enflure
swim	nager
swim trunks	maillot de bain
swimming pool	piscine
swimsuit	costume de bain
Switzerland	Suisse
synagogue	synagogue
synthetic	synthétique

T

table	table
tail	queue
tail lights	feux arrières
take	prendre
take out (food) (v)	emporter
talcum powder	talc
talk	parler
tall	grand
tampons	tampons
tape (adhesive)	scotch
tape (cassette)	cassette
taste (n)	goût
taste (v)	goûter
tax	taxe
taxi	taxi
taxi meter	compteur
taxi stand	station de taxi
teacher	professeur
team	équipe

teenager	adolescent
teeth	dents
teething (baby)	poussée des dents
telephone	téléphone
telephone card	carte téléphonique
television	télévision
temperature	température
tender (adj)	tendre
tennis	tennis
tennis shoes	baskettes, chaussures de tennis
tent	tente
tent pegs	piquets de tente
terrible	terrible
terrorists	terroristes
testicles	testicules
thanks	merci
theater	théâtre
thermometer	thermomètre
thick	épais
thief	voleur
thigh	cuisse
thin	mince
thing	chose
think	penser
thirsty	soif
thongs	tongues
thread (n)	fil
throat	gorge
through	à travers
throw (v)	jeter
Thursday	jeudi
ticket	billet
tight	serré
time, on	à l'heure

timetable	horaire	track (train)	voie
tire	pneu	traditional	traditionnel
tired	fatigué	traffic	circulation
tires	pneus	train	train
tissue,	kleenex; mouchoirs	train car	voiture
facial	en papier	transfer (n)	correspondance
to	à	transfer (v)	prendre une
today	aujourd'hui		correspondance
toe	orteil	translate	traduire
together	ensemble	transmission	liquide de
toilet	toilette	fluid	transmission
toilet paper	papier hygiénique	travel (v)	voyager
token	jeton	travel	agence de voyage
toll	péage	agency	
toll-free	gratuit	travelers	voyageurs
tomorrow	demain	travelers	chèque de voyage
tomorrow,	après demain	check	
day after		treasury	trésorerie
tonight	ce soir	tree	arbre
too (much)	trop	trip (n)	voyage
tooth	dent	tripod	trépied
toothache	mal aux dents	trouble	trouble
toothbrush	brosse à dents	T-shirt	T-shirt
toothpaste	dentifrice	Tuesday	mardi
toothpick	cure-dent	tunnel	tunnel
total	total	Turkey	Turquie
touch (v)	toucher	turn signal	clignotant
tough	dur	tweezers	pince à épiler
tour	tour	twins	jumeaux
tour, guided	visite guidée		
tourist	touriste	**U**	
tow truck	dépanneur	ugly	laid
towel	serviette de bain	umbrella	parapluie
tower	tour	uncle	oncle
town	village	unconscious	inconscient
toy	jouet	under	sous
toy store	magasin de jouets	underpants	slip

underscore (_)	souligne
understand	comprendre
underwear	sous vêtements
unemployed	au chômage
unfortunately	malheureuse-ment
United States	États-Unis
university	université
up	en haut
upstairs	en haut
urethra	urèthre
urgent	urgent
urinary infection	infection urinarire
us	nous
use (v)	utiliser
uterus	utérus

V

vacancy (hotel)	chambre libre
vacant	libre
vacation	vacances
vagina	vagin
valid	bon
validate	composter
valley	vallée
Vaseline	Vaseline
vegetarian (n)	végétarien
velvet	velours
venereal disease	maladie vénérienne
very	très
vest	gilet
video	vidéo
video recorder	magnétoscope
view (n)	vue

village	village
vineyard	vignoble
violence	violence
virus	virus
visit (n)	visite
visit (v)	visiter
vitamins	vitamines
voice	voix
vomit (v)	vomir

W

waist	taille
wait (v)	attendre
waiter	garçon
waiting room	salle d'attente
waitress	serveuse
wake up	se réveiller
walk (v)	marcher
wall, fortified	remparts
wallet	portefeuille
want (v)	vouloir
war	guerre
warm (adj)	chaud
wash (v)	laver
washer	machine à laver
watch (n)	montre
watch (v)	regarder
water	eau
water, drinkable	eau potable
water, tap	eau du robinet
waterfall	cascade
waterskiing	ski nautique
we	nous
weather	temps
weather forecast	météo
Web site	site web
wedding	mariage

Wednesday	mercredi	**word**	mot
week	semaine	**work (n)**	travail
weight	poids	**work (v)**	travailler
welcome	bienvenue	**world**	monde
west	ouest	**worse**	pire
wet	mouillé	**worst**	le pire
what	que	**wrap**	emballer
wheel	roue	**wrist**	poignet
wheelchair-	accessible à un	**write**	écrire
accessible	fauteuil roulant		
when	quand	**X**	
where	où	**X-ray**	radio
whipped	crème chantilly		
cream		**Y**	
white	blanc	**year**	année
who	qui	**yellow**	jaune
why	pourquoi	**yes**	oui
widow	veuve	**yesterday**	hier
widower	veuf	**you (informal)**	tu
wife	femme	**you (formal)**	vous
wild	sauvage	**young**	jeune
wind	vent	**youth**	auberge de jeunesse
window	fenêtre	**hostel**	
windshield	essuie-glace	**youths**	jeunes
wiper			
windsurfing	planche à voile	**Z**	
windy	venteux	**zero**	zéro
wine	vin	**zip code**	code postal
wine shop	marchand de vin	**Ziplock**	sac en plastique
wing	aile	**bag**	à fermeture
winter	hiver	**zipper**	fermeture éclair
wish (v)	souhaiter	**zoo**	zoo
with	avec		
without	sans		
women	dames		
wood	bois		
wool	laine		

TIPS FOR HURDLING
THE LANGUAGE BARRIER

Don't be Afraid to Communicate

Even the best phrase book won't satisfy your needs in every situation. To really hurdle the language barrier, you need to leap beyond the printed page, and dive into contact with the locals. Never allow your lack of foreign language skills to isolate you from the people and cultures you traveled halfway around the world to experience. Remember that in every country you visit, you're surrounded by expert, native-speaking tutors. Spend bus and train rides letting them teach you.

Start conversations by asking politely in the local language, "Do you speak English?" When you speak English with someone from another country, talk slowly, clearly, and with carefully chosen words. Use what the *Voice of America* calls "simple English." You're talking to people who are wishing it was written down, hoping to see each letter as it tumbles out of your mouth. Pronounce each letter, avoiding all contractions and slang. For bad examples, listen to other tourists.

Keep things caveman-simple. Make single nouns work as entire sentences ("Photo?"). Use internationally-understood words ("auto kaput" works in Bordeaux). Butcher the language if you must. The important thing is to make the effort. To get air mail stamps, you can flap your wings and say "tweet, tweet." If you want milk, moo and pull two imaginary udders. Risk looking like a fool.

If you're short on words, make your picnic a potluck. Pull out a map and point out your journey. Draw what you mean. Bring photos from home and introduce your family. Play cards or toss a Frisbee. Fold an origami bird for kids or dazzle 'em with sleight-of-hand magic.

Go ahead and make educated guesses. Many situations are easy-to-fake multiple choice questions. Practice. Read timetables, concert posters, and newspaper headlines. Listen to each language on a multi-lingual tour. Be melodramatic. Exaggerate the local accent. Self-consciousness is the deadliest communication killer.

Choose multilingual people to communicate with, such as students, business people, urbanites, or anyone in the tourist trade. Use a small note pad to jot down handy phrases and to help you communicate more clearly with the locals by scribbling down numbers, maps, and so on. Some travelers carry important messages written on a small card: allergic to nuts, strict vegetarian, your finest ice cream.

International Words

As our world shrinks, more and more words hop across their linguistic boundaries and become international. Savvy travelers develop a knack for choosing words most likely to be universally understood ("auto" instead of "car," "kaput" instead of "broken," "photo," not "picture"). Internationalize your pronunciation. "University," if you play around with its sound (oo-nee-vehr-see-tay), will be understood anywhere. The average American is a real flunky in this area. Be creative.

Here are a few internationally understood words. Remember, cut out the Yankee accent and give each word a pan-European sound.

Amigo	Communist	Mañana	Restaurant
Attila	Computer	McDonald's	Rock 'n' roll
(mean, crude)	Disco	Michael Jackson	Self-service
Auto	Disneyland	Michelangelo	Sex / Sexy
Autobus	(wonderland)	(artistic)	Sport
("booos")	Elephant	Moment	Stop
Bank	(big clod)	No	Super
Beer	English	No problem	Taxi
Bill Gates	("Engleesh")	Nuclear	Tea
Bon voyage	Europa	OK	Telephone
Bye-bye	Fascist	Oo la la	Toilet
Camping	Hello	Pardon	Tourist
Casanova	Hercules	Passport	U.S. profanity
(romantic)	(strong)	Photo	University
Central	Hotel	Photocopy	Vino
Chocolate	Information	Picnic	Yankee,
Ciao	Internet	Police	Americano
Coffee	Kaput	Post	
Coke, Coca-Cola	Mama mia	Rambo	

French Verbs

These conjugated verbs will help you assemble a caveman sentence in a pinch.

TO BE	*ÊTRE*	eh-truh
I am	*je suis*	zhuh swee
you are	*vous êtes*	vooz eht
(formal, singular or plural)		
you are	*tu es*	tew ay
(singular, informal)		
he / she / one is	*il / elle / on est*	eel / ehl / oh<u>n</u> ay
("one"—or **on**—is colloquial for "we")		
we are	*nous sommes*	noo suhm
they (m / f) are	*ils / elles sont*	eel / ehl soh<u>n</u>

TO HAVE	*AVOIR*	ah-vwar
I have	*j'ai*	zhay
you have	*vous avez*	vooz ah-vay
(formal, singular or plural)		
you have	*tu as*	tew ah
(singular, informal)		
he / she / one has	*il / elle / on a*	eel / ehl / oh<u>n</u> ah
we have	*nous avons*	nooz ah-voh<u>n</u>
they (m / f) have	*ils / elles ont*	eelz / ehlz oh<u>n</u>

TO SPEAK	*PARLER*	par-lay
I speak	*je parle*	zhuh parl
you speak	*vous parlez*	voo par-lay
(formal, singular or plural)		
you speak	*tu parles*	tew parl
(singular, informal)		
he / she / one speaks	*il / elle / on parle*	eel / ehl / oh<u>n</u> parl
we speak	*nous parlons*	noo par-loh<u>n</u>
they (m / f) speak	*ils / elles parlent*	eel / ehl parl

TO WALK	*MARCHER*	mar-shay
I walk	*je marche*	zhuh marsh
you walk	*vous marchez*	voo mar-shay
(formal, singular or plural)		
you walk	*tu marches*	tew marsh
(singular, informal)		
he / she / one walks	*il / elle / on marche*	eel / ehl / oh<u>n</u> marsh
we walk	*nous marchons*	noo mar-shoh<u>n</u>
they (m / f) walk	*ils / elles marchent*	eel / ehl marsh

TO LIKE	*AIMER*	ehm-ay
I like	*j'aime*	zhehm
you like	*vous aimez*	vooz eh-may
(formal, singular or plural)		
you like	*tu aimes*	tew ehm
(singular, informal)		
he / she / one likes	*il / elle / on aime*	eel / ehl / oh<u>n</u> ehm
we like	*nous aimons*	nooz eh-moh<u>n</u>
they (m / f) like	*ils / elles aiment*	eelz / ehlz ehm

TO GO	*ALLER*	ah-lay
I go	*je vais*	zhuh vay
you go	*vous allez*	vooz ah-lay
(formal, singular or plural)		
you go	*tu vas*	tew vah
(singular, informal)		
he / she / one goes	*il / elle / on va*	eel / ehl / oh<u>n</u> vah
we go	*nous allons*	nooz ah-loh<u>n</u>
they (m / f) go	*ils / elles vont*	eel / ehl voh<u>n</u>

TO DO / TO MAKE	*FAIRE*	fair
I do	*je fais*	zhuh fay
you do	*vous faîtes*	voo feht
(formal, singular or plural)		
you do	*tu fais*	tew fay
(singular, informal)		
he / she / one does	*il / elle / on fait*	eel / ehl / oh<u>n</u> fay
we do	*nous faisons*	noo fuh-soh<u>n</u>
they (m / f) do	*ils / elles font*	eel / ehl foh<u>n</u>

TO SEE	*VOIR*	vwar
I see	*je vois*	zhuh vwah
you see (formal, singular or plural)	*vous voyez*	voo vwah-yay
you see (singular, informal)	*tu vois*	tew vwah
he / she / one sees	*il / elle / on voit*	eel / ehl / ohn vwah
we see	*nous voyons*	noo vwah-yohn
they (m / f) see	*ils / elles voient*	eel / ehl vwah

TO BE ABLE	*POUVOIR*	poo-vwar
I can	*je peux*	zhuh puh
you can (formal, singular or plural)	*vous pouvez*	voo poo-vay
you can (singular, informal)	*tu peux*	tew puh
he / she / one can	*il / elle / on peut*	eel / ehl / ohn puh
we can	*nous pouvons*	noo poo-vohn
they (m / f) can	*ils / elles peuvent*	eel / ehl puhv

TO WANT	*VOULOIR*	vool-war
I want	*je veux*	zhuh vuh
you want (formal, singular or plural)	*vous voulez*	voo voo-lay
you want (singular, informal)	*tu veux*	tew vuh
he / she / one wants	*il / elle / on veut*	eel / ehl / ohn vuh
we want	*nous voulons*	noo voo-lohn
they (m / f) want	*ils / elles veulent*	eel / ehl vuhl

TO NEED	*AVOIR BESOIN DE*	ah-vwar buh-swan duh
I need	*j'ai besoin de*	zhay buh-swan duh
you need (formal, singular or plural)	*vous avez besoin de*	vooz ah-vay buh-swan duh
you need (singular, informal)	*tu as besoin de*	tew ah buh-swan duh
he / she / one needs	*il / elle / on a besoin de*	eel / ehl / ohn ah buh-swan duh
we need	*nous avons besoin de*	nooz ah-vohn buh-swan duh
they (m / f) need	*ils / elles ont besoin de*	eelz / ehlz ohn buh-swan duh

French Tongue Twisters

Tongue twisters are a great way to practice a language and break the ice with local Europeans. Here are a few French tongue twisters that are sure to challenge you, and amuse your hosts.

Bonjour madame la saucissonière!	Hello, madame sausage-seller!
Combien sont ces six saucissons-ci?	How much are these six sausages?
Ces six saucissons-ci sont six sous.	These six sausages are six cents.
Si ces saucissons-ci sont six sous, ces six saucissons-ci sont trop chers.	If these are six cents, these six sausages are too expensive.
Je veux et j'exige qu'un chasseur sachant chasser sans ses èchasses sache chasser sans son chien de chasse.	I want and demand that a hunter who knows how to hunt without his stilts knows how to hunt without his hunting dog.
Ce sont seize cent jacynthes sèches dans seize cent sachets secs.	There are 600 dry hyacinths in 600 dry sachets.
Ce sont trois très gros rats dans trois très gros trous roulant trois gros rats gris morts.	There are three very fat rats in three very fat rat-holes rolling three fat grey dead rats.

English Tongue Twisters

After your French friends have laughed at you, let them try these tongue twisters in English:

If neither he sells seashells, nor she sells seashells, who shall sell seashells? Shall seashells be sold?	Si ni lui ni elle ne vendent de coquillages, qui les vendra? Les coquillages seront-ils vendus?
Peter Piper picked a peck of pickled peppers.	Pierre Pipant a choisi un picotin de cornichons.
Rugged rubber baby buggy bumpers.	Des pare-chocs solides en caoutchoue pour les voitures d'enfants.
The sixth sick sheik's sixth sheep's sick.	Le sixième mouton du sixième sheik est malade.
Red bug's blood and black bug's blood.	Sang d'insecte rouge, sang d'insecte noir.
Soldiers' shoulders.	Epaules de soldats.
Thieves seize skis.	Les voleurs s'emparent de skis.
I'm a pleasant mother pheasant plucker. I pluck mother pheasants. I'm the most pleasant mother pheasant plucker that ever plucked a mother pheasant.	Je suis une plaisant plumeur de faisanes. Je plume les faisanes. Je suis le plumeur de faisanes le plus plaisant qui ait jamais plumé de faisanes.

French Songs

You probably know the nursery songs *Frere Jacques* and *Sur le Pont d'Avignon*. Here are a couple more French songs and their meanings. Ask a friendly local to teach you the tunes.

LA MARSEILLAISE

Allons enfants de la patrie,	Let's go, children of the fatherland,
Le jour de gloire est arrivé.	The day of glory has arrived.
Contre nous de la tyrannie	The blood-covered flagpole of tyranny
L'étendard sanglant est levé,	Is raised against us,
L'étendard sanglant est levé.	Is raised against us.
Entendez-vous dans nos campagnes	Do you hear what's happening in our countryside?
Mugir nos féroces soldats?	The ferocious soldiers are howling.
Qui viennent jusque dans nos bras	They're nearly in our grasp
Egorger nos fils et nos compagnes.	They're slitting the throats of our sons and our women.
Aux armes citoyens,	Grab your weapons, citizens,
Formez vos bataillons,	Form your battalions,
Marchons, marchons,	March on, march on,
Qu'un sang impur	So that their impure blood
Abreuve dans sillons.	Will fill our trenches.

CHEVALIERS DE LA TABLE RONDE

This is a great drinking song often sung when friends and families get together.

Chevaliers de la table ronde,	Knights of the round table,
Goûtons voir si le vin est bon.	Let's taste if the wine is good.
Goûtons voir, oui, oui, oui	Let's taste, yes, yes, yes
Goûtons voir, non, non, non	Let's taste, no, no, no
Goûtons voir si le vin est bon.	Let's taste if the wine is good.
Goûtons voir, oui, oui, oui	Let's taste, yes, yes, yes
Goûtons voir, non, non, non	Let's taste, no, no, no
Goûtons voir si le vin est bon.	Let's taste if the wine is good.

J'en boirais cinq à six bouteilles,	I will drink five to six bottles,
Une femme sur les genoux.	A woman on each knee.
Une femme, oui, oui, oui	A woman, yes, yes, yes
Une femme, non, non, non	A woman, no, no, no
Une femme sur les genoux.	A woman on each knee.
Si je meurs je veux qu'on m'enterre	If I die I want to be buried
Dans une cave où y'a du bon vin.	In a cave where the wine is good.
Dans une cave, oui, oui, oui	In a cave, yes, yes, yes
Dans une cave, non, non, non	In a cave, no, no, no
Dans une cave où y'a du bon vin.	In a cave where the wine is good.
Les deux pieds contre la muraille	The two feet against the wall
Et la tête sous le robinet.	And the head under the spigot.
Et la tête, oui, oui, oui	And the head, yes, yes, yes
Et la tête, non, non, non	And the head, no, no, no
Et la tête sous le robinet.	And the head under the spigot.
Sur ma tombe je veux qu'on écrive	On my tomb I want it to be written
Ici gît le roi des buveurs.	Here lies the king of the drinkers.
Ici gît, oui, oui, oui	Here lies, yes, yes, yes
Ici gît, non, non, non	Here lies, no, no, no
Ici gît le roi des buveurs.	Here lies the king of the drinkers.

French Gestures

Here are a few common French gestures and their meanings:

The Fingertips Kiss: Gently bring the fingers and thumb of your right hand together, raise to your lips, kiss lightly, and toss your fingers and thumb into the air. Be careful: Tourists look silly when they over-emphasize this subtle action. It can mean sexy, delicious, divine, or wonderful.

The Eyelid Pull: Place your extended forefinger below the center of your eye, and pull the skin downward. This means: "I'm alert. I'm looking. You can't fool me."

The Roto-Wrist: Hold your forearm out from your waist with your open palm down, and pivot your wrist clockwise and counter-clockwise like you're opening a doorknob. When a Frenchman uses this gesture while explaining something to you, he isn't sure of the information or it's complete B.S. He'll usually say, "*Bof!*" or "*Comme ci, comme ça.*"

The Hand Shave: Move the back of your hand gently up and down the side of your face as if checking a clean shave. This denotes a boring person, show, talk, or whatever, and is often accompanied by the expression "*La barbe*" (the beard).

The Shoulder Shrug: Move your shoulders up towards your ears and slightly lift your arms with palms up. This basically means, "I don't know and I don't care."

The Nose-Grab-and-Twist: Wrap your hand around your nose and twist it down. If someone does this to you, put down your wine glass—it means you're drunk.

To beckon someone: In northern Europe, you bring your palm up, and in France and the south, you wave it down. To Americans, this looks like "go away"—not the invitation it actually is.

Numbers and Stumblers

- Europeans write a few of their numbers differently than we do. 1 = *1* , 4 = *4* , 7 = *7* .
- Europeans write the date in this order: day/month/year.
- Commas are decimal points and decimals are commas. A dollar and a half is 1,50 and there are 5.280 feet in a mile.
- The European "first floor" isn't the ground floor, but the first floor up.
- When counting with your fingers, start with your thumb. If you hold up only your first finger, you'll probably get two of something.

APPENDIX

Let's Talk Telephones

Making Calls within a European Country: About half of all European countries use area codes (like we do); the other half uses a direct-dial system without area codes.

To make calls within a country that uses a direct-dial system (Belgium, Czech Republic, Denmark, France, Italy, Portugal, Norway, Spain, and Switzerland), you dial the same number whether you're calling across the country or across the street.

In countries that use area codes (such as Austria, Britain, Finland, Germany, Ireland, the Netherlands, and Sweden), you dial the local number when calling within a city, and you add the area code if calling long-distance within the country.

Making International Calls: You always start with the international access code (011 if you're calling from America or Canada, or 00 from Europe), then dial the country code of the country you're calling (see codes below).

What you dial next depends on the phone system of the country you're calling. If the country uses area codes, drop the initial zero of the area code, then dial the rest of the number.

Countries that use direct-dial systems (no area codes) vary in how they're accessed internationally by phone. You always start by dialing the international access code, followed by the country code. Then, if you're calling the Czech Republic, Denmark, Italy, Norway, Portugal, or Spain, simply dial the phone number in its entirety. But if you're calling Belgium, France, or Switzerland, drop the initial zero of the phone number.

Country Codes

After you've dialed the international access code, dial the code of the country you're calling.

Austria—43	Belgium—32
Britain—44	Canada—1
Czech Rep.—420	Denmark—45
Estonia—372	Finland—358
France—33	Germany—49
Gibraltar—350	Greece—30
Ireland—353	Italy—39
Morocco—212	Netherlands—31
Norway—47	Portugal—351
Spain—34	Sweden—46
Switzerland—41	United States—1

Useful Phone Numbers

Emergency:	Dial 17 for police
Emergency Medical Assistance:	tel. 15
Directory Assistance:	tel. 12
(some English spoken)	
Train (SNCF) Information:	tel. 08 36 35 35 35
(some English usually spoken)	

Embassies

U.S. Embassy/Consulate:
- tel. 01 43 12 22 22
- 2 rue Saint Florentin, 75001, Paris
- Métro stop: Concorde
- www.amb-usa.fr/consul/consulat.htm

Canadian Embassy/Consulate:
- tel. 01 44 43 29 00
- 35 avenue Montaigne, 75008, Paris
- Métro stop: Franklin-Roosevelt

Tear-Out Cheat Sheet

Keep this sheet of French survival phrases in your
pocket, handy to memorize or use if you're caught
without your phrase book.

Good day.	*Bonjour.*	bohn-zhoor
Do you speak English?	*Parlez-vous anglais?*	par-lay-voo ahn-glay
Yes. / No.	*Oui. / Non.*	wee / nohn
I don't understand.	*Je ne comprends pas.*	zhuh nuh kohn-prahn pah
Please.	*S'il vous plaît.*	see voo play
Thank you.	*Merci.*	mehr-see
You're welcome.	*De rien.*	duh ree-an
I'm sorry.	*Désolé.*	day-zoh-lay
Excuse me (to get attention).	*Excusez-moi.*	ehk-skew-zay-mwah
Excuse me (to pass).	*Pardon.*	pahr-dohn
No problem.	*Pas de problème.*	pah duh proh-blehm
Very good.	*Très bon.*	tray bohn
Goodbye.	*Au revoir.*	oh reh-vwahr
How much is it?	*C'est Combien?*	kohn-bee-an
Write it?	*Ecrivez?*	ay-kree-vay
euro (€)	*euro*	oo-roo
one / two	*un / deux*	uhn / duh
three / four	*trois / quatre*	twah / kah-truh
five / six	*cinq / six*	sank / sees
seven / eight	*sept / huit*	seht / weet
nine / ten	*neuf / dix*	nuhf / dees
20	*vingt*	van
30	*trente*	trahnt
40	*quarante*	kah-rahnt
50	*cinquante*	san-kahnt
60	*soixante*	swah-sahnt
70	*soixante-dix*	swah-sahnt-dees
80	*quatre-vingts*	kah-truh-van
90	*quatre-vingt-dix*	kah-truh-van-dees
100	*cent*	sahn

I'd like...	*Je voudrais...*	zhuh voo-dray
We'd like...	*Nous voudrions...*	noo voo-dree-ohn
...this.	*...ceci.*	suh-see
...more.	*...plus.*	ploo
...a ticket.	*...un billet.*	uhn bee-yay
...a room.	*...une chambre.*	ewn shahn-bruh
...the bill.	*...l'addition.*	lah-dee-see-ohn
Is it possible?	*C'est possible?*	say poh-see-bluh
Where are the toilets?	*Où sont les toilettes?*	oo sohn lay twah-leht
men / women	*hommes / dames*	ohm / dahm
entrance / exit	*entrée / sortie*	ahn-tray / sor-tee
no entry	*défense d'entrer*	day-fahns dahn-tray
open / closed	*ouvert / fermé*	oo-vehr / fehr-may
At what time does this open / close?	*À quelle heure c'est ouvert / fermé?*	ah kehl ur say oo-vehr / fehr-may
Just a moment.	*Un moment.*	uhn moh-mahn
Now.	*Maintenant.*	man-tuh-nahn
Soon.	*Bientôt.*	bee-an-toh
Later.	*Plus tard.*	plew tar
Today.	*Aujourd'hui.*	oh-zhoor-dwee
Tomorrow.	*Demain.*	duh-man
Monday	*lundi*	luhn-dee
Tuesday	*mardi*	mar-dee
Wednesday	*mercredi*	mehr-kruh-dee
Thursday	*jeudi*	zhuh-dee
Friday	*vendredi*	vahn-druh-dee
Saturday	*samedi*	sahm-dee
Sunday	*dimanche*	dee-mahnsh

MAKING YOUR HOTEL RESERVATION

Most hotel managers know basic "hotel English." E-mailing or faxing are the preferred methods for reserving a room. They're clearer and more foolproof than telephoning. Photocopy and enlarge this form, or find it online at www.ricksteves.com/reservation.

One-Page Fax

To: _____ @ _____
　　　　　　　hotel　　　　　　　　　　　　　　　　　fax

From: _____ @ _____
　　　　　　　name　　　　　　　　　　　　　　　　　fax

Today's date: _____/_____/_____
　　　　　　　　　day　month　year

Dear Hotel_____

Please make this reservation for me:

Name: _____

Total # of people: _____ # of rooms: _____ # of nights: _____

Arriving: _____/_____/_____　Arrival time: (24-hr clock):_____
　　　　　day　month　year　　　　　　(I will telephone if I will be late)

Departing: _____/_____/_____
　　　　　　day　month　year

Room(s): Single____ Double____ Twin____ Triple____ Quad____ Quint____

With: Toilet____ Shower____ Bathtub____ Sink only____

Special needs: View____ Quiet ____Cheapest____ Ground floor ____

Credit card: Visa____ MasterCard____ American Express____

Please fax or e-mail your confirmation of my reservation, along with the type of room reserved and the price. Please also inform me of your cancellation policy. After I hear from you, I will quickly send my credit-card information as a deposit to hold the room. Thank you.

Signature _____

Name _____

Address_____

City_____ State ____ Zip Code _____ Country_____

E-mail address _____